The Notes

The Notes

or On Non-premature
Reconciliation

LUDWIG HOHL

TRANSLATED FROM THE GERMAN BY TESS LEWIS

FOREWORD BY JOSHUA COHEN

YALE UNIVERSITY PRESS ■ NEW HAVEN & LONDON

A MARGELLOS
WORLD REPUBLIC OF LETTERS BOOK

Copyright © 2021 by Yale University.

English translation copyright © 2021 by Tess Lewis

Originally published as *Die Notizen oder Von der unvoreiligen Versöhnung* © Suhrkamp Verlag Frankfurt am Main 1981.

All right reserved by and controlled through Suhrkamp Verlag Berlin.

Yale University Press books may be purchased in quantity for educational, business, or promotional use. For information, please e-mail sales.press@yale.edu (U.S. office) or sales@yaleup.co.uk (U.K. office).

Set in Electra and Nobel type by Tseng Information Systems, Inc., Durham, North Carolina.

Printed in the United States of America.

Library of Congress Control Number: 2021935404

ISBN 978-0-300-22005-6 (hardcover : alk. paper)

A catalogue record for this book is available from the British Library.

This paper meets the requirements of ANSI/NISO Z39.48-1992 (Permanence of Paper).

10 9 8 7 6 5 4 3 2 1

CONTENTS

FOREWORD

The Swiss writer Ludwig Hohl (1904–1980) spent the bulk of his final decades — the decades during which he received his only ac-claim — living poor in a Geneva basement strung with clotheslines, from which he hung his pages like laundry out to dry. He'd finish a page and then decide where to hang it, clipping, reclipping, trying to find the perfect order, or at least trying not to give up on the hope of a perfect order . . .

A few forays into fiction aside, Hohl's writing consisted of notes — not aphorisms or adages, proverbs or *pensées*, but, as Hohl insists in his original German, *Notizen*, comprising quotations of the work of other writers (Montaigne, Spinoza, Goethe, Rilke), glosses on the work of other writers (Proust, Kafka, Balzac, Mann), ruminations on the meaning and purpose of "work" (for Hohl, it's virtually a synonym for "life"); his thoughts on Switzerland and the Swiss (not a fan); his thoughts on pharmacists (his epithet for the bourgeoisie), dogs and cats and death and dying. I feel an inclination now to reproduce some of these notes, but I won't, or I won't before acknowledging that Hohl was opposed to their being read out of sequence. Unlike, say, Karl Kraus or Lichtenberg or La Rochefoucauld, Hohl believed or claimed he believed that his *Notes* were philosophical propositions, numbered nuggets of prose that, if read in the sequence he intended, constellated a system. In Hohl's assessment, any reader who skipped around, picking-and-choosing, should expect to become as confused as a reader of Wittgenstein's *Tractatus* who tries to assimilate its #6.41 ("The sense of the world must lie outside the world"), before assenting to its famous #1 ("The world is everything that is the case").

But I am here to tell you that this isn't true, that you'll be confused no matter what you do, whether you skip around or read through page by page.

And now I'll quote some Hohl:

> II, 194: Those who have no self-discipline—to me this seems certain—are incapable of intellectual or spiritual achievement. They are no doubt perfectly suited for the usual occupations: the office director or the house rules, etc. provide the discipline. But for spiritual and intellectual undertakings, where can one find systems with bosses and rules and requirements to help them be realized?

> I, 283: Morality exists to release man from his duties.
> Before he had to answer for each step he took, to take them in accord with his purpose—now he only has to be in step, mechanically, with a ready-made schema and he is absolved of all guilt.
> —but also from changing the world.

> VI, 27: True poetry is the opposite of fiction.
> Nietzsche said, "the poets lie too much." Hölderlin "yet what remains, the poets provide." Do these two serious ideas contradict each other?

> VII, 11: The most frequent thought that occurs to me at the sight of another person: "How does it survive?"

> I, 44: There are two fundamental misconceptions about knowledge: first, that you can impart it (the way you pass on names or scientific theorems); second, that you can preserve it (in your memory or on your bookshelves).

> II, 108: It's simply a matter of beginning *somewhere*, not at the beginning: because there is no beginning.

Whether Hohl truly believed that he'd created a system, or just wanted to believe that he had, or just wanted his readers to believe that he had, is immaterial. What is material is Hohl's claim that humanity's essential "work" in the world is to restore the order that it lacks (from I, 49: "*Work is the realization of knowledge*").

Hohl aspired to systemization out of a mistrust of fragmentation (of his mind, of his time, of bodies of knowledge) and out of a sense of resentment that the twentieth century he lived through forced honest writers like himself to admit that full-circle narratives and resolvable plots were no longer descriptive of life, or no longer desirable, or no longer possible. I read his *Notes* as the record of a man attempting to reconcile the reality of fragmentation with the fantasy of logical method, which in his lifetime became the purview of technology.

Die Notizen—Hohl's primary collection, written in the 1930s— bears the subtitle *oder Von der unvoreiligen Versöhnung*, which Tess Lewis translates as *On Non-premature Reconciliation.* This subtitle is so important to Hohl that he states in his preface that if the reader can't understand it, "he would be well advised to put the book down, at least for a time." Reading and re-reading that advice, I can't help but wonder how long of a break Hohl would've recommended: a week? A month? And what should I do in the meantime? Should I just wait (VII, 164: "I'm someone who is utterly incapable of waiting; but how often have I waited in my life . . .") or is there some way to keep on "working"?

The first thing you might notice about the phrase "non-premature reconciliation" is the implication that there's such a thing as "premature reconciliation," and that Hohl has chosen to express its opposite through a negation. In other words, the opposite of "premature reconciliation" is not Punctual Reconciliation, or Accurate-as-a-Swiss-Watch Reconciliation, but "non-premature," the apophatic *un-voreiligen.*

The book's most concise definition of what this might be is characteristically roundabout, found in IX, 10: "Switzerland suffers from premature reconciliation, which, to be precise, is nothing other than superficiality." This sentence, "to be precise," tells us that "non-premature reconciliation" is "nothing other" than the "non-superficial" . . . the deep . . . the thorough . . . the genuine . . . the authentic . . . the uncompromising . . .

History is full of writers whom critics have described as "uncompromising," but that epithet is never meant literally: show me one writer, one person, who has never compromised, and I'll show you an illiterate child. Hohl, though, might be the one writer to have taken "non-compromise" as his fundamental subject. He is obsessed, unhealthily obsessed, with how people—not just Swiss people—are constantly settling for less; for the watered-down and adulterated, the simplistic and easy. To his mind, reconciliation with less (not *resignation to* less) is inevitable—after all, we all must die, and death is less than life—but it's incumbent upon us to hold out as long as possible. The more we surrender to the cheap entertainment, to the false political comfort, or to the consoling political lie, the more difficult we'll find it to recognize our function in a greater social system, and the ways in which our personal lapses can license our neighbors', until our entire society has unconsciously conspired to ignore its higher principles, Netflix, and chill, opening the door to all manner of exploitation (I, 65: "Crowds barely think. That is why they must be led by thinkers, not exploiters").

I realize this sort of seriousness seems old-fashioned nowadays, and that when it comes up in conversation you're supposed to either mock it with cynical irony or contextualize it in identity-terms as the outdated standards of a straight white European male desperate to resuscitate a corrupt cultural past that might not even have existed.

But mockery and politics are "premature reconciliations" too: reductive reactions that will keep you from grappling.

Maybe you feel differently, but in my experience, people today are simultaneously too busy *and* too lazy. Excuses are everywhere and they're mostly enjoyable, at least until you're reminded of what they ward off: thoughts about death and what happens after.

I often think that poetry will survive if only because we'll always need something to read at funerals. And I think that Hohl's prose-work will survive too for the very same reason: we'll always need some truths whose measure we can fail.

Joshua Cohen

For the past fifty years, one of Switzerland's best kept literary secrets has been the writer Ludwig Hohl. Although praised by Elias Canetti, Robert Musil, Max Frisch, Friedrich Dürrenmatt, Adolf Muschg, George Steiner, and Peter Handke, among others, Hohl has remained a writer's writer, if not a writer's writer's writer. Hohl's prickly, demanding, uncompromising, relentless, and sui generis intellect is not for the faint of spirit. Yet those willing to take on his magnum opus, *The Notes; or, On Non-premature Reconciliation* have often fallen under his spell. As Dürrenmatt wrote, "Other writers have their mistresses. I have Ludwig Hohl."

Born into a pastor's family in the small town of Netstal in the canton of Glarus, Hohl was eventually thrown out of the gymnasium because of his "rebellious disposition" and his frequent talk of women, cigarettes, and Nietzsche. Hohl was essentially an autodidact and his relationship with his native land was always fraught. After a falling out with his parents, he spent his early twenties in self-imposed exile in Paris and Vienna, then lived in The Hague from 1931 to 1937. It was there, between 1934 and 1936, in a state of "extreme spiritual desolation" that he composed the bulk of *The Notes.* Described as a "massive, fiercely rugged thought-quarry" straddling the border between philosophy and literature, *The Notes* is a meticulously ordered compendium of over a thousand observations, anecdotes, reflections, recollections, mini-essays, and quotations, bound together under his philosophical conceit of *Arbeit* or *work*, by which he meant the unrelenting and wholehearted use of one's creative forces.

In his *work* and his works, Ludwig Hohl was a high priest of differentiation, a master of fine distinctions. He devoted his life to the single-minded pursuit of subtleties of meaning; his was a quest to capture, express, and understand ineffable nuances. For him, both God and the devil were in the details.

Indeed, the rigor of Hohl's intellect is established right in the subtitle of *The Notes.* It would be easy to explain Hohl's "non-premature reconciliation" as the refusal to lower one's standards for the sake of expediency, but it is a more expansive, more existential attitude. As Joshua Cohen points out in his foreword, Hohl warns the reader that extensive engagement with this work will certainly be necessary to understand the subtitle. And yet, if its meaning still eludes the reader after such protracted grappling, "he would be well advised to put the book down, at least for a time." Hohl will not meet his readers halfway, though he does offer them a few footholds. He explains in IX, 10, for example, that premature reconciliation is a kind of superficiality, an eagerness "to offer harmonious solutions when confronted with spiritual or intellectual discord," especially if one can avoid experiencing discord oneself. Elsewhere he presents plagiarism as a variety of premature reconciliation. The plagiarist's reluctance to find his own answers, his reaching for convenient and appealing formulations of ideas he has not thought through himself, is symptomatic of this weakness of character. Another aspect can be found in "Optimism," a story that Hohl wrote in Paris in the late 1920s but did not publish until 1943. In it, the talented, starving young artist Juliano responds to professional setbacks by compromising his standards or comforting himself with grand plans that he never realizes, nor in fact, ever really tries to realize. He is unable to face the reality of his situation without consoling illusions that he would one day, soon, produce real works of art.

If Hohl harbored any consoling illusions, he did not let them get in the way of his writing. During his desolate years of wild production in The Hague, he filled thousands of pages with cramped writing, using whatever paper he could find. Despite his family's disapproval of his bohemian lifestyle, they supported him with occasional funds that kept him and his wife barely above water. Even so, he had to pawn his typewriter on more than one occasion and was regularly forced to write letters home asking for money to buy paper, an irony of fate given that his mother's family owned one Switzerland's most prominent paper factories. Nonetheless, he left Holland in 1937 with a bundle of handwritten jottings he called a "four and half kilo primeval forest of variations and attempts." The typed manuscript assembled from these forest leaves, which he titled the "Epische Grundschriften" (the epic foundational texts), formed a precursor to *The Notes.*

He spent years culling these entries and dividing them thematically into the twelve categories that reveal the range of his interests: "On Work," "On the Accessible and the Inaccessible," "Talking, Chattering, Keeping Silent," "The Reader," "Art," "On Writing," "Varia," "Pharmacists" (his shorthand for the consummate bourgeois philistine), "Literature," "Dream and Dreams," "On Death," and "Image." He then added commentary in a smaller font as well as footnotes to qualify or explain, to trace echoing or overlapping notes across the twelve sections and to recall notes from his very first publication of the sort, *Nuancen und Details* (Nuances and details), which appeared in 1939. Reading the resulting work is like entering the skeletal structure of a literary-philosophical geodesic dome: the notes are intricately interwoven in patterns that repeat with variations and form an elegant whole punctuated with light and openness. They are, in a sense, the inventory of one man's soul.

Although Hohl published some poems, essays on literature, stories, and novellas, much of his life was dedicated to revising and reordering *The Notes* and composing a kind of sequel, *Von den hereinbrechenden Rändern: Die Nachnotizen* (From the invading margins: The after-notes). He spent most of the last two decades of his life on the edge of poverty in a windowless basement room strung with a web of clotheslines on which he hung and continuously rearranged his notes and after-notes along with newspaper articles and photographs.

Because of poor sales and friction with his early publisher, only four sections of *The Notes* were published in his lifetime. In the 1970s, Hohl was taken on by Siegfried Unseld of the esteemed Suhrkamp Verlag, who began publishing his works regularly, although *The Notes* in their entirety did not appear until a year after Hohl's death.

For Hohl, having all notes in one volume was essential for them to be properly understood, and the single volume seems a breviary or a numbered labyrinth of thought. Various admirers and critics have stressed the aphoristic or epigrammatic character of Hohl's notes. And yet, to isolate any one of them as a pronouncement is to impoverish it. Hohl constantly refined and tested his thoughts by reordering them and adding footnotes to map interconnections between them. Viewed in different contexts, his concepts acquire new layers and unexpected shadings as one reads one's way through the twelve sections. In this aspect, Hohl's *Notes* resembles Giacomo Leopardi's *Zibaldone*. Yet while the evolution of Leopardi's thought can be traced sequentially, Hohl's thinking tended to progress in a spiral. Indeed, the echoes between the various notes, especially those on his central topics—work, intelligence, art, understanding, truth—illustrate his belief in writing as an endless striving toward an impossible goal: definitive expression. Writing, no matter how authoritative, is only ever provisional. Note XII, 83 offers his most succinct summation:

> *Eternal task:* to capture *it* (IT) in words that are always new. For words lose their substance, one after the other. (We *hear* the words of Spinoza but who *understands* them? How many understand the connection, the tremendousness, inherent in those commonly used words?)

The interconnectedness of the notes is a crucial element their significance. So it was with great trepidation that I faced the necessity of abridging the work to meet space constraints. I have tried to cut only those notes that would not upset the equilibrium of various themes that Hohl develops through the work.

Some notes have simply not aged well. Hohl admits as much in a footnote to an entry in which he rages against the ghastliness of the common first name Piet in Holland. "Again, I must emphasize the time frame in which these texts were written: 1934–1936. I've had to leave out a number of less than amiable notes on Holland or, better, on Dutch conditions and characteristics, since the enormity of the events that have occurred since then would make misunderstandings inevitable. (1944.)" "Less than amiable" is quite an understatement. The misery and isolation that Hohl experienced during his years in The Hague deeply colored his view of the Dutch and more than a few insulting notes survived his culling. Dogs are another frequent target of his condescension, but this antipathy—along with his loathing of editors—he excuses as being both productive and objective in note VIII, 112:

> Do I write things that are filled with rage? Exaggerations that come only from rage are lifeless; instead, exaggerate and attack where you can be productive: I'm not persecuting people on their account. Faced with certain phenomena—like editors and dogs (in principle)—rage is *objective*.

Prickly notes on national stereotypes or chauvinistic remarks about women that were common currency in Hohl's time seemed an unnecessary distraction from the true core of this work, as did the sheer volume of his complaints about philistine pharmacists in section VIII. While he treasured the guileless receptivity of children, he was ruthlessly judgmental of people he considered inadequate parents. The notes censuring broad social groups for selfish procreation struck me as superfluous to his central argument. Similarly, his pronounced antipathy to Rilke, especially *The Book of Hours*, grows repetitive without offering new insight into Rilke's poetry or Hohl's interpretation of it. I cut those notes as well. I endeavored to keep enough to offer a sense of Hohl's less than amiable attitudes, while turning the reader's focus to notes that engage more creatively—by Hohl's own measure—with his main topics and themes.

I also eliminated notes that seemed too obscure for current readers. I pared down Hohl's extended discussions of lesser-known Swiss writers of the nineteenth and early twentieth centuries, along with his heated dismissals of dialect and works written in dialect. "Dialect impedes intellectual progress" (IX, 37) is one of many such pronouncements that did not make the cut.

Finally, I necessarily, but as judiciously as possible, sacrificed a number of worthy notes that address Hohl's essential themes. Variations and nuances have been lost as a result, but enough of these notes remain to provide a complex view of Hohl's literary-intellectual-spiritual enterprise.

The greatest challenge in translating the notes was rendering Hohl's dance between absolute clarity and concision and intentionally labyrinthine, even tortuous sentences—sentences that are choreographed to simultaneously express and challenge his thoughts as they trace his arduous mental struggle to refine and order his intuitions into coherent, consistent units.

I endeavored to retain his idiosyncratic punctuation as much as possible. The dash—in German *Gedankenstrich* means thought-line or thought-stroke—is used sparingly in English, but plays an active, even muscular, role in Hohl's texts. Sometimes he uses the em dash to bind or contrast two ideas more forcefully than a mere conjunction would.

Rapid change *is* possible—but not on command. (II, 260)

He frequently calls in a double em dash for special emphasis.

Yet imagination helps us with everything——helps us in the end even to imagine what we *have* (for that is the most difficult to imagine). (XII, 97)

It's tempting to see typographical symbols as notation in the dance of Hohl's intellect. Indeed, he enlists the gamut of punctuation marks almost as rhythmic markings. His one overt mention of punctuation appears in a note comparing it favorably to silence.

> Keeping silent acquires meaning only from the surrounding talk; it is like a punctuation mark, it cannot stand on its own. Like an em dash that binds two ideas.
>
> Punctuation marks are important; does this mean that those who have written poetry using only punctuation marks have written poems?—To be precise then, punctuation marks are more than simply keeping silent, because they allow for variations while just staying silent does not (there's the period's crude, earthy silence and the semi-colon's higher, more transparent silence, the comma's clear, plain, merely postponing silence, the deep, forceful, extensive silence of the ellipsis or the em dash's silence like an arrow shooting into the distance, among others); ordinary silence is equivalent to *one* punctuation mark repeated ad infinitum. (III, 7)

Five notes later, Hohl reinforces the notational aspect of silence and, by implication, of punctuation.

> I would like to sing the praises of eternal silence—but, to be precise, by this I mean Bach's music, Montaigne's talk, and other things that make a wonderful sound. (III, 12)

Hohl uses the colon not only to introduce an item or a list, but also to signify a kind of logical progression or intensification. In a discussion of the paralysis that grips a writer at the thought of not being understood, the colons in the final sentence emphasize the inevitable movement from lazy and conventional to all but dead, false, inadequate, and finally, inarticulate.

> This [paralysis] can occur even when writing a letter: you improve a passage and yet you know that you've made it less comprehensible to your correspondent . . . (What to do? Should you

restore the passage's previous version, a version you know to be
lazy—conventional: therefore in large part moribund: therefore
false: inadequate, sign language?) (IV, 15)

Whenever possible I tried to preserve the intricacies of Hohl's
style and the way his sentences' internal drama charts the path of his
thought. Nevertheless, it was occasionally necessary to delete dashes
and rearrange clauses for smoothness because as concentrated as
Hohl's prose is, it is rarely awkward or stumbling. German allows for
more flexibility than English in the ordering of sentence clauses, and
so permits more fleeting suspensions of Hohl's main thought.

> Die *ungeheure* Veränderung in meiner Denkweise soll nie ver-
> gessen werden: Einst hatte ich—erst in meinem dreißigsten Jahr
> wurde es mir klar—ohne es zu wissen dem Bürgertrug geglaubt,
> die Philosophen seien——für die Philosophie, und das Leben
> regiere sich selber, sei für das Leben, und ganz . . . ; und stehe
> der Philosophie, die als unabhängiger Luxus irgendwo installiert
> sei, *gegenüber!*

A literal translation preserves the sense of epiphany experienced by
the thirty-year-old Hohl, who had fully bought in to the bourgeois
mindset that relegates philosophers to the margins of life, but it creates a choppier sentence in which the reader could easily lose her way.

> The *tremendous* change in my way of thinking should never be
> forgotten: before I had—it only became clear to me in my thir-
> tieth year—swallowed whole the bourgeois delusion that phi-
> losophers were good for——philosophy and that life, which
> rules itself, is good for life and completely so . . . ; and philoso-
> phy, an independent luxury fixed somewhere outside life, is its
> *counterpart!*

My final version, while smoother, loses some of the impact of Hohl's
realization that he had allowed himself to be duped by the prevailing
bourgeois anti-intellectualism.

> The *tremendous* change in my way of thinking should never be
> forgotten: it only became clear to me in my thirtieth year that I
> had swallowed whole the bourgeois delusion that philosophers
> were good for——philosophy and that life, which rules itself, is
> good for life and completely so . . . ; and philosophy, an indepen-
> dent luxury fixed somewhere outside life, is life's *counterpart!*

I often found myself trying to strike a balance between semantic precision and accessibility while building a bridge between the German
and English syntaxes.

The density of thought and allusion in Hohl's individual notes
lends them a specific gravity that I sometimes despaired of preserving
in translation. I returned again and again to particular notes, or passages within a note, in an attempt to convey a new aspect or nuance
that had eluded me on previous readings, while avoiding any obtru-
sive explanation or interpretation of the note. One of the fragments
assembled in Note II, 264, under the heading "Fragments and Variations on the Central Issue," plays on various kinds of knowledge, recognition, apprehension, and comprehension.

> Wer weiß, ob nicht die Bäume in ihrem Geist das einzige Streben
> kennen, die Sonne zu erreichen (sie materiell zu berühren): da-
> raus entspringt ihre Form; man sieht endlich: ein schöner Baum.

Aside from the perennial difficulty of translating *Geist* into English
(we have no word that encompasses its various meanings; our equiva-
lents capture only certain aspects, such as mind, spirit, and intellect),
there are echoes of Rilke, Plato, and Goethe, to name the three most
obvious, that must be preserved. There is also an intertwining of the
physical and metaphysical worlds that is resolved through authentic
apprehension. And finally, the texture of the initial clause *Wer weiß,
ob nicht . . . das einzige* is rather unwieldy in English if translated
"straight." Hohl's German is complex, but not off-putting, and to be
true to his style, I replaced the negative *ob nicht* (if not) with "perhaps . . . but one kind." I felt it was essential to keep the colon after

man sieht endlich (one finally sees) because what we see is not just a beautiful tree, but a tree in its true physical and spiritual glory. In other words, we achieve truer vision.

> Who knows, perhaps trees recognize, in their spirit, but one kind of striving, to reach the sun (to touch it physically): whence their form; we finally see: a beautiful tree.

Only to the extent that we are able to recognize the spiritual striving of the plant world will we be able to truly see—and appreciate—it and its beauty. The ideal of striving might thus become our own. (Hohl repeatedly cites the chorus of angels at the end of *Faust II*: "He who ever strives / Him we can redeem.")

Hohl cites many of his touchstone authors, including Goethe (his "daily bread"), Kleist, Pascal, Balzac, Montaigne, Valéry, Lichtenberg, and others. Unless otherwise indicated, all translations are mine. In the somewhat idiosyncratic subject index drawn up by Hohl I have included only the notes contained in this edition. Faced with the intractability of the term *Geist*, I have retained it in German for the entry that covers the notes in which I've rendered it as spirit, mind, or intellect.

In German literature, Ludwig Hohl was a glacial erratic. He was an absolutist whose thinking was both thorough and provisional; in fact, it was thorough precisely *because* it was provisional. He never ceased reexamining his statements and observations, refining and qualifying them, observing how they changed in different contexts and testing them to see whether they grew weaker or stronger through repetition. An accomplished scaler of peaks, he saw many parallels between mountaineering and serious thought. As his philosophical novella *Ascent* illustrates, he believed the view from the peak to be important, but more impactful and formative is the climb, and the spirit with which one approaches the mountain most crucial of all. Our perspective is always skewed, always partial. Ideas, like mountains, are there to be scaled repeatedly.

In this volume abridged by necessity, we cannot follow Hohl from the very deepest and narrowest of valleys to the highest peaks, but we can, nearly step for step, follow his arduous journey upward with its setbacks and switchbacks, endure the gusts of inclement weather, marvel at the unexpected sights, and finally reach an elevation sufficient to appreciate the magnitude of his achievement.

Tess Lewis

The Notes

The Notes were written over a period of three years, from 1934 to 1936. At the time I was living in Holland in a state of extreme spiritual desolation. The original manuscript, finished in early 1937, was significantly longer than the final version and presented the texts in chronological order. In the following years, I reworked the manuscript strictly by theme, with no regard for the date of each note's composition. (The last note of Part XII, for example, was written before the first note of Part I.) The notes' distribution, therefore, followed the principle of simultaneity insofar, of course, as that is at all possible in practice. This new method of organization sprang from my desire to give structure to the whole—a structure almost no one seems to have recognized to this day. The process of selecting, ordering, and cutting the notes was a long one. The new material added during that process (primarily footnotes) consists of only a few pages: an insignificant amount compared with the whole.

Due to unpleasant circumstances, the entire work was never previously published in a single volume. Parts I through VI appeared in a first volume in 1944; parts VII through XII in a second volume in 1954. This division was completely arbitrary and must have given readers the impression that the second volume was a sort of appendage to the first or at least was written later. Over the past few years, various sections have been published separately and have completely obscured any sense of the whole. And yet the work—such as it is—cannot be fully comprehended if one has not grasped its unity. This is not a collection of aphorisms.

If the reader, after extensive engagement with the work, still fails to understand the subtitle—*On Non-premature Reconciliation*—he would be well advised to put the book down, at least for a time.

I recognized that my style is often laconic long before I was criticized for it. And I have to admit that it's precisely the most concise passages I tend to prefer.—I was never swayed by considering whether or not a passage was complicated or novel enough or suitably "poetic" for certain people. For me, it was about something else altogether . . . : a phrase's incandescence, perhaps, or its firmness.

Criticism, as it is generally practiced, whether laudatory or damning, is mere diversion.—When critics summarily dismiss this work—as too muddled or too laconic, too dark or too sensuous, too autodidactic or too literary, too shapeless or overly constructed—I happily turn to the lines from Goethe that I chose almost forty-five years ago as an epigraph for the finished manuscript of *The Notes:*

> Sie sagen, das mutet mich nicht an!
> Und meinen, sie hätten's abgetan.

> They say, "It don't please me a bit!"
> And then believe they're done with it.

Ludwig Hohl
Geneva, October 1980

I

ON WORK

Ψυχῆς ἐστι λόγος ἑαυτὸν αὔξων

Heraclitus

1

Human life is short.

It's a fatal mistake to believe—or, more exactly, to preserve the childish belief—that life is long. If we were constantly aware of the brevity of our lives, everything would be very different.

Life certainly appears long from the perspective of childhood; considered from its end, it seems incredibly brief. Which is its actual duration? It depends how early and how often you've considered your life brief.

(A life is not measured by the clock, but by what it contained.)

For our actions to be worthwhile, we must undertake them fully conscious of life's brevity.

If we lose this awareness, we may appear active but will live in a perpetual state of *expectation* (in most cases, external forces compel us to engage in apparent busyness and leave us no escape). However, if you maintain complete consciousness of life's ephemerality, your primary desire will be to *do* something immediately (—and with a very different kind of seriousness than the one with which you do things when governed by external forces). Yet it is only *doing* of this sort—activity you engage in out of inner compulsion and not because of external pressures—that gives life, that can save.

Precisely *this* kind of action is what I call work.

For the sake of clarity, I will insert this passage (from *Nuances and Details* II, 51). Although not a definition in the sense that it explains the essence of work, it functions like a definition in that it ruthlessly excludes everything I do not recognize as work.

"Work is always an internal process; and it must always be directed outward. Activity that is not directed outward is not work; activity that is not an internal process is not work."

Then the passage specifies that it can be directed outward in several senses: "But what if internal matters, internal zones of work are involved? Then the activity must be directed outward relative to the internal: this interior becomes exterior again. (Thus clarity is an exteriorization of the unclear, thought an exteriorization of presentiment, the spoken word an exteriorization of thought.)"

As an illustration: the artist X, who for three months has been preoccupied only with the "movements of his soul" instead of creating visible works—after he has reached a point at which he is able to create visible works, of course—is not working. Conversely, Mr. Average, whose activity for the last ten years has been similar to that of a mill grinding, is not working: his activity is not an internal process.

I have addressed what constitutes an internal process in other passages. (To put it succinctly, the activity must be dictated by necessity.)

I point in particular to the following lines in *Nuances and Details* (II, 11):

"Are circumstances preventing you from deploying your activity? Then put effort into changing the circumstances: that will be your activity."

To conclude this brief clarification of what leads to work and the practice of it, it seems worth citing that passage again but in full:

"What is missing in the 'depths of our soul' I'd propose, are *colorful images:* that is what ails us.[1] It is up to us to decide which way we will take to reach these *colorful images.* There is truly only *one* way and a hundred false paths. (Most of the false paths consist of hoping for some kind of happiness, of *waiting* for happiness in one way or another.) The right way is to deploy our activity to the fullest extent that we can, taking into account the means at our disposal (the circumstances in which

---

1. I subsequently came across this sentence in Katherine Mansfield's correspondence: "For it seems to me that we live on new impressions—really new ones."

we find ourselves) and the effect we have on others (as well as on ourselves). A bit of knitting will not suffice (if it did, we would be pitiful beings indeed). Are circumstances preventing you from deploying your activity? Then put effort into changing the circumstances: that will be your activity. Surely we should, as the book of Jonah teaches us, be 'merciful' with our nature (with *all* of nature), that is, we should not hope to overwhelm it (the great change we dream of will only come in its *own* time), we should let it 'rest' (a provisional term for the sake of brevity); but there is only *one* right way . . ."

2

This person refuses to work. We can offer him this or that object, use every means of influence in our power—: work is the only realm in which no one can help another.

We can help each other with sowing and mowing, with copying, with moving one's limbs or one's tongue, with all such actions, but not with work.

3

What does human worth consist in then, in this world of perpetual flux?

Still, this difficulty in determining human worth is only an apparent difficulty; this ostensibly serious question is an illusory one. It is a question asked by those who are not *in place*; of what interest is it to them? A swindle! Those who are *in place* see it more clearly. Human worth consists in *the desire for worth*.

Yet we must immediately caution against two misconceptions—unclear thinking that leads to confusion:

First, wanting worth is not the same as simply *saying* one wants it (just as love has nothing to do with prattling on *about* love).

Second, wanting worth is not the same as wanting to amass worth, to fatten up, to gain power.

(In primitive times, these two may well have been the same, just as they still are among animals. The constant, fundamental underlying urge is surely to live *more*, to live a larger life. Nonetheless, human consciousness has been developing for thousands of years and man has been aware for millennia now that it is impossible to acquire a greater quantity of life by increasing his weight, mass, or physical strength. Those who want worth cannot desire it disingenuously, in other words, they can never act *in disregard of levels of consciousness already achieved*.)

—Wanting worth is not the same as saying one wants worth: but it is the same as working.

And yet, how would I be understood, today, in our era of *dervishes*, if I were to say: "Human worth consists in working":

Tourne, tourne, le derviche!	Spin, spin, dervish!
Que la force centrifuge	May centrifugal force
Cravache aux quatres horizons	Spur his arms, his eyes, his reason
Ses bras, ses yeux, sa raison!	To the four directions of the wind!

(Fernand Lot)

—in our era, when turning in a circle for ten hours at a stretch or treading the floor until it wears away is considered work?

It's important to emphasize the fact that most people don't flee work into laziness—not into apparent laziness—but take refuge in completely moribund busyness rather than simple immobility. True laziness these days consists in dead movement.

In some cases, apparent utter immobility would surely be preferable, because legitimate movement can break out of it, can find a new beginning in it.

"Activity, movement": is work, then, not the same as movement (and movement, therefore, also the same as work)?

Work is movement . . . , but it is *our* movement. We have the fatal ability to mimic others, a water wheel, for example.

A real water wheel works as it turns: because turning is *its own particular* motion, its complete possibility. Even a cat works as it moves, is completely present in its movements, progresses through its movements. As do children above all. He who does not completely grasp the elevated praise of children in the New Testament—one of the most peculiar and perhaps most modern passages in this fascinating scripture that has been more powerful than any other book for almost two thousand years—, he who fails to fully understand this immediate, unmediated, intensive praise of children but feels compelled to struggle for an explanation—such toilsome explication being roughly the opposite of complete comprehension—, he, too, has failed to understand what work is.

4

We build. And yet we have no idea where the general contractor is. Fulfill only your particular task, which you can surely find.

5

In the realm of art:

"Aren't there influences there that could hinder your development?"

—When I am hard at work, nothing can hinder me.

6

All work tends to change, of its own accord, to a state in which it no longer is work.

The task of the true worker is therefore above all to effect this change, to always be aware of the precise moment when this change is necessary.

As has often been said and must always be repeated, most people have fled from work not into immobility, but into utterly moribund movement.

7

They hurry to the train station in a mad rush and climb onto a freight train. Rarely do we see anyone walk very slowly and then take an express train.

8

We cannot live in a way that is neither positive nor negative but neutral, latent, expectant—we cannot "simply live"; no more can we use words that are neither our own nor someone else's. But when you are not living positively—living your own life—you are *already* living negatively—living the life of another. Just as a word used by me that is not *my* word, is already plagiarism.[2]

9

"Lord, give each his own death!" Rilke cried.

I would rather have heard, "Give each his own work." (And the expression "one's own work" is one I'm adapting here because what I call work is always individual.) "Give?" The question is who should give it. Why do we need someone to hand it out since those who work already have it? (Aside from the fact that gods are not wont to give men the work that befits them, quite the opposite.)

One's own death . . .—that is wonderful, perhaps the highest thing one can attain. Yet the question remains, how can one attain it? One's own death—yes, that is a coronation: but what good is calling out to someone: "Get yourself crowned!" Shouldn't you instead show him the way that leads to coronation?

Your own work will necessarily lead to your own death.

---

2. By "my word" I mean one for which I am fully responsible. Cf. VI, 30.

10

Method:

Immersing oneself in things: let swimming be a metaphor for this! To act without jolts or collisions. Wild thrashing, especially on land, is useless. Better to begin immediately even if gingerly. The element will support you and that is the main point.

What makes for a good swimmer is not strength, but trust in the element, trust *that has already become physical.*

(The best swimmer is the one who can immerse himself in the element with the most confidence. Fish shoot like arrows using little strength.)

11

Activities must follow hard one upon the other, must be intertwined with the next.

My acquaintance X once claimed that you must find a new woman before your relationship with the former has ended. That, at least, is true of one's productions.

12

This is why one should never stop working:

External circumstances, favorable or not, inhibiting or inspiring, are constantly alternating and doing so in a completely unpredictable fashion. A long period of almost debilitating difficulty may be followed almost immediately by an extremely productive phase. Anyone who has not kept in constant practice during this fallow period — even if only the most modest, perhaps only imperceptible, results could be expected! — will need *time* to find himself in the changed circumstances and to become active. He will have become rusty, as it were. And in the meantime, the favorable circumstances may well have disappeared (aren't the most splendid economic cycles the most ephemeral?). In any case, the loss is a frightening one.[3]

13

Mr. Jones: a gentleman who likes to claim that he has his feet on solid ground.[4]

14

Once I finally managed to define Mr. Jones—as the man who announces during some non-event: that is, not when crossing a swamp or a river (at least then such an announcement would have some significance) nor when crossing a maze of glacier crevasses made treacherous by a layer of fresh snow, but rather upon hearing that a new planet has been discovered or during a discussion of Johann Sebastian Bach, of art dealers made rich by Van Gogh, of the meaning of dreams: the man, then, who announces during some complete non-event that *he has his feet on solid ground*—I reflected deeply on what it signifies.

This "solid ground" does not mean the physical ground. Nor does it mean *real* ground: the ground we construct for ourselves. (Because we don't picture that ground as being beneath our feet, but on those rare occasions when we think about it, it hovers before us on some distant horizon.) His solid ground cannot be any ground at all.

3. The hare sped past in an instant and the lazy hunters called for their guns.—One day a passing school of fish was spotted. But the fishermen, who had been indulging in food and wine, first had to repair their nets, search for their equipment, caulk their leaky boats.—No one knows at what hour of the night the bridegroom will come. Suddenly he appears and behold: those who were meant to greet him had fallen asleep; their lamps had gone out.

4. Hohl uses "Mr. Jones" as shorthand for a kind of Mr. Average, a common bourgeois, a figure not quite as objectionable as the "pharmacist" who symbolizes the consummate bourgeois philistine. (Trans. note.)

Having figured it out, I must summon the courage to say it. It signifies that Mr. Jones will never, *under any circumstances, engage in work.* But expressed in his appalling way. How was I able to penetrate the colossal inanity of his statement and get to what actually must be said? Indeed, I'm almost surprised myself. (Someone talks of having his "feet on solid ground" and we ascertain first, that he's not talking about earthly things, but about the region that is difficult to access, the invisible realm of real life and second, that in this context what should be said is almost exactly the opposite of what words can express, twist and turn them as you will!) I am absolutely sure of my conclusion, there is no possible doubt. The context of this obscure formulation—by which I mean the external circumstances, because there was no actual context—the fact that in many different circumstances Mr. Jones's facial expression, tone, attitude, remained exactly the same, suddenly made it all clear to me; and I had a hundred opportunities to verify my conclusion.

15

I have never seen a triune unity or trinity as one but have often seen a dual unity or two as one. Whenever you want to see or expect to see one of the two mysteriously connected faces of these things, then it's almost always the other one that is facing you; and in those moments when one gives way to the other, they shimmer together, one in the other.

These two essences were: doing and knowing, knowing and doing, as they are conjoined in work.

And once again, work with regard to place: "work is always an internal process; and it must always be directed outward."

16

When they hear someone claim that, say, this way of writing is easier than that way or that hoarding money one's entire life long is easier than actually producing something, they call out: "Well then, if it's easier, do it!"

When I say that climbing Mount Everest or even the Aiguille Doran is harder than trotting around the world, they say "so, first trot around the world, then we'll believe you."

I'd have to trot around a good many things if I were to go all the places idiots tell me to.

17

No one can work in several places at once.

To push off, you need ground solid enough to offer resistance. When a fitter climbs a ladder in order to install something in the ceiling, you can't change anything at the ladder's feet at the same time unless you're prepared for him to fall. If one of our actions effects creative changes—that is, work—then our other actions in daily life must be purely routine—that is, the opposite of work—so that they provide a *foundation* that makes work possible. It is a matter of uniting and focusing all our abilities in *one* area—the one in which we can achieve our best results—and not expending any energy, or as little as possible, on other areas (secondary duties) that require attention. In other words, it means that our mundane tasks should be completed *automatically.*

This immediately brings to mind Immanuel Kant, an extremely productive man—that is to say, an extraordinary worker—who is said to have to have risen at five o'clock and gone to bed at ten o'clock every day for over thirty years. And every day he passed the same house at exactly the same time, so that people called him "the clock." It would be too easy and short-sighted to attribute this lifestyle to a natural penchant for pedantry. In fact, it was closely associated with his immense capacity for work. An examination of all lives filled with extraordinary work will reveal similarities. (Here we throw a passing glance at the habits of Rodin, Cézanne, Balzac, and Spinoza;

Thomas Mann's work habits were also said to be highly "pedantic.") In some districts of large cities, as in Montparnasse, you occasionally come across sensational artistic types. Nothing in their appearance is conservative; their lives are a series of innocent scandals. Lenin did not resemble them in the least but instead worked in libraries for years, almost decades, filling notebooks with miniscule handwriting, and lived an outwardly bourgeois life. Yet he changed the world. Cézanne, the most revolutionary of artists, led the life of an anxious little pensioner, withdrawn, sparing of gesture, yes, almost sparing of . . . spirit. Fireworks shoot off in all directions. The cannon is calm and precise.

How does Mrs. Jones spend her day? (Mrs. Jones who, especially in northern European countries and in the moneyed classes, has many sisters.) She devotes herself to running her household. And this household is lavish! That is, not really; it's quite small, in fact, and once the meals have been seen to and the housekeeping more or less completed, then she has accomplished all that can reasonably done. Nonetheless, for Mrs. Jones, running the household is a creative activity! No task is completed automatically. Mrs. Jones is always making alterations from the way she cooks the meals and shops, to the arrangement of the carpets. There is always something provisional about her household. She changes the sequence of her tasks and also the order of steps in each individual task so that complications, surprises, novelty arise constantly. Through this inventive, creative way of fulfilling her duties, she does in fact spend ten hours a day running her household even if it is only a household of two in a small apartment, and even if she has a maid. On top of it all she complains about the amount of work she has to do.[5] It's a disgrace.

5. We're familiar with the explanations along the lines of: "That's beyond Mrs. Jones' scope . . . , we also need simple, common folk . . . , etc." They are wrong. We also need simple folk: did I claim that Mrs. Jones should be greater than she is capable of being? Did I claim that Mrs. Jones should have written Goethe's works? Creative

Someone is always ready to object that Mrs. Jones spends her days this way because she doesn't have anything important, doesn't have any real work to do. But I counter with the objection—an objection that is every bit as valid—that precisely because she spends her time in this way, she will never be able to find a higher occupation or anything real to do. All of her better energies are used up, squandered. One can waste one's creative energies at any point, even when one is not creative. There is only one hope for Mrs. Jones: a powerful external constraint though some kind of imprisonment (which Mrs. Jones manufactures for herself to a certain extent by making herself ill).

[. . .]

It is true everywhere and always: as soon as processes are automated to a certain level, creative energies (energy as such) emerge on a higher level.

One day, in prehistoric times, a creature invented the first machine, or more exactly: found, discovered (it was, no doubt, the lever). Can we assume that he discovered it because he was more intelligent than the other creatures? No, instead he found it by chance (this *first* opportunity to mechanize some of his necessary tasks): but as soon as it was at his disposal, he *became* more intelligent than his fellow creatures. That is, his powers were no longer limited to the level on which that mechanization occurred and he could put them to use on the next highest level. In other words, his powers had become— compared to those of the creatures he left behind, the wholly animal—what we call *creative*. They were put to use on a different level, and yet were nonetheless the same powers that animals employ in vain with their endless, nearly fruitless pawing. (While the creature

---

work, in the universal sense in which I understand it, is not limited to those who work on the most elevated levels, but includes everyone, each to his abilities. Mrs. Jones, too, could lead a worthy life—it is not only possible, it is imperative that she lead a worthy life, it is such an absolute necessity that it has made her ill for years. Because her soul is ailing, she suffers constant physical complaints no doctor can heal. (None of those doctors who examine Mrs. Jones' spleen, but not her life.)

that is fully animal will spend days trying to move the rock that has fallen in front of his cave—scratching and scraping, pushing and shoving—the creature who has found the lever can dispose of it in a moment and put his powers to other uses.)

18

Human work, work that can change the world, is performed in three stages:

1. the great idea
2. the individual conceptions of the overarching idea. Or, rather, the application of the great idea in smaller ideas, in parts of the whole
3. the individual application of these smaller ideas.

In short: the great idea, the smaller ideas, the small acts.

Unfortunately, most people never move beyond the first of these three stages; they remain stuck on the great idea or simply on some aspect of the great idea; it takes on a hue of "idealism," of fantasy. Think of the Church and the masses it renders inactive. Benjamin Constant saw this clearly when he wrote, "Fools turn their morality into a compact, indivisible whole, so that it will interfere as little as possible with their conduct and leave them free in all matter of details."

—Are these three stages meant to represent the whole of human activity? They do; there is nothing else.—Where then can we find the great act?

"Does the great act follow of its own accord?" No. It has already occurred.

19

The smaller ideas that come from a great idea are therefore situated on a higher level and the individual actions that come from the smaller ideas are, in turn, higher still, assuming that they, too, came from a great idea.

Fools will say, "Hmm, and the highest of all is the great act?" To put it as clearly as possible: No great act *has yet* been committed, that is, a great act that is other than what has been described; the third of the three stages is the highest stage, the culmination. The three stages are simply the three human stages that, together, constitute the great act.

As an example, let us look at the great act that consists in building an unusual structure:

You have a magnificent idea for a building—the vision of a magnificent structure (and who hasn't *at least once* seen in his dreams a majestic building, whether a palace or a cathedral?); that is the first stage. And the majority of people advance no further, fashioning a comfortable relation with the vision they call an "ideal" and which is far removed and quite separate from what are considered serious matters (the way a mountain is separated from others by a deep valley). ("Fools turn their morality into a compact, indivisible whole . . .") That vision is not taken any more seriously than the art of baking pastry, decorative icing, lavish ornamentation that, as they say, "prettify" life or make it more "agreeable," but are never able to effect any changes where life is miserable and beauty sorely needed, where there is great suffering and relief is needed.

You convert your great idea into individual ideas (that are not large at all!); that is the second stage and one that is, in fact, rarely reached. *This* is how *this* wall will be and this is how the roof will be and this the threshold; 20 cm, 85 cm, 2 meters 65, 7 × 33, an angle of 42 degrees. Yet all these measurements—there are no exceptions!— must be those of a building that befits the magnificent idea, not just any house! The threshold cannot be *just any* threshold! The thickness of the walls, the length of each beam, all the measurements must tally and together yield the magnificent building, not just any structure.

Then you complete the threshold, the walls, the doors, everything, the way they were drawn up in the individual ideas (and here "drawn" can be understood in its literal sense). That is the third stage. Its completion, as everyone knows, consists exclusively of innumerable tedious and *ordinary* small acts. When all the small acts have been done and the windows and railings have been installed, is there some great act left that must be completed? What would it be?

This teaching may strike those not given to reflection as banal. I believe that telling the young this again and again is not so much useful, as of vital importance and that there is perhaps more love for humanity in this lesson than in any other. The moral of this teaching is nothing other than the dominant thread running through Goethe's work, at least of the late Goethe. *Who* might accomplish the great act if it were to be realized exactly as the young imagine it? It *isn't* so hard, we're not so lost, so dependent on chance, on "luck" — no, we can make manifest more or less what we are. ("He who ever strives . . .")

"The heights charm us, not the steps to reach them; with our eyes on the summit, we are happy to walk along the plain." But who would reach the summit, if they had to do so in one great act, that is, without stages, without steps (in other words, in one great leap)? — And he who has reached the summit by stages, must he still accomplish the great act?

20

Once more:[6]

6. Doesn't this representation of human work with a clear three-stage structure contradict other statements I've made on the same subject, such as the passage in which I speak of work as an inscrutable duality of interiority and exteriority? — You can always present different structures of the same subject. A house may be divided into cellar, ground floor, first floor, and so on, yet at the same time it is comprised of cement, stone, wood, and iron: where is the contradiction? You can view Mont Blanc from Courmayeur and from Chamonix; and you can see it properly from Chamonix and badly from Courmayeur, or badly from Chamonix and properly from Courmayeur. An aviator, on the other hand, will see the mountain as an utterly different

The great idea,
The small ideas,
The small acts,
—and no fourth stage, nothing else.

(You have the great idea to change your life [and doesn't almost everyone have it?]; well then, divide this great idea into appropriate parts [how many manage to do even this?]; accomplish each of these things [slowly, one after the other, according to your opportunities, to *your* abilities alone]. Your life will be changed.)

I can anticipate the objection. In my mind's eye, I see a man slowly shaking his head (not entirely side to side or up and down) as he states his objection: much of what you say is true and may well apply perfectly to daily existence; yet in history, particularly in world history, there are situations in which *only* a great act is possible, indeed, is essential, a truly great act, that cannot be called anything else, and not individual acts! Instead, a concentration of powers that are otherwise employed in different directions into a synthesis, in *one* instant, that becomes a kind of explosion, a leap. (Think of a Napoleonic battle, etc.)

—I refute this as well. That great acts exist in a certain sense is absolutely clear and cannot be denied: they exist when seen from a distance. We, who are far removed, see in it a great act. But in reality, from close up, while it was taking place, things were completely different. May our powers of observation grow! The hero of history did not prepare himself for a leap: the many moments—the small acts—he strung together carried him toward the act: the final moment required no more gravity from him than any of his preceding acts. (This corresponds to what I have said elsewhere: writing *The Ethics* was not difficult for Spinoza at the point he had reached.) The many moments that lay behind one surely exert at times pressure strong enough to give rise to a further remarkable moment in world history (which is then succeeded by another long series of anonymous moments), although without requiring from the actor any kind of *leap* in that world historical moment: he merely performs a single, precise act, just as he had before. This becomes particularly clear

---

expanse. Nonetheless, all three observers can deepen our understanding of Mont Blanc. Furthermore, the alpinist examines the mountain for possible ascents, differentiating between an easily traversed flank, a difficult ridge, an inaccessible rock face. The geologist, in turn, offers us a very different picture with no consideration of how it can be climbed.—And yet, it still Mont Blanc.

when we consider the declaration made by one of the most powerful revolutionaries in a decisive moment: "Here I stand; *I cannot do otherwise.*"

Oh, fellow humans, my friends, life is not that hard!

21

There are always a few who spend their lives striving to become part of History. Everyone becomes a part of History without even trying.

22

Yes, yes, I'm told, all this (with the three stages) is already well-known, perfectly obvious, clear as day. (I don't need to add that my conversational partner is Mr. Jones, the pharmacist.)

Suitably well-known, then?

—Of course. (He turns up his nose, gives me a haughty, put-upon look.)

—Completely clear and true and obvious? Doable, in other words?

—(He gestures without a word.)

—In that case, why are you still such a bumbler?

23

This person limits himself to particulars and changes the whole. That one preaches the universal and alters neither the whole nor the particular.

24

I am not afraid of repeating myself one more time: after the three stages mentioned above, there is no great act. This is the sentence I would like to see etched in stone, not simply written on paper.

. . . the idea that the fourth stage is a great act is a *delusion*, the delusion that has caused the most harm. Only the short-sighted are unable to perceive its true measure. Why is John Doe still such a sad case, such a nullity, so—*worthless?* He says: "If only *everyone* would do this or that . . . (not go to war, live differently, or some such), but what can one single person do? (If the great act were accomplished, were fulfilled, well then, of course . . .)" And he remains the same old John Doe, such a very sad case, so negligible, so worthless. (A man who, like most others, doesn't lift a finger, who changes absolutely nothing, leaves nothing behind.)

John Doe is a man who plays no part in the world and accordingly leaves nothing behind when he dies. Nevertheless, he had a great idea, John Doe did, he desired it ardently! We cannot participate in the world through a great idea, through ardent desire. *It is impossible.*

25

The shield of Achilles shines, as do those of ancient warriors—shines through the centuries. Up close, its luster was dimmed by dust and sweat and blood. What is it that gleams in the man who acts? Only his faith, his distant vision . . . ; never the visible, the detail, or what is close by. The single steps that make great ascents possible are each unspeakably difficult.

I have seen men on mountaintops. Any claim that their climb was easy is vanity and falsehood.

Each step is an overcoming of resistance and each of these defeats brings pain.

26

From high elevations:

On my high-altitude ascents, I don't believe I ever took a single step with joy. That could be an image of the whole.

I could certainly be filled with happiness, with joy, at the thought of the whole, that is, of the goal and meaning of the ascent, of undertaking the ascent, of the climb itself. The individual steps are simply arduous. It is the same with writing: I don't remember a time when each of the intermediate steps—sitting down (sitting down *again!*), picking up my pen, in short, each element—was not arduous.

In some cases, however, the arduousness could be overpowered, masked by the contentment that comes from considering the whole, and its effects suspended—just as the arduousness of the individual steps on a mountain climb can be drowned out.

The only thing one can hope for is that the details of the individual steps are so well integrated in the whole that they occur almost unconsciously.

Those who deny this have no memory. Or they lack the capacity for rigorous observation in the most complex and immediate situations.

I have no doubt about why the individual steps of a high-altitude ascent are so arduous compared to the entire climb. The whole is new, the individual step is old.—Only what is new, what is transformative and productive brings man joy. Only life delights life. (Death brings no joy to life.)—We make something new in part of old bricks: in this case, of steps.

27

. . . Nearly frightened to death, he turned away from the ridge and began his descent; and only as he made his way downward, half-hour by half-hour, did the stupor of fear gradually abate.—What had occurred? A figure had emerged from behind the bare ridge. A figure emerged even though he knew very well that no one could be there. No one had been there, no one had reached the ridge but he; he alone had followed the paths that circled the mountain, without end or number, that came from many directions, that began anew and multiplied in higher elevations, winding extensively through the mountain range, ceaseless paths that had finally led him up to this topmost ridge at the extreme edge of earth and sky . . .

As time passed, he forgot the incident—partly. But the ceaseless paths had not died out; they led him on, or he led them. They increased again, rose up, in ever greater number, rising ever higher as time passed. They grew in *number* and spiraled ever higher up the mountain.—He wanted to follow these *paths*; he couldn't not want them. He had forgotten the incident on the ridge.—And finally, spiraling ever higher, they led him back to the same ridge. (It took a long time, but in the end, they finally led him *there*; they couldn't lead him anywhere else.) But there . . . a figure emerged.

And he fled again. He hurried down the mountain, but not with such haste, not driven by as a great a fear as the first time. When he had gone some distance, he dared look back: the man on the crest had disappeared.

This occurred many times until he could finally bring himself to remain on the ridge and look.

Then he recognized himself in the figure.

And yet, this person was another who doubled the climber. He acted independently of this figure; he was able to look in another direction; he had been given a new power and would necessarily change the world.

It was not just a reflection, his double, but also—his son.

28

Egoism is not another world—just a smaller one. It is not the opposite of going out into the world but a preliminary phase.

"My longing has grown too great to find fulfillment on earth— that is, in *my* life. Therefore, I must necessarily turn toward others. And toward THINGS," says the wise man.

29

What is highest?
I don't need to give this question a moment's thought. True work.
—And perception?
—True work is perception.
—The highest knowledge?
—Most true work *is* the highest knowledge.

The highest is its synonym, just as genius is another word for consummate socialism. Just as miracle and creative power are one and the same.

30

Under certain circumstances, when it serves one's interests, harming another can be a positive act. Harming another when it does not serve one's interest is always a negative act.

Only a stupid man will do the latter. —An "evil" man? Evil is a derivative concept; no one is certain what it means; it changes from one period to another, from one place to another. "Stupid" is a primary concept.

"Under certain circumstances": namely, when one ends up in a position of achieving a greater result than the other, unharmed, would have been capable of achieving.

31

The truly active man cannot be presumptuous. Presumption sets in only when the actions are incomplete, when they begin to show their flaws.

32

When an action applies only to me or only to another, it is not a positive action. It is not work.

For a positive action applies to the best result I can achieve, through me alone or through others or both, but sooner or later always *for* me *and* for others, for others and for me.

33

He who does good only for recompense is just as lost, or perhaps even more lost, than one who does ill for profit. The latter is short-sighted, the former a fool.

34

The inactive man can only end up enraged or ill.

"Inactive": to a large extent insufficiently active. For no one is ever consummately active; nor is any one completely inactive either.

"Enraged or ill": depending on one's character, whether one tends to be more irascible and uninhibited or cultivated and channeled by ethics.

35

In a letter I wrote "X. has put himself in a *losing position*," and meant that if I were to hear that further misfortunes had befallen him, I wouldn't be the least surprised since they would be nothing other than the natural, the expected outcome; I meant that this person was in a situation where he could only lose. The situation was as follows: for several years X. had more and more come to *expect* something, had become ever more inclined to wait for some advantageous external change that would improve his life. Although the only external advantage we can expect with impunity is the opportunity and instruments to increase an activity we are (already) engaged in, the aforementioned person had handed the world a bill implying that the world owed him something and was therefore obligated to repay him, in other words to reward him through personal relations, new circumstances, all from outside, through others.

36

The world consists of roads, of which only very few have been traveled. All the impalpable space around you is filled with roads that you cannot recognize as such. We do not need to build roads.

Having the courage to recognize one of these roads is an accomplishment.

37

Others always talk of Hölderlin's "fate" and his tragedy. And yet, Hölderlin is one of the rare victors . . .

38

In the end I still believe in one thing: the world. THE WORLD IS THE GREATEST OF ALL PERSONALITIES.

39

Men improve themselves slightly and late.
Even so, some do improve themselves.
The others . . . let it go.

40

One knows perfectly well if one is working or not.

41

And then he discovered a new intoxication, that of work.

42

One who truly works can no longer stop working.[7]

43

"Vivre avilit" (Living debases), wrote Henri de Régnier in a poem and this phrase was highly praised, was called "fulgurant" (searing). This strikes me as false.

The phrase does indeed have a superficial, a proverbial accuracy. It is accurate when applied to what most men *call* living and thus can serve as a sort of testimony about this type of "living." To atrophy (to dwindle, to waste away) makes you ugly. Living leads to the exact opposite, the increase of all things, including beauty. Indeed, most people lead another kind of existence and are unable to rise to action, unable to receive the countless images that flow toward us, augmenting our being.

Perhaps we can still recall what another, more famous old man said about the course of life: one grows *older*, not *wiser*. Is it any surprise that these words come from the elderly Hamsun? To this great poet's[8] opinion, I will contrast the saying of a third old man who was no less of a poet than Hamsun and most certainly a greater spirit:

"It wouldn't be worth reaching the age of seventy if all the world's wisdom were nonsense before God."[9]

---

7. This sentence also strikes me as at once the freest and the most exact translation of Heraclitus's *"The Logos of the soul is one that increases itself"* (115). Eva Brann, *The Logos of Heraclitus* (Philadelphia: Paul Dry Books, 2011). [Trans. note: This is the epigraph to this section, which Hohl left untranslated in his edition.]

8. I'm thinking here of those several wonderful pages in his endless stories.

9. Goethe, *Maxims and Reflections.*

44

There are two fundamental misconceptions about knowledge: first, that you can impart it (the way you pass on names or scientific theorems); second, that you can preserve it (in your memory or on your bookshelves).

45

That we can't take anything from our lives into death is something everyone knows. Yet who knows the equally important truth that we haven't brought anything of any *value* into our lives? The only thing anyone could bring are conditions; value, if one desires it, must be *generated*, hour by hour, minute by minute.

Because value cannot be preserved. This is precisely the meaning of all change: the constant renewal of value that cannot be preserved.

You burn: the flame is the value.

46

And that is why the only ones who deserve our sympathy are those who still desire change although all change is for naught—they desire it *in order to maintain what is unchanging*.

47

You cannot know something completely and not act. Knowledge turns *imperceptibly* into action.

We so often hear the statement "he knows perfectly well, but he doesn't do it." More cheap wisdom, easy on the ears of the unthinking, fundamentally untrue.

"J. himself *knows* it all, he knows that his relationship with this girl is not good for him, that the cost is too high, that he would do better to end it."

—No, he doesn't know it. Or else what does "to know" mean? If J. were to recognize clearly that the relationship is not good for him, he would end it and do so without difficulty. However, since he is clinging to the relationship only these two cases are possible:

Either he has not reached the point of recognizing what we know; or he sees something we don't that is inseparable from the situation.

48

We know that there is nothing higher than knowledge. But it is absurd to shout at someone: "Know!" Knowledge is the summit, but what are the paths leading to it? For the mountain climber on the plains, there is nothing more wonderful than the summit; and yet his thoughts are concentrated solely on the path. What is the path for one who wants to reach the summit of life? Doing the right thing!

But which act is most right? When you are young you are faced with so many!—So seize one in which you see what is right! What is right in this act will expand and become a beacon that will guide you to what is even more right.

49

Variation:

What is clearer to me than anything else: there is nothing higher than knowledge and mankind's only true salvation lies in knowledge:

But to then tell someone "Know!" and believe you have accomplished something is sheer delusion.

It is essential to do the right thing; *Work is the realization of knowledge.* Fed with knowledge, work feeds knowledge in turn. Knowledge does not feed itself.

50

We know through our senses. Yet the point of all our senses is to act.

51

True work would be like the melody of an organ if the melody of an organ were to create ever more and ever greater organs.

Yet how can it be that all this suddenly ends in death?

This—is not at all the case. After all, in connecting with everything we have ever more of the opposite of death. Work is nothing other than translating what is mortal into what continues.

II

ON THE ACCESSIBLE AND THE INACCESSIBLE

(Mankind–Development, Transformation, The Historical–Education–Relations,
The Social–The Biological)

> Ordering and classification are the beginning of mastery and the truly dreadful enemy is the unknown.
>
> *Thomas Mann*

1

Where is the path?—
Give it your all! Then it will be easy.

2

Of the two great principles, some see only the one: that there must be change. They live solely in *this* impulse to change, as if it were the first and only and most perfecting principle, and they rise and fall with it: that is the simplicity of youth.

Others, in contrast, see a chain of innumerable changes that have already occurred and through it all they see the immutable. They believe, in the end, that the will to change is vanity: that is the simplicity of age.

But strength of spirit lies between these two and partakes of each. For human greatness—that is, spiritual greatness—is essentially founded on the number *two*. The wise man sees all that has not changed since the time of Heraclitus and will never change (this includes most of the world), but he also knows that strength of spirit is impossible without the will to change the world for the better. And he recognizes in the meeting of these two principles—of our mutability and the world's immutability—something that is inexpressible but unites all great spirits across all borders.

3

The world is anything but an "Either-Or" or a victory on the first attempt.

4

The question is not so much whether a man is healthy or ill but what he does with his good health or illness.

5

If men changed at the right time . . . , neither too early nor too late, then they would possess life. That is the secret.

6

There is (on the whole) only *one* error. For we all agree that we must preserve higher things and eradicate (fight against) baser things. Our error is that we mistake the external forms for the things themselves and try to preserve the forms that once *contained* greatness (the Good, the Just).

7

Whoever wishes to preserve external forms must not aspire to becoming a custodian of higher things; whoever wants to preserve higher things must not wish to preserve external forms.

8

Where is the abyss? *In each false step*; but not in multiplicity or in polyphony.

9

"It's another matter altogether with *wisdom* (which neither may nor can deny established scientific knowledge); here, all our efforts are focused on reaching the same heights *again*. For wisdom [. . .] cannot be communicated."[1]

However, the *forms* of wisdom are always different and the forms lead to action — they extend over the most various spheres: here it is speech, the use of language; there it is attitude, agreement or disagreement. Forms always arise in connection with their respective (ever-changing) times.

Thus the fraction of eternal wisdom we can access, that is, the immutable external form of wisdom that is inseparable from the means of expression *of any* kind available at any given time, is also ever-changing.

10

Three levels. — "I know too much to be able offer advice." This occurs often and is an important and correct response. Someone who knows ten times less would immediately offer advice, advice that is fresh and perhaps not at all bad. How should one react to such a situation? Would the higher level of value then be simultaneously less valuable? — This second level is not the final one. There is a third level: when someone knows "everything" (relatively speaking) and still offers advice. This is good. He will mention all the other things, the counter-arguments, but once they have all been listed, each jus-

1. *Nuancen und Details* II, 47; compare *Nuancen und Details* III, 1.

tified and complete, he will present one more prominently, as dominant, and will list the reasons why all the others should be subordinate to it.

11

In the mountains. We saw the paths of others, brilliantly illuminated, but not our own.

12

. . . narrow is the space in which we can extend a hand to the happy.

(The strictest art form—a good deed—lifelong work that brings only a single moment of light—other examples, as well.)

13

Life. First you count up the bad moments. Then you count up the happy moments—and you become happier.

[. . .]

15

There is actually no great difference between things that are most distant from each other or situated at opposing ends, like the North and the South Poles. Instead, the greatest difference would, for example, be found in the reception and celebration of a pilot in a great metropolis and a night spent above the ocean—that night of utter solitude, unchanging and terrifying, in which the greatest triumphs are achieved, in which *feats* are accomplished (a mental feat: the difficult transoceanic flight that had as yet rarely been completed but was the undoing of many is part of this order, at least in part—or perhaps it merely offers an image . . .).

—Do you want to celebrate this man?

He was already no more.

The one he had summoned to cross the ocean overnight cannot descend among men.

[. . .]

17

A person's strength of spirit can be measured in a state of fear. To be sure, everyone can be overcome with a powerful fear—yet the decisive question is whether or not one can hear the voice of reason when afraid. The professor making his way along a mountain ridge that appears dangerous to him: it is understandable that he would be overcome with fear. But his inability to hear a seasoned climber's simple explanation of the lack of danger and clear instructions on how to eliminate all risk reveals a lack of mental strength rather than a high degree of fear. Faced with extreme danger, the strong in spirit seek refuge in reason, it is in reason above all that they seek salvation!

18

In *changing questions*, we see that things were different in the past.—Not that better times arrived once the earlier questions were answered and then new questions arose: it is only in the changing questions that we can recognize incidentally, if we look closely, that the earlier questions have been resolved.

19

Shift in Consciousness

From a newspaper report: "The snow crunches, the thermometer announces 10 degrees below zero. Suddenly a voice rings out in the silence: 'Put out your fire and . . .' It is the *night watchman.* A. is one of the few Swiss locales where a night watchman . . . still makes his rounds . . . hour after hour. On his back, his fire horn gleams."

I try to imagine how one of our grandmothers or great-grandmothers would have read this report. For her, the night watchman is an iron-clad institution, like the contours of the landscape or the starry sky; and she reads a report about night watchmen exactly as she would a report about a storm raging in Asia, about the red cliffs in *those* mountains, or about the darkness of night *there*. But we are no longer in a position to think that way: we try to imagine this municipal council, to understand why it did not follow the lead of other municipal councils but decided instead not to eliminate their night watchman. *Deciding:* somewhere decisions are made, by people — not the landscape. The great-grandmother would be shocked if someone spoke to her about this figure, so deeply anchored in her image of the landscape, as if of a more or less arbitrary institution. She has not developed to the point where she could think that way.

This difference in conception is the historical phenomenon and it indicates an important development.

From the unfathomable confusion of these things — questions of the world's development, of our responsibility in this development, of the meaning and value of the innovations — only one thing rises with shining rectitude and unshakable certitude:

Whatever I can conceive of, I *must* think. Where light has begun to glimmer, it can only grow stronger (— regardless of how things had been before or in other times or in other places, regardless of how well or badly or differently things had been configured in other places and other times!).

Where one can conceive of something, a path will appear sooner or later.

20

And once more: nothing men can think is impossible. It's simply that one idea is closer, another is farther off.

21

All good happens only through necessity, that is, voluntarily. Good does not occur through coercion, that is, through compulsion.

22[2]

The question of the meaning of life will become more important over the coming decades. And—as many have recognized—it will ultimately be resolved through our ability to love.

The great questions about friendship . . . (And other questions that serve as gateways.)

Certain people *cannot* reach a state of complete denial, that is, of finding everything meaningless! Even if all were utterly rotten and indolent, there would always be children or adolescents one could help (—didn't I receive help, joy, assistance at different times in my life? What experience, what knowledge could possibly offset, undo this fact?). That is enough to give meaning and it all starts anew.

At the end of the world, the scurrilous will see everything only in a scurrilous light despite having attained knowledge. Hölderlin said it: "Only they believe in the divine / who are themselves godly."

How could a world in which a Balzac existed (was able to exist) possibly be meaningless?

23

The path is always the same (as are the stations):

First, we see that no one will help us, no one will come to our aid (we recognize this when we are in need; we see nothing at all absent need).

Second, we ask ourselves: would we act differently if the roles were reversed (differently than those who offer no help)?

2. Cf. "Interview with Prof Viktor E. Frankl," *Weltwoche*, 22.3.78.

Third, the answer to that question depends on another, more important question: does the world have meaning, is life worth living?

And consider the fourth, it's not necessary to be very different from others (from the way others appear on the outside). The flame of our devotion need burn in only *one* location, must *still* burn, must *always* burn. We can devote ourselves to the young as mentioned previously; we can devote ourselves to the love of an adult (it is here, in a more questionable manner, that D. H. Lawrence sought the solution); we can devote ourselves to the love of an idea, to the idea of love (of human progress on the highest level). One of these three things must obtain: if not, the world has no meaning and only idiots will continue to "live"—that is, to vegetate until they die.

24

You must find your reward within, there can naturally be no other goal for your efforts. And you will find your reward within when you can say: "I have lived for the benefit of another," *provided that* living for another's benefit accords with your constitution. (For you may not demand that your reward come from others! Such reckoning would be counter to all laws.)

25

A human being has a duty to be prosperous.

26

We only have *moments* of closeness.

27

The greatest in any realm are always those who come from elsewhere.

This became particularly clear to me when reading Balzac's

novella *Z. Marcas.* My reading of the story was cut short close to the end because a few pages were missing from the book. I have still not read those final pages, nor any report on the story and yet I've never had the slightest doubt how the story would end (because it's a story by Balzac, we can draw conclusions about it as confidently as we can about nature): the main character did *not* come to power. He could not. Why is that?

Because Balzac portrays himself in this character; because Z. Marcas resembles Honoré de Balzac too closely.

—But didn't Balzac, in fact, come to power and achieve pre-eminence as a writer?

—pre-eminence *as a writer!* And he achieved it because he was a man very much like Z. Marcas, that is, a man who aspired to another kind of power, to worldly power. We attain our greatest powers by turning away from our origins—we attain them through exile.

> Aren't the most beautiful roses those that grow soonest after the crossbreeding of species?—And does their beauty last as the hybrid lives on or does it not rather tend to decrease? The question is how long a hybrid cross can last—specialists could inform us. One can surely find the clearest and most simple examples in the realm of biology.

Who knows? Perhaps the greatest men in terms of worldly power—such as Napoleon or Lenin—were destined, through some part of their being, large or small, to become something completely different—an artist, say, or a thinker. And perhaps they achieved their invincible strength only through being transplanted into another region.—"Who knows?": maybe it would better to say "Everyone knows—"

Pure mathematics cannot flourish in mathematics. It's necessary that a poet or a thinker be grafted onto a mathematician. Then the poet or the thinker will blossom immeasurably, by virtue of the graft, and we will have a great mathematician.

28

Tests for the two primary kinds of vision:

For psychological vision: the interpretation of dreams (truly natural interpretation, not according to external guidelines).

For economic-political vision: accurate prognoses.

Inversely: no one's political vision will be proven through explanations, no matter how extensive and detailed, of why events that have already taken place were unavoidable. Even if such a presentation is highly poetic, it will not be proof of keen political vision as long as it does not include accurate predictions. —And no one will display keen psychological aptitude by trying to absorb or hypnotize others or by tacking some moral onto their story.

29

He sees in great distances, incredibly far and incredibly near (which is one and the same): that is what I call psychological vision.

He sees in the middle distance; he therefore lacks the ability to judge the *overall* circumstances and conditions: this is economic-political vision.

30

All great spirits have a system somewhere, even Goethe; but the system is an earthly stopgap (a constraint).

In spirit, all would unite; and yet Goethe had to reject a few (Kleist, Beethoven), even Goethe.

31

The dreadful expanse of the *highest* plateau . . .

32

Is art instruction or an offer of beauty?
It is both and neither:
It *offers affirmation*.

When we look at a landscape, an exalted landscape—it sways, it is elevated[3]—
we suddenly recognize what happens in art: a landscape, a heavy, earthly, massive
landscape is (not represented but) set into motion before our eyes. We see that something in it is elevated (even if that is a man's fate, all the same). Only Dionysus is
the foundation of art. The Apollonian is a mixture; it cannot be opposed to the Dio-
nysian.

What nonsense it is to talk of artists "making things up"! They
have set themselves a *spiritual task*: that is art.

We have seen how, in the dunes, the ridiculous piles of sand
made by men became veritable mountains (planted with trees and
furnished with a flight of stairs—a small mountain like the others, the
prior ones, those found in nature): no village schoolteacher can comprehend this. This is the work of mankind. (And the schoolteacher
will be the first to venerate the mountain, as will the others.)

Your image is inadequate. We are of a higher level.

(What reproach is possible for an image so completely lacking?)
. . . but I can read the old fables of mankind.

33

The word, the written:
It should be seized and passed on before it becomes congealed

---

3. Cf. V, 2.

and glazed over again . . . as long as it maintains the angularity of earth-born metal.

[. . .]

35

Countless people would have believed in Faust if they had seen him at the beginning, in his study—that is not difficult. But who would still have believed in him and his intellectuality and spirituality if they had seen him *on his travels . . . ?*

(yet that makes no difference to Faust because he was not satisfied through men, but through divine hosts.)

36

"He who ever strives . . ."

This is perhaps the most decisive turn in life (some learn this too late, others never; Heinrich von Kleist died from having never achieved it); the turn from aiming at summits in one's youth to the confident knowledge that no genuine effort remains fruitless.

For youth lives in the conviction that only conquering summits has value (and only the highest summits at that; as if there were a highest one!). As a result, when they do not conquer summits they lose faith in their steps.

On the *mystical* nature of every serious human effort: the path is not straight, as the young believe; the reward (the path's goal) cannot be seen: we do not see the summit it is meant to lead to, but a banner lures us onto the path or, in the best case, a secondary summit of no significance.—Along the way we find precious stones—or we glimpse the summit that becomes more and more true: our actual summit is the path itself.

The greatest beings are simply those who *know paths best.*

37

I believe that thought conquers all—thought is a small worker: the greatest among them. (The smallest: but their legions can be deployed most broadly).

[. . .]

39

But night has *one* great quality: we can see farther at night.

40

Intuition and Connection to the Past

Disciplined attempts to recall things from the previous day that have already been swallowed up by the night can reveal wonders. There is the perception of those *traces of light* left by the transmission of what I no longer have, of what I still had just recently; and the memory of the *place* (the place in time) when I still knew; in addition, deeper within me, there is a kind of *form* for the things that have disappeared, so that when someone tells me these things (assuming, of course, that I was not the one who recalled them into being, as we will not waste any words here about the simple case of direct recollection), I can say, "Yes, that is how it must have been," precisely because the things recounted immediately fit into forms already present in me . . .

A very similar marvel occurs when we remember or try to remember things at a much further remove from us, things from more distant pasts—we can speak of remembering here because memory does not end or begin with an individual person but extends over generations. Suddenly the essence of what we call "intuition" is illuminated for us.

In this context we recall Goethe's sayings:

"The task of the tragic poet is none other than to verify a moral-psychological phenomenon in the past through a comprehensible experiment."[4]

"Only someone to whom the present is important will write a chronicle."[5]

"When you lose interest, you also lose memory."[6]

That is why you can recognize the possibilities of a present in terms of the selection of pasts it takes into account (and the first question is whether it takes any past at all into account; if it doesn't take any into account, then it is nothing). Think of one nation today that is primarily preoccupied with the Battle of the Teutoburg Forest and other things from the primeval forests.—Goethe's saying: "Tell me whom you frequent and I will tell you who you are; if I know how you occupy yourself, then I know what you may become,"[7] is equally valid for the choice of past eras or past minds.

41

When you have something significant to say, you must also assume the risk inherent in saying it. Oh, those who are always lamenting: "I was right, after all, but—if only I hadn't said anything!"

Petty, inadequate, shortsighted!—Was harm caused? The good that comes of saying it will always be greater!

One should perhaps specify "something of primary significance." Because things of secondary significance, which are not essential to one's productivity, can be kept to oneself so as not to lose prematurely the means of fulfilling one's fundamental task.

---

4. Goethe, *Maxims and Reflections.*
5. Ditto.
6. Ditto.
7. Ditto.

4²

"Is it such a great secret, what God and man and the world are?
No! But no one wants to hear it; so it remains secret."[8]

For example, telling those who are arguing over whether man
(his fate) is a product of his environment or the result of his (innate)
personality, his will, and his own efforts. The truth is so simple, so unmistakable: he is both, as much the former as the latter, and if either
is to a certain degree flawed, things will turn out badly.

—Only you can create a better situation!—There is some truth
to this; but precisely because I didn't refute it, it is not true.

43

A man is swimming against the current (unless he is in *calm
water* . . . ?): he does not move from his spot. Does he know if this is
due to a weakness of will or to external circumstances? How could he
know? He only sees that he is not moving forward.

However, in practice, in certain practical situations, what is important is that he not let himself be swayed by the thought that the
problem lies in him—when it is not the case—and his will become
truly weakened.

44

The way our own strength expands is imperceptible: a larger
body.

The reason human capacities are limited is that an individual
only ever has a small number (if any) of others who believe in him

8. Goethe, *Venetian Epigrams*, LXV.

completely. Thus a person rises to a certain level, but no higher. He does not advance into the inexpressible, into the spirit (*also* capable of working "miracles" in all acts). If such a person had many others, perhaps ten or twenty, who had complete faith in him, he would gain powers (should he be so compelled) that would make everything possible.

[. . .]

46

He who is not given his due generally claims more than he deserves. The reason for the abundance of messiahs in certain (small, predominantly commercially minded) countries: those who do intellectual work are not afforded fitting recognition there. (A look at France, which is essentially devoid of messiahs, makes this even clearer.)

[. . .]

48

On Sorrow

All of life, whether enjoyment or effort, is but pursuit and if one does not have a private sense of being within an order, one is unhappy.

This means that there is no other (real) happiness than the one granted a Balzac in his joyless, harried life—with legitimate effort exceptionally well-ordered.

Shouldn't one then never stop fighting against sorrow (of the common variety), against illness and suffering, because after all—? Woe to those who set foot on that path!

(Apart from the fact that one kind of sorrow can quickly turn into another.)

49

Naturally, one must always seek ways out—but not false ones. For the exits we seek on the wrong path only lead us deeper into the hole. (When you fall into a crevasse: first come up with a calm plan.)
[. . .]

51

Certainly, one grows through the burden one carries (only through the burden); but if the burden is too great, one collapses in an instant.

It is a sin not only to be unwilling to shoulder one's burden, but also to willingly take up a greater burden than one is able carry.

52

There is only *one* misfortune: having nothing to do or being forced to do something false.

Any activity that does not increase the abilities of the one performing it is a false one.

53

Action: of the same stuff as light, it can also not take things further; a different *quantum* of light; an accumulator of light.

54

"Be forbearing with nature" is an injunction that should not be misunderstood. We should not exhaust horses already tired from running and be patient when they rest; yet we do not allow raging pestilence to last. The same goes for laziness in you.

55

When excusing oneself for an omission ("But it was because . . . ,"
". . . there was a reason"):

You need not tell me that there are reasons for every action (or
non-action), but why you chose those particular ones.

56

One of Karl Kraus's most important statements is: "Good opinions are worthless. What matters is who holds them."

57

If one does not value progress as such (actions that improve)
but is fixated on the achievement of a goal or an ideal state (and this
means: the nearest image rather than the higher one)—then one is
just as stupid as someone who does good in the hope of a reward; and
just as bound to experience failure.

58

The way. Work toward raising the emotional state of one's usual
(daily) life to that of the state one is in when *traveling*—to that state
of openness, of readiness to offer oneself, of being able to see things in
their full proportion, of internal tension and fecundity of thought—
that is life.

(Life is always an immediate enhancement of life, an increase
of life.)

[. . .]

60

Spiritual strength is only possible through the struggle against
opposition.

More and more, I see this phenomenon in all of history whereas I had initially recognized it only in my own experience—and in the end, it is no longer surprising, but is simply an integral part of thought centered on the fundamental theorem of productivity—there can be no life without productivity.

61

War.—On the often misconstrued dictum that war is the father of all things.

—A long period is now necessary for the few worthy beings who have survived today's warfare, the few whom *chance* has spared, to recover from the ordeal.

—There is such a thing as productive combat: the struggle engaged in on internal grounds for spiritual gain. The struggle is only positive when fought between two similarly intentioned parties (not between those with good and those with evil intentions: then the only possible good would come from destroying the ill-intentioned—an outcome that is doubtful—and not from the struggle itself), between two sides of one person, for example, because they are similar (they carry the same weight), but not between a scholar and a gorilla, between a poet and an avalanche.

62

The study and the example of physics have an appeasing aspect; their light accompanies intellectual discoveries.

63

Strength. "I have the strength, what I need is faith!"

This formula seems right but isn't always. Strength is nothing other than accumulated belief.—What is a strong muscle? Accumulated belief subdued in the corporal.

[...]

65

Crowds barely think. That is why they must be led by thinkers, not exploiters.

66

Class-consciousness, yes, the theory is all too correct. But there is yet a third class, that of Socrates, that of the implacable.

67

The Writer's Self-Criticism

True self-criticism must be internal, close to the source, under *its own* spell.

False, harmful self-criticism comes from outside, from that space where there was doubt about the possibility of reaching others and this self-criticism is *only* destructive.

68

One should speak proverbially (or employ proverbs) only if one reawakens them, lets new life flow into their desiccated limbs (something that is rarely possible and is more difficult than expressing oneself without them altogether).

For words, too, are constantly withering and constantly need to be rejuvenated.

69

At arm's length, one has no strength.

70

Theology

"Spinoza sneeringly suggests that Blacks no doubt think of their god as Black and donkeys, if they had a god, would think of their supreme being as a donkey. This mockery is not worthy of the great thinker." This statement, however, is not worthy of a theologian.[9] (Although he calls Spinoza a great thinker: what can theology possibly do with such greatness of thought?) Spinoza presents a simple and incontestable fact and yet it is clear that a theologian, for whom God is absolutely central, cannot accept it—for how could God then be modified by a distant creature (being thought of now as Black, now as a donkey)? How can this not be seen as mockery? All theology is based on the fundamental notion of a point, a central point—whereas all true thought has always conceived of the world as change, as movement, as *flux*.

Goethe explicitly taught that in phenomena, the interior is *not distinct from the surface*; the earth, the planetary systems, the "center of gravity" and all the rest teach us this. What is the *center* of gravity? (Mathematics are there to make physics comprehensible; physics to make phenomena comprehensible.) If we live on earth, what does the central point matter to us? As a mathematical point, it could certainly serve to help us understand the *direction* at any given moment of one force or other, but the forces are in us or in the earth (in the earth's expanse). If we could compress the earth slightly: everything would change. If we could change its position: where, then, is the point? Yet God is "the force"?—And any smaller body's center of gravity: the mathematical point of some imagined resultant, which cannot be set against the millions of forces emanating from that body's position as king and god, as *reality?* If you change the form of a body, the center of gravity will shift. If you hit it with a hammer, it may break into a

9. Emil Brunner, *Neue Schweizer Rundschau* (probably 1934), p. 480.

thousand more. — What is essential is not the point or central point, but the tremendous abundance of things in the stream of eternity.

Yet this false theological doctrine, probably the falsest of any the human spirit has brought forth — the doctrine of a central point as the dominant force over life and reality — persists today. In the central point lies the highest ruler. Theology's Copernicus has not yet been born. Theology burned his first followers at the stake and then made a few concessions — but only a few (as it now accepts Spinoza, calling him a "great thinker"). But never on the essential matter. Today theology can no longer deny that the earth revolves around the sun and that the earth moves with the sun — but that makes no difference. It is not essential. It will go on for some time, the movement will continue — and then it will stop. The reign of the central point that never moves begins somewhere far out in space and we all revolve around it. It gives us life!

71

Goethe, too, was not a central point, but was a consciousness that raised itself powerfully above the flux and looked out beyond the limits of time.

72

There is that beautiful formulation by Hamsun that there is no one cause, but a series of causes.

73

The Great Idea and Good Thoughts

(A Comparison)

A great idea consists of two elements: on the one hand, it is what we usually think of and is effective in the realm of familiar concepts;

we will accept or reject it depending on how it clashes with our own thinking. On the other hand, it is a torch that sheds light a great distance.

Good thoughts are something else altogether. They are not comprised of two parts. They lack transcendence; their impact is limited to the immediate present. There is nothing of the torch or searchlight to them.

This can be clearly illustrated with a comparison of Forel[10] and Freud. Freud provoked violent attacks and Forel . . . his ideas can only be praised. But how paltry they seem, how completely they fail *to touch on the real,* his concepts of the "pathological," of "sick" and "healthy" (of genius, that *may even occasionally . . .*), of "poisons"! And nothing in his work can mitigate or save these feeble notions. By contrast, we may disagree with Freud, and yet he touches us because he is the man who had a great idea. We cannot set one part of his thought against another. Forel is typically the kind of man who had *only* good minor ideas. And here we see the striking difference: a great idea is, first of all, a torch that lights a great distance, that *illuminates* even opposing regions; the respectable doctor, on the other hand, is content to advance with modest steps. If his thoughts are good, they earn praise; if they are bad, the good ones that preceded them cannot salvage them.

A great idea can also be expressed through smaller thoughts; whether good or bad, something transcendent illuminates them.

If they are good, the transcendent still illuminates them; if they are bad, the transcendent shines into them and improves them.

Those who have only good thoughts deserve our thanks for each one of them. The others don't. Those who think great thoughts do not need it, they are unavoidable. Even their worst antagonists may try to hide by creeping into the most remote mountain ravine—the reflection of their light shining down from above will reach them.

10. Auguste-Henri Forel (1848–1931), a Swiss psychiatrist and neuroanatomist who was active in social reform. (Trans. note.)

74

Psychology

First, we must distinguish two groups: the non-psychologists and the false psychologists. The latter, for whom Vienna proved a particularly favorable breeding ground, resemble men brandishing axes and running after random passersby who have done nothing to provoke them and from whom they cannot expect anything.

—Imagine a hundredweight of iron lying on the bottom of the sea with some floating object (a piece of wood or a balloon, a mine-shaped buoy) bound to it with a chain. The length of chain is equal to the perpendicular distance from the surface to the seabed. The sea is murky. We will use this image to illustrate higher human intelligence (or psychological aptitude).

—Or, as a test of psychological aptitude, we could use the sign a poet would hang in his window: the sign was almost always hanging in the window; the poet only ever took it down for brief moments. When it hung in the window, it meant the poet was receiving visitors, but if it was not there, it meant he was not particularly eager for visitors as they could, under certain circumstances, disturb him . . . Kitty Spleen, who understood the system, came up with one of her innovative and oh so insightful ideas—to great acclaim from everyone around her, especially the pharmacists. She decided that it would be more practical for the poet to hang up the sign only when he did not want to be disturbed at work. However, when he was ready to receive visitors, which, after all, was almost always the case, then he should not hang anything . . . etc.

And Kitty Spleen could not or would not understand that there would no longer have been any point for the poet to hang up a sign to keep from being disturbed: because the sign itself disturbed him.

Kitty Spleen had no psychological aptitude, which is no worse than a false aptitude. "False aptitude" is an incorrect term since there is no such thing as a false aptitude. One is able or unable to climb a tree or to grasp the connection between two things. Naturally, by "false aptitude" I meant an inability, but one different from Kitty's in that she adopts the external trappings of aptitude. In a word, I was thinking of those who have read Freud et al. and seek to apply what they've read to every situation without having understood it in the slightest.

—Let us return to the mine-shaped buoy. We must distinguish three levels: 1. Those who understand, fully or in part, the relation between the surface and the seabed and who continue to investigate it. 2. The "pedagogues": the clueless who splash about on the surface of the water. 3. And precisely those who throw stones in the water, shoot at the fish, and trouble the (already murky) sea.

75

The Others

Someone reproached me for thinking only of myself. Earlier, this would upset me (in itself a sign that the reproach was not justified), later, when I had more confidence in my relation to things and had gained some insight, I could reply: "Yes, and I must and will think much more and more often about myself. Some have already reached others—they can leave themselves out of it. But me, I must think myself through my own self in order to reach others."

However, most people are nowhere at all.

76

They say: "The child is so well-behaved today!"

Hmm, no, not in most cases, unfortunately . . .—what do they know about whether the child is truly well-behaved or not? The child is simply not lacking anything today, is not in distress.

I, too, would like to lead people to think of others, but to really *think* of others. Not to wrap themselves in sanctity and sanctimoniousness, that immutable and eternal attitude, and to believe that is sufficient for the well-being of others.

—instead, think of others.[11]

77

. . . what kind of socialism we would have if in others we only saw other people and not ourselves?

78

A discovery is always disproportionate, a discovery is monstrous—it stands in the world like an enormous golden calf.

79

The endless, extended circling of every creative thought: in a mind, as in humanity.—One must merely be shown the direction, then one will eventually arrive everywhere. It will take a long time, but you will finally reach the place that had been indicated for so long.

80

Great intelligence combined with any talent, applied with determination, will *always* result in accomplishments and discoveries.

Great intelligence is rare, talent is common, but for both to be applied with determination is rarest of all.

11. "Kierkegaard reminds us that to help other human beings we must meet them where they are." *Nouvelles Littéraires* 11/3/34.

81

Illegality

The great sciences have still not been consecrated. (The area and framework in which the greatest discoveries take place is new and vague; the university department for them has not yet been built; or if it has, then it is demolished and fallen to ruin.)

To which scientific field did Freud's discoveries belong? They were expelled from the consecrated sciences.

The works and discoveries of Copernicus were also expelled from the consecrated sciences. They have nothing to do with science, it was declared, but are blasphemy.

What kind of science did Socrates pursue?

The new science was born illegitimately (from two earlier sciences whose union was not sanctioned).

What kind of science was it that Lenin (the obscure Lenin) pursued for decades and ultimately used to build an entire world? His were ravings of a marginal fanatic, it was said, dangerous perhaps (like a weaver of secret intrigues; it does not take much to be dangerous). Perhaps he wasn't even "dangerous," but he certainly wasn't serious . . . and didn't have much of an audience.

It is the same with forms (in art).

Whenever a significant work was created, the professors constructed a theory to consecrate its form; a form the inept subsequently fill in.

Pregnant form, too, is always born illegitimately.

But every great writer will have an effect through spirit and mind.

82

Someone says, "Me, the head of a school? I consider my mind to be in a better condition than that!"

The multitude of humanity, growing in strength, creates a nation. When it grows weak or degenerates it is unable to create a nation or allows the existing one to collapse. The mind follows an opposite course: it founds a school when it has become decadent. When it is strong, it doesn't yet have a school or it blows one up.

83

No action that we perform with goodwill can be lost. (A poem.) But goodwill cannot counter knowledge.

84

What is a pessimist?
A bad person.
(But most pessimists are not pessimists.)

85

There is a place (and an extreme place it is), where it is our free choice to say "good"—and it will be good—or "bad"—and it will be bad.

(Accordingly, in this place it is decided whether one belongs to the good or to the true pessimists, that is, the bad: those who resent everything and want to revenge themselves on everything because . . .)

86

Exclusivity befits only those who accomplish great things or else those of very limited ability.

87

Every great and truly productive thought represents the world in an absolute manner. Every *image* is an absolute. Time passes and eventually shows that this construct, too, is contingent.

88

At best, only our *vocation* can be completely spiritual; it is a mistake to believe that any *life* can be led independent of the political principle (except in the final stage of sainthood, which is not life, but annihilation).

89

With politics as with the body. People say that we cannot live independent of politics — those who claim that they do are mistaken. A man who does not want to exercise disdains everything associated with physical activity. This attitude would (perhaps) be fine, if spiritual strength enabled us to live without a body, without being dependent on our bodies.

And yet, despite everything . . . there are a few for whom the body becomes of almost no importance; Kant, for example, and Hölderlin.

90

If, after all your writing and your mountain climbing you have got no further than to recognize at the end of your life that your time would have been better spent farming than writing or climbing mountains, then you have certainly not got very far.

91

It is not hard for a stupid man to have a strong will: the will is measured against minor oppositions.

92

A great capacity to feel pleasure and creative power are sometimes separated by only a hair's breadth.

93

On Greed

The man who always aimed a bit too high . . . or more exactly, who shoots at a target beyond the range of his particular weapon. If his weapon could shoot to a height of twenty meters, he would shoot at something twenty-five meters high. If on the following day, however, he had a weapon that could shoot to a height of fifty meters, he would not limit himself to an object thirty or forty meters off the ground but would shoot at a target fifty-one meters off the ground and hit nothing. And so on.

He missed the eight o'clock train and returned home in despair; once he finally reached a decision, he didn't choose a train the next day but instead, "to win at least a partial victory," decided to catch the eleven o'clock train that was already gathering steam in the station. He rushed to the station, missed the train and ruined his night's rest; and so he always missed the train.

94

One of the main axes in all events: the overcoming of sorrow by externalizing it.

[. . .]

96

There is a reason happiness is so seldom discussed (in letters or other communications) aside from the fact that one must be productive (that is, one must deal with the bad, not with the good, which does not require our efforts): by the time we can name something it is almost always over—suffering, for example, but good things, too.

97

A good deed, that is what we *must* live at least once, yes, live . . .

Indeed, everything depends on good deeds (to be sure: even if we are not able to sort out or improve the world in a decisive way, even if the world will always continue on its dubious way like a death ship).

Good deeds, after all, can only improve our days and bad ones make them worse (even though no good deed can set the world right, without them it would no doubt very quickly become unbearably bad, as bad as the plague). If everyone were to do just *one* in their lives! One good deed they could *name*.—Otherwise their lives don't amount to anything.

Giving a small amount of money, or even a large one, to the poor once a year, at Christmas, say, does not count as a good deed. This act is commendable, to be sure, but so negligible when compared to the sheer mass of indifferent and thus harmful acts committed in one's life (or to the roles one plays, one's impact on others) that this good deed soon fades into insignificance. In your profession, in your social situation broadly speaking, you do not act for the good (and all indifference becomes evil since the flow of life, channeled by evil, never ceases): the fact that negative effects outnumber positive effects by many thousandfold proves this. *The good deed must be performed in your essential being.* (An apparently minor act, in terms of quantity, will be multiplied by ten thousand.)

98

Values are everywhere the same: in good music and in the just actions of a simple woman.

Thus from the summit of some worthy accomplishment one looks out onto other worthy regions. (There have, for example, been great politicians who were good judges of art.) Yet each elevated region does not have a view onto every other: because forms are different and difficulties of *form* are enormous. And because all actions must be directed outward, toward these very difficulties of form, form is external.

Form is external: but by no means superficial!

99

You human! You must know the good to measure things against the good. If you take care only to ensure that you don't commit a bad action here or there: that is no life.

100

A man wandered alone through a leafless forest and said (to those who were not there): "Here I see the grove again and here, again, is Socrates (or Plato, or Aristotle); only the students are missing." He thought a while and confirmed: yes, perhaps the conditions are the same, but the circumstances that made a Socrates (a historical Socrates) possible are missing.

We are all subject to circumstances; but they determine only the external dimensions of our work, not its spiritual significance, only its historical impact, not the level of our own achievement.[12]

101

"You're too late." "It's too late."

No one who is true can arrive too late. His arrival can only be opportune or inopportune.

102

Goethe's admonition is:
Gather your strength for what is significant!

---

12. Compare *Nuancen und Details* III, 14.

103

On Growing Old

"Age does not bring wisdom; age brings nothing but age." If Hamsun had not written this, I would dismiss it as nonsense and add that one does not grow old if one does not wish to and that one will always become wiser if one wishes to.

Oh, those golden years of youth. You grow old, everything passes away! But I ask: *Where is the gold?* Because it wasn't in youth.

The gold is in my glance back and the gold does not age. It does not pass away because I can always look back.—It's terrible to see what confusion folk wisdom has again sown in the simplest things. Do children have gold? Yes, when they look at some distant object. Does something pass away? What passes then? Muscular strength? Then it only becomes gold once you have seen it. Health? That, too, you don't see when you have it because you are surely looking at something else, at long voyages, for example, at distant islands with a golden glow. And now that good health is out of reach and you see it and *delight* in it, you possess it more than you did before.

If one can or even should speak of possession . . .

In any case, growing older is a process of constant accumulation: what is valuable in you increases, as it did with Goethe—as long as you do not let yourself be distracted by the chatter of crowds and, instead of seeing what there is to be seen, begin to covet something that is not appropriate to your situation. One can forgive this mistake in children who always want to have what the grown-ups have, long pants, for example. But how can it be excused in adults and the elderly? Hamsun was right: they grow ever more foolish.

How, then, do you expect to grow when you are always working against your own growth?

The tree accepts its law completely, but you are like a tree that blends a stream of poison with the flow of its sap. Thought, one's way of thinking, is a grave and particular element in man, no less important than the material elements, than the tree's roots or its bark.

And yet the tree knows that there is only one ascension, only a great growth upward and a further expansion; and subsequently only death.

"The tree—; but is growth and decline not clearly visible in the *human body?*"—The important thing in every comparison is a proper transposition. You do not consist solely of a body, do you? You are also made of many potentialities. Sometimes a tree will grow in height, sometimes in width. Sometimes it will produce lush foliage, sometimes fruit.

"A great growth upward." What is meant by "upward"? This does not contradict the previous direction; life cannot retrace its steps, it can only *continue*. Certain prophets may have preached the vision of a world in which the spirit plays no positive role, in which there is no question of continuing forward, only of crawling back to the earth.

But for the two most renowned of these prophets, Rousseau and Hamsun (one could include D. H. Lawrence to a certain extent), theirs was primarily a reaction against shallowness, against spiritual fraudulence, and not representative of their complete view of the world. In Hamsun's *Growth of the Soil*, Isak is certainly a positive character compared with certain fools that are or were to be depicted in darkest hues and corrected or stamped out, however, the true creator of the future is not Isak, but Geisler, if there are any at all (more precisely: Geisler is one side of such a creator), just as Christopher Columbus and Leonardo da Vinci were, along with all the other "moon-wanderers" about whom Thomas Mann wrote so beautifully. Isak cultivates only a small patch of land, but the other figure (of whom Geissler represents only one aspect) cultivates an entire world.

And what of Hamsun himself? He, too, cultivated the earth for a certain time, but even if he had done so for much longer, of what importance is his husbandry compared to his writing? All Hamsuns and Rousseaus refute themselves.

104

Human grandeur—human hope; the *way* to greatness—lies in the recognition of our insignificance, of our relativity, that is, our relation to the unfathomable night that surrounds us, not in the mastery of it, *not in the mastery of the whole*, but in the neatness with which we align our existence, in the precision of *our own* machinery. Man is like a small clock lost in the inorganic chaos of the Sahara. His grandeur lies in the precision and rectitude with which he functions. And in the light he sheds on his small circumference.

Man is like a small clock—that runs—in the Sahara; and like a lamp—a single lamp—in the unfathomable night. But he is not like an eagle with a large enough wingspan to grab, contain, and carry off the Sahara.

When man recognizes this and strives first and foremost to perfect himself, he will become greater; but if he sees himself as an eagle, he will only be reduced. (It is a bit like the young Mozart who will become great if he tries to play music, but if he tries to wrestle an elephant . . .)

Today, it is both more difficult to recognize this most fundamental aspect of our condition and more necessary than before because the important scientific discoveries, implemented as technological inventions, are blinding.—I do not doubt that one day we will land on the moon (or could reach the moon if it were in our interest). But the fact that humans can reach the moon will not make them greater since the infinite space that surrounds them will be no smaller (subtracting a number from infinity still leaves infinity). Humans cannot rival the universe in terms of *dimension*, but they can in terms of clarity. The poet—a human being *par excellence*—is no match for the power of an avalanche. The pen with which I write these words is not the same as a bomb. As a bomb, what good would it be? But if it serves as a pen, then it will be more than a bomb. For what is a bomb compared to the power of planets or even of the ocean? Human grandeur lies in *comprehension* (in the elements of understanding), not in power.[13]

---

13. "Greatness of soul is not so much a matter of striving upward and forward as knowing how to order and circumscribe oneself." Montaigne.

105

And yet, there are a few things to which, decidedly, no true answers will be found (nor should it be otherwise). The concept we once
designated with the Greek word "logos" suits them.

(As well as the question of whether it is necessary that unhappy beings exist,
people, that is, who are unable to find salvation in productive activity.)

. . . Furthermore, this struggle should remain obscure. Some
things can only be made clearer when one distances oneself drastically from them.

106

Art

Art requires less than I once thought.
—not such complex accumulations, nor such an inscrutable
combination of many things: but instead *one* element and a clear
step.—not a parade of troops as far as the eye can see, but an ambler's
walk.
[. . .]

108

It's simply a matter of beginning *somewhere*, not at the beginning: because there is no beginning.

For those fools with their systems, their "wasted lives," their "too old," their "too
high for me," their "yes, but can it be done?," "how can it be implemented in daily
life?": there is no HOW to implement—the how is already realized, the how first of
all—what must be implemented is what is right.
In reading a book, in studying a branch of science, in all important undertakings.—One must also be wary of writers who take five pages to say nothing and
whom one only understands after reading a thick book.

109

There is always some delay — no matter how he runs, the chain of realities is always one link ahead and he lags behind. One can imagine the fitting image of a geometric series in which things advance: he says 4, but there already were 8; he quickly says 9, 10, 11, but there were 16; he speeds up: 20, 25!, he shouts, but there were 32 . . . He never catches up; he runs faster but things move more quickly too, and more quickly than he does. How will it end? Will he save himself before it is all over?

Surely not in this fashion. Not by constantly increasing his pace, since he has been slower from the very beginning. Only by changing his method: by not running downward, but instead coming from above; and in this case this means by recognizing the mathematical law. Knowing an operation of a higher order, he can descend boldly, as if from the clouds, and land where the series thunders to earth powerfully and arduously.

110

The Mirror

You yourself are perhaps invisible; but in some cases we see your essence in a mirror.

There are several such mirrors (and since they do not belong to you, you cannot get rid of them). For example:

How do you die?

Which one of the fairy tales you heard as a child was most important to you?

To which historical periods do you feel a connection? (If none, that is also a mirror.)

Whom do you love? (If you love no one, that is also a mirror.)

And many more. There are mirrors everywhere and it would take your entire life for you to become clever enough to evade them all; and even if you achieved this, that, too, would be a mirror.

111

On Overcoming Sorrow

A bird—early in the morning as I lie sleepless and uncomfortable in bed—begins to shriek with murderous and horrifying impudence from the roof (just over my head). Its cries wash over my ears like a tidal wave, it's maddening. I am no longer a child and in my despair (my desperate situation), I know: there is only *one* remedy, and I resort to it: immediate acceptance, complete agreement and already I can feel the effects wane. The cry becomes like the floor of my room, to which I pay no attention, like my feet, which also do not disrupt my thoughts. And at the same time, I sense that, century after century, it can be no different with all of man's external circumstances (all such considerations must take into account our physiological limits; not as a revocation, but as a necessary addition): as soon as he adopts a new foundation, man will continue to think without interruption.

I once evoked a cork: it could not be drowned and so it must be God. It is, I now know, only man.

112

I met a man who gazed for a very long time into the void—into the heavens—until he saw something: a projection of his ailing eyes. And this he called Lord God of Hosts, Jehovah, and other names as well.

113

On God

When mankind's greatest inventions are listed, one is usually forgotten: God.

The most remarkable thing about this God business is that those who seriously affirm His existence and those who seriously deny it understand each other very well.

"God" is—or, more exactly, was, in those eras when He was still a reality—an ingenious abbreviation of many things.

I would gladly love God, if I only knew *whom* to love. One can love a person or a truth but not a point of intersection. Because removed from the things conjoined, He has no existence; as for the things, we have them already.

114

The Church

Paul: one of the greatest writers who has ever lived and surely one of the worst (most pernicious).

. . . If you have love and *neither* speak with the tongues of men and of angels, *nor* do (or can) you give your body to be burned, *nor* do (or can) you bestow all your goods on the poor, *nor*—(compare the original[14]), if you have only that love without doing anything: then—yes, then:—you are *nonetheless* blessed!

Is it not, in fact, better to choose that kind of love straight away?

People have done precisely this since then—they have chosen spiritual love.—It wasn't long before they used incense to fulfill that office—it served just as well and was more practical.—Now pure love is THERE. Incense has and spreads pure love—its perfume and threads of smoke wend their way toward the heavens. Men can commit or omit whatever they want.

The Church has not been indolent since . . . , but was indolent from the very beginning.

—still, what of the meaning Balzac and Dostoevsky found it to have? (Dostoevsky does not signify much on this question because he was only great and infallible as an artist. Spiritually, or more exactly, intellectually, he did not create a significant work, that is, despite exquisite subtlety in parts, he did not succeed in sublimating

14. Paul's First Letter to the Corinthians (Trans. note.)

on the whole. Instead, he remained trapped in the pathological.[15]) Balzac, a spirit so *just*, so impartial, a man with so much *space* in his thinking? The meaning that Balzac saw in the Church despite his insight into evil? For him, it was the Church's creation of certain cultural goods or, even more, the fact that it enabled the *duration* of certain conditions and thus enabled those very things whose existence depends on duration. A vessel that is perdurable and makes duration possible: but at the same time stifles what is new in its clayey embrace. (Each era must choose which of the two fundamental human conditions it will give priority to.)

115

When a drunken, trembling old dentist said: "Be kind to each other!—As for the rest . . . ," he was voicing part of wisdom. Wisdom in its entirety does not lead to something else, but consists primarily in preparing the way, in getting rid of obstacles.

116

The world decays rapidly and if you do not constantly regenerate it within yourself, you are impoverished.

Once again: be wary of *those who have long been saved.*

117

One must achieve the (external) goal one has long been striving for in order to see that it involves something completely different.

118

On Crippling Preparation

More precisely: on the crippling effect of *false* preparation. Because there is also preparation that is utterly necessary, that is proper.—Yet wouldn't it be better not to call this "preparation"; it

15. "If there is no God, everything is permitted."

is preparation in only one respect, namely when it is itself the execution; therefore, one would do better to demand that there be no preparation, only the execution.

Here is the principle:

One activity feeds another when it is done for its own sake and not for others. When, however, it is not done for its own sake, it benefits neither itself nor others.

> It is in this context that the note "A *human being has a duty to be prosperous*" is to be understood. — This sentence should also be read in this context: "Every day should be a celebration."
>
> "Is it possible for every day to be a celebration?" — That depends entirely on you. Your activity must be *inspired*, anything else is a false path.
>
> Or: "One cannot live in constant rapture." Can't one? One must simply direct the rapture properly!

119

Once more: The artist is merely a greater *quantity* than any other person — not *different*. When we study the law that governs the artist — for which the condition of greater quantity is so suitable — we find results that are valid for all people.

Therefore: life is like the work of art and the work of art is like authentic life. Achieving one or the other consists in proper conduct, in bearing witness, that is, representing an interior through the exterior; in short, it consists in affirming life and consequently: in augmenting life; it is communicating with others, working.

120

Illness has three causes: 1. Overwork, 2. Lack of work, 3. Improper nourishment.

(These three elements can be tangled in a knot of illness.)

[. . .]

122

That the world is changed very little through the human spirit or human actions is something we know perfectly well. But: *however small* the changes effected by the human spirit may be, we know that *all of life is contained in them* and they alone comprise its value.

One cannot be spiritual and not want to change. The very essence of the spirit is its desire for change. (Even for an Epicurus! You need only look closely.)

123

The collision of measureless principle with measure: this is the source of brilliance.

(Brilliance does *not* come from the unification of two formed things; and not from the collision of two chaotic things.)

124

Admiration and love are not the same thing. And it must be clearly stated that love is more: since it encompasses admiration.

125

Each new religion built more or less by *one* man is, however, just as much a product of a century's suffering (even in cases in which the founder is most prominent). Otherwise what point would there be for the man who conceived the doctrine to preach it? His appearance would remain without effect, the myth would not become real. At best, those hearing him would say nothing more than: "he spoke well" (in a literary way) — and continue on their way.

126

When the claim is made; "We calculated so precisely—everything was precisely calculated—and yet, things turned out differently," then one thing is certain: the calculations were not precise.

127

Taking stock of individual perceptions, discoveries, and output is only necessary in politics and activities similar to politics, not in art (philosophy included) and not in the sciences: because in these fields what counts is discovery pure and simple and completed production in all its details. (When you discover the cause of an illness, any child can take stock of it; when you discover a treatment for it, every physician in his right mind will use it.)

And people still take stock: in the sciences, there are sometimes grounds for it, in art, it's a sin.

128

An important question: are human beings appallingly stupid or not?

Sometimes they seem to be terribly stupid and sometimes (going by certain signs, certain minor details) not.

Spinoza answered the question thus: they are not that stupid but determining what is right is very *difficult.*

I believe that it is almost a sin to speak like this (no doubt the only sin Spinoza ever committed). It seems to me that it is *not* difficult to live properly—not for those who are always active and advance step by step—but human beings are simply appallingly *lazy.*

They are so lazy, they would rather spend an hour in prayer than spend a single minute thinking.

129

In antiquity there was sophism and today we have theology. But sophism still brought some good (the skill with which they handled concepts; Burckhardt, among others, wrote well about this), theology only profits from it.

130

"*God.*" Not all those who have invoked this name spoke non-sense (even in modern times, in earlier eras this is a given): one need only think of Spinoza—or of the excellent final few pages of Hesse's *Knulp* (an otherwise rather boring book). This word has no doubt been used by those who endow it with a particular significance no less often than by those who claim that there is no God and do not associate a concept with this word, that is, by people not qualified to deny Him (the very same who then call on God at the moment of their death or secretly pray or make promises to Him etc. when they suffer a toothache).

If one's denial of God is based on a true conception of the world, then one cannot call on him in distress—however great one's distress may be—and make promises (out of some "instinct" or whatever they call it); one will always know that He is not there as long as one's mind is not clouded.

Human reason is not child's play; it does not vanish as soon as things get serious but is itself a serious matter—more serious, more powerful than all else but one thing: the world.

131

The power of a spiritual site increases proportionally with the length of the way that leads to it.

—The man with the greatest inner obstacles who then, at a late hour (to the surprise of those who know him only superficially), is nonetheless able to make the most important decisions: this man then becomes, through the knowledge he has accumulated (in the process of overcoming his internal resistance), almost *invincible* (in his rising up; in his persuasiveness).

132

Variation: I will continue to repeat that the greater the resistance a revolutionary has had to overcome within himself, the greater his power. Every inner obstacle he has confronted and overcome increases his store of knowledge and here knowledge is a weapon.

(Or: . . . knowledge is power.)

Here one might think of Luther—whether one cares for him or not is another matter, for this argument he is a clear example. Or of Saint Paul.

Those who might be considered revolutionaries *by nature*, who always immediately appear to be revolutionaries, the breezy and lightly fluttering, who rise up effortlessly everywhere because they are weightless, because they have never encountered any internal resistance, who show up self-evidently as soon as there is a change to be made—they never achieve much. All great revolutionaries are made of heavy material.

133

Panthalis

> Not only merit but fidelity, too, preserves our person.
>
> *Faust II, act 3*

This statement, with a powerful note, this immeasurably wonderful statement, which Goethe has the chorus leader Panthalis deliver, is like a dividing sword, a final judgment that divides all human

beings forever, assigns them their place in one of the only two worthy
groups, or relegates them to the third group, with all the rest . . . :

He who has acquired no name, nor noble end pursues
Belongs to the elements, so now begone!
I wish most ardently to be with my Queen;
Not only merit but fidelity, too, preserves our person.

So then: either merit (accomplishment—work) or loyalty. The
rest—belong to Nature's elements; they were briefly on this earth, did
not participate, they disappear again. They are the absolute negative
of which Mephistopheles could *rightly* say: *might just as well have
never been . . .*

Why not go further and say: only creative power need not be
loyal (examined more closely this means: not in the usual sense, not
loyal to something visible, something that can be *named*)?

Is that going too far?—What about someone who is not loyal and
yet does not accomplish anything? Aimless wandering—wandering
far and wide, but not reaching the distant goal: were he to reach it,
that would be an accomplishment, an adventure—an *unproductive*
adventure.—But this is to say:

When you stay in the realm of the Faustian Mothers until you
must depart, your departure will be a creative one.

"Aimless wandering far and wide": and these common human
beings try to ensure that the Mothers are behind them and that they
do everything for the Mothers. This is an unmistakable sign that they
are devoid of creative power—and therefore, because they also were
not *loyal*, they are devoid of worth . . .

But what is the value of one who is "loyal" and who remains in
the realm of the Mothers? He prepares the way for future flights of
the imagination! Because premature flights *will not* soar. They are
nothing.

Enthusiasts—grains of dust, flakes in the air: they float over the abyss but do not unite anything. They have no *location* and no *effect.*

Yet isn't the only, the definitive value (in the human sense of the word) the work?—whereas the location only has value (again, in the human sense of the word) with regard to the future work by allowing its necessary conditions to reach full maturity?

What, then, is Goethe's woman, his house?—An additional comment is required: time ("with regard to the future work") can contract until it is no longer time, but presence; the "location" is then no longer a "foundation," but a *means of preservation.* These two elements are always necessary for an act of creation: the created and creation. The created comes in two forms: first, as an aggregate—the past; second, in countless small fragments scattered throughout the creative act (they all actually play the same role, one need only discern them at a microscopic level)—the preserving present.

To say the same thing again using different words: for those who know how to apply time properly in their thinking, who know how to think time, and that means how to think time *away*, all of French history relates to the French Revolution as Goethe's woman relates to Goethe (this is not a quantitative comparison, but an essential one). In both cases, what has been created furnishes creative power.

By "person" Goethe meant what we usually call "worth": more precisely, the human form that is worthy.

When Goethe says "person," he expresses himself with a subtle and productive nuance but at the cost of being less comprehensible—two elements that generally go together.

I have twice appended "in the human sense of the word" to "worth." The opposite would be: in the sense of the All, measured against the universe. But how can one essentially measure anything against Creation (as they call it): for "Creation" worth is always one, yesterday, today, and in the future. One cannot expect change from an entity that always remains the same. But one can advance humanity.

It would be pointless to want to change the universe, to advance it, eternal unity that it is, because there is nothing outside of it.—But human beings gain worth to the extent that they are able to insert themselves in the All, more exactly, to participate intentionally in this inclusion.

134

One cannot have the will to greatness without greatness. Where there is an authentic will to greatness, there is greatness.

135

On a Kind of Duality

Just as we cannot think of something other than in space and time, we are similarly unable to hold certain of its characteristics in mind *simultaneously* (one characteristic appears to negate the other even though the thing in question has both).

So it is with this central and terrible question: we know that we can change nothing (so infinitesimally little, that we can justifiably say: nothing); and we know that we must constantly change, that we *only survive through change*: we change and live because of this change and yet we change nothing. These two things cannot be considered together; they cannot be thought simultaneously and cannot be reconciled—and yet, each in itself is clearly part of our reality and our experience. The first is a kind of knowledge (one we might call pure) and the second is knowledge of what we must do (—and is also a pure knowledge).

I once formulated it this way: "Life wants transformation and will achieve the preservation of what is essential. Death wants preservation and will achieve decay."[16]

16. *Nuancen und Details* II, 51.

136

One essential thing we must never forget: that it is up to *us* to change the world, not up to others. *Always up to us.*

137

When YOU change yourself, the world changes.

138

The idea that the "earthly"—our life—is merely a preparation is lovely but easily misunderstood and dangerous. Dangerous when it leads us to believe in the existence of a "hereafter."

Preparation for what, then?

Yes, for what! (For all other preparations in their endless chain . . .)

139

And yet and yet . . . there is only *one* way to improve the world and that is to change the world—never the opposite.

Freedom is found where one is attuned to necessity—nowhere else.

The *bourgeois* are those who say, "it's necessary" of things that have long ceased to be necessary and in doing so they disrespect necessity.

A genius is one who always recognizes necessity as soon as it has become necessity (or at the most: what is about to become necessity).

And where, then, does that leave *the good?* No need to worry! The concept of the good derives from that of *necessity* (the good is secondary, necessity primary). Whatever complies with necessity is good. Human values are persistent; when challenged, they only increase.

Knowledge brings tremendous *strangeness* to the natural world.

140

Man must first recognize his break from nature to become part of nature again.

141

Always keep in mind that development advances only in the one direction, never in the other.

142

To resist a truth one has recognized is to kill.

143

And, always in that same important context:

When you do one thing simply in order to do another—it does you no good.

144

With regard to the statement: "A human being has a duty to be prosperous."

Wasting time is for bunglers. For those on a superior level, it is a matter of living each moment fully—according to the nature of *the particular moment.* Wasted time, like time well spent, will be full, full in its own way. Complete sleep will yield utter wakefulness; a time of consummate reading, of consummate social activity will yield a time of consummate activity in work, and so on.

The value of production (for productive people) is in productivity itself, not in what is produced.

In other words:

Production and productivity, when compared solely with regard to their inherent values, are one and the same.

Or: productivity is the highest form of production.

145

Socialism in its consummate form and spirit are surrogates for each other; that is, consummate socialism replaces spirit and true spirit replaces socialism.

146

"Very well, but what of others?"

Are those who receive the "work" not others? From what sign do you recognize the other? From the fact that he receives help!

147

I have spoken at length about the vital importance of the ability to communicate, to reach others—:

But there is a certain relationship to one's surroundings that the creative spirit should never have.

This statement must be understood in the following context: the powerful were all dreamers once.

148

Because it is said that someone "had no enemies," I am far from concluding that he had even one friend. Nullities do not make much of an impression on other nullities.

149

I believe everyone has the obligation to be thankful to anyone who has accomplished something for their accomplishment. (Just as we feel anger against every nonentity for not doing anything.)

Honor and gratitude are also due to those who have accomplished something in fields opposed to one's own and perhaps even in fields one finds repellent. — To every true connoisseur of any profession, of any industry, of any relation between worldly things, *to every real connoisseur of any circumstances whatsoever.*

150

Take note again and again (something Balzac, too, emphasizes) of the way small things teach greater ones.

In one particular application of this observation:
"If men were willing to be frank with themselves, they would perhaps recognize that misfortune never once befell them without their having received some warning, either obvious or veiled."[17]

151

People are not always aware of what they reveal.

Certainly, on the *true* path our knowledge is without limits; but here, precisely, are the limits . . . *of such* a path to knowledge.
The latter path is the individual, humanly accessible path; the former is the path of integral knowledge: the superhuman path, so to speak. Yet one could ask: why do I use the indicative instead of saying "our knowledge *would be* without limits"? Because the true path is not extra-human; because for the briefest of moments — when we have reached a summit — we do perceive it. Hence the statement: We only have *moments* of closeness.

[. . .]

153

"Whoever wants more than one friend, deserves none at all." (Hebbel). — One's works? They are letters to a friend. In general, ex-

17. Balzac, *Une Ténèbreuse Affaire.*

traordinary natures cannot have a friend near them (in any case, the limits of people's spheres of life make this unlikely: only those who are similar connect); their works are letters to a distant friend.

154

The Intellectual Laborer's Relation to the People

It is not a matter of lowering himself to their level, but of raising them up to his. This is something those who want above all to promote dialects, who eulogize thatched roofs and, whenever possible, behave "like plebs" do not like to admit. Here, too, there is only *one* proper way — just as there is with respect to children — : to encourage others to do what is good *for them* and this is not achieved through occasional ingratiation. "Oh, the connoisseur of human nature! With children he behaves like a child, / But the tree and the child seek what is above them."

I quoted this Hölderlin epigram from memory; but when I looked it up, I found something even more striking: the title, which I had forgotten or never even noticed. It is "False Popularity."

About those "who want above all to promote dialects": — they should instead offer a language that leads forward (one that a greater number of people speak; that enables one to say more and to say it more precisely).

As for "eulogizing thatched roofs": — they should instead provide roofs that leak less.

[. . .]

156

I believe that just as things would lose their form (their perceptibility) in an absolute light, an absolute (universal) consciousness would erase consciousness (at least on a human scale, but what other scale can there be?).

However, this does not mean that we should remain in twilight; we should always strive toward the light. In accordance with the fundamental principle, development advances in only *one* direction.

One of the worst things about Holland (aside from the language) is that people love twilight and in the evening they wait as long as possible before turning on any lights (perhaps primarily out of stinginess).

The "dawning of consciousness": I am fond of this expression. But how does it dawn? Only insofar as we emerge from the darkness into the light.

Despise all darkness: the north, the night, ignorance, etc.

157

Sorrow. "He is alone with his sorrow." To be precise, one is always alone with one's sorrow. — One who suffers sorrow absolutely is necessarily absolutely alone (cf. on this topic the final pages of Malraux's *The Royal Way*).

Only a few have at their disposal strong remedies against sorrow: they alleviate it through a powerful countercurrent.

What is called "shared sorrow" is not shared by any means; but is sorrow lightened by joy (that comes from concord).

Taking part in sorrow does not mean that one takes on a part of it: but one overcomes (lightens) sorrow though something greater.

Joy, now *that* one can share! This is a strange phenomenon and it can provide the basis for an important observation: it reveals the fact that sorrow and joy are not opposites (opposites are indeed similar) but are of *different natures.*

158

One of the most difficult things to do: to think the number two. (The young are utterly incapable of this).

At a certain stage of development, prominent men fall into a distressing state of intellectual impotence on account of this mistake (this flaw in their thinking—

there is no other): they have not mastered the concept of "matter"—or "world"—or "woman" (all three names fit the concept). (Men of no importance have always grasped it. But they understand nothing else.)

159

On the number two. Everyday everyone should think of the fact that the most powerful and most spiritual institution (I do say *institution*), the papacy, sentenced those who claimed that the sun did not revolve around the earth, but the earth around the sun, to be burned at the stake.

. . . then we would be in a different world, like heaven compared to this one.

160

This is the question: why are all the great teachers of mankind unemployed?

161

He who can help but does not behaves basely.

Consequently: those in whom this behavior predominates are base—unless one is prevented from offering assistance for the sake of a higher quality of assistance. (A higher quality is here exactly the same as a greater quantity, but this is difficult to recognize.)

Another principle says (and Hebbel understood this clearly—"understood this very forcefully" would be better: you can know with quite different levels of force): *One must apply one's strengths where they will achieve the highest result* possible. (Hebbel said that we belong to our greatest strength.)

162

A child has a primary validity (as opposed to an effective validity), all-important but only as mountains or plants are. Effective validity is not less than, is nothing other than a bit of primary validity plus something we learn in the second stage, the degree of awareness about the state of the world; the means. When this awareness acquired in the second stage *rejoins* the primary validity, it produces art or productivity in general (effective validity). Alone it is nothing.

163

It takes exceptional strength to maintain one's spiritual dignity when in financial distress (defenseless because of misery); the artist can do it, the common man cannot; so the common man must change the world. (For spiritual dignity is everything, or at least, the primary concern.)

In earlier times, the problem was solved through religion. Religion with heaven and so on bestowed a treasure on which the individual could draw; just as the artist draws on riches. *Now that we can think differently,* religion is no longer a solution. Only through dense, absolute faith could it solve problems; we cannot return to an old faith but only move to a new faith (one that includes all new findings without eliminating a single one); here rules the iron law of irreversibility,[18] of sequence: once we are aware of something . . .

164

"A saint," my friend? One who has been sanctioned, I would say.

165

I would like to know what the saints have done, if anything, that is more than what Balzac or (the later) Rilke have done.

18. Cf. 141, 142, 156, 19.

What can be considered holy, if not such a life as Balzac's? If you place the periods of his life side by side (there are only two): the infinite, inexpressible weight of the first part,[19] in which he had only a star for a friend and the terrible, prolonged, apparently superhuman creative unloading and endless hardship of the second (from the ages of thirty to fifty); then death intervened when he had reached his prospect. What can one do but weep at such a sight? He is another Benassis.[20]

166

Passing a church.

Well, they built it there, a *massive stone building*, for——; for nothing. This enormous stone building, with all its splendor and signs of sublime gravity, stands for something that does not exist: anyone who understands this would be ripe to change the world radically. (Consider how much less firmly based on reality other institutions must be.)

Effective means to persuade people that God does not exist can surely only be created out of precise knowledge of what drives believers; no one who is far removed from this could create the means—he would be talking to the wall, doors would be shut in his face. Only someone with profound experience of faith could do so. One who sees: that he never actually believed in God (which does not reduce the importance of his experience in any way) and that no one does; that he had only been making enormous efforts to convince himself and to call up the presence a powerful, clearly delineated You: he performed magic (he tried to, in any case: he engaged with magic). He rose above his circumstances toward a higher *name*, a name for

19. "I have always bent under a terrible weight . . . nothing can give you an idea of my life before the age of 22. *I am astonished at no longer having to fight destiny.*" (Balzac's letters.)

20. *The Country Doctor.*

his inner life.—Between not believing (Barrès did not believe), and not knowing that God does *not* exist . . . there is a vast expanse.—For some it is not *believing*, but *letting themselves be caught up by certain dynamics.* (Barrès and those more powerful than he: Dostoevsky, late Tolstoy, etc.)

167

The greatest sorrows are always secret ones. Yes, in my experience, always and without exception.

From this it is clear that one way to overcome one's sorrow, or at least lessen it, is to acknowledge it, to oneself first and foremost.

Since almost every sorrow, as soon as it is seen clearly, proves to be one that many others share, it is then alleviated to an even greater extent because as its visibility increases, it is even easier to bring it out of the shadows.

The path? (There is always the question of which path to take, which particular path, which is the *next* path; knowing the general direction, having a *great* idea, an overall idea is not enough.[21]) Accept sorrow, embrace it completely. Because as long as you fight it, an element of denial is present and as long as your affirmation is not complete, sorrow cannot emerge from the shadows and it remains partly secret, in other words, active.

168

When a sorrow arrives, one can choose between only two alternatives: loss or gain; it is utterly impossible to retain one's previous position.

21. Cf. I, 18–24.

169

For this simple, unproductive being, sorrow can mean only loss: a person who has not understood that sorrow need not mean loss—he grasps sorrow as a material reality, determined and immutable, like a boulder—or understood that sorrow is much more an opportunity: for gain or loss. In other words: sorrow itself is not decisive, but *what we make of it* is. For those who fail to see this, who believe that sorrow is the determining factor, it is, in fact, true: they have already opted for loss.

In each sorrow, it is a matter of developing one's highest potential (of achieving the highest results, of making sorrow productive) . . . not for sorrow to stare at the world with enormous eyes like the little horse in my story by the same name from 1929. This path is not impossible: it is too difficult, rarely passable. And it is easily misunderstood: it is solely a path for art. The little horse was not reality, but my writing was; for the little horse, my writing was irrelevant.

170

. . . and nevertheless, he preserved his essence.

But until man can recognize that one does not preserve oneself through preservation but instead by directing oneself outward (expending oneself)—! By investing oneself in continually new areas, one becomes eternal, but one expires when trying to remain in one single one.

Like the flame. The flame, which the greatest thinker of antiquity recognized as an image of the universal. (Or: named when asked what the first principle is.)

171

There is nothing higher, nothing more intensive than the complete participation in life. When this is achieved or almost achieved there is an extraordinary trembling, glittering, a radiance that is always the same,—Bach, Napoleon, any average person in the midst of consummate sexual relations (which, as Lawrence stresses, is a rare thing), every artist whenever he has truly created—no: each time he *creates*. (And the converse: *in this* we find the criterion for true art! Almost everything fails that is coldly created, clever, empty stuff.) And all people, every time they participate in anything fully ("affirmatively"? Participation is always affirmative!); only the domain, or more exactly, the scope differs: with Bach, the scope is always immense, with the average person, it is small.

> In the latter case: the complete participation in any occurrence—the possession of an "adequate idea" of . . . or complete adherence to . . .—is usually called "love"; I am loath to use a word that is misused nineteen times for every time it is used halfway correctly—we can hardly expect better in our secular age. "Love" is the most prostituted word I know.

172

Trade

In order to be able to say "I no longer have a trade"—a phrase one does not say oneself, art says it—one must have achieved a high level of mastery and have a great learned a great deal, if not everything.

In art, learning is forgetting.—A young man is trapped in his great respect for craft; *this* paralyzes him. (Yet he does not know it.)

He stands in a gorge, overshadowed by enormously high mountains. He shouts, "Spirit is all!" but in reality the gigantic mountains appear to him as a conglomeration of crafts—and it is more or less to compensate that he shouts the opposite so loudly—; he sees the external.—Because he *could* now make his creation! He could begin the climb. Respect prevents him. Now he will act as if he were walking on stilts—he has none—now as if he were wearing crampons—on a path—now as if he were on a rope, now as if he were climbing up a chimney. Always falsely undertaken and without moving an inch.

People then declare when they read or see what the eighteen-year-old has written or painted: he has no trade! But it would be more accurate if they were to say: he has too many trades. But that would not be constructive. So, once again: the path to overcoming a trade leads through the trade. It is a kind of unlearning, to be sure, but rather than say "throw it away!," one should merely say "learn!"

The comparison with the high mountains cannot be taken any further. — The young man walks in place as if he were wearing seven coats of armor; one day he throws off the armor (or the idea of it) and takes strides. — Before he was rude, made offensive gestures, and stood in one place; now he conquers the path and makes only those gestures suitable to surmounting it. This is the point where the mountain can no longer teach, for in the mountains it would have been possible to master the path and also make superfluous gestures, *in art this is not possible.*

Swimming would be clearer example, especially swimming with the goal of breaking records. But no analogy is completely satisfactory here. Only "life," that is, art's counterpart, its companion, its extension, its sister can instruct us in this matter. The fact that only fitting gestures master the path and each unsuitable gesture *makes it impossible* to master the path cannot be expressed but only *experienced* in art and "in life."

Perhaps it can be expressed after all, namely, as implied above, not using swimming in general as an analogy, but competitive swimming done with the goal of setting records and in which the essential motion is not movement for its own sake, but for winning the top medal. — And yet, this analogy is also insufficient because one can imagine a flawless swimmer who nonetheless does not set any records; conversely an exceptionally naturally gifted swimmer could perhaps set records with proper form (that is, not using "only fitting gestures"). We would need a nobler and more elevated list of records . . . one that would take into account only those who swim in an integral manner (= establish records measured against the powers a swimmer disposes of at the time). — There are, in any case, two movements, one superior, one inferior. In art, when the inferior movement is completed integrally, the superior one begins immediately. There must be an even more satisfactory analogy, to wit in the mechanical world . . . a gas meter whose indicator for larger units is set in motion only when the indicator for smaller units reaches a certain speed . . . Dynamos that only create electricity when all their components are appropriately set in motion. For the briefest of moments they emit rays, but otherwise spin for a thousand miles providing none.

173

The *totality* oppresses him; because of the whole that he did not possess, he did nothing.

174

Humanity's power is realized in the individual, not in the whole.

175

The Eternal Trade

People always say "on the whole" or "overall"; but everything comes down to details. Anyone can write a novel "on the whole," but it takes a Dostoyevsky to be up to the detail. Anyone can improve the world "overall"—that is, imagine a better world—but conceptualizing particular ideas (of how it is to be changed) is more difficult; still only *the latter* changes the world. Nothing can be changed "overall"; in this realm, ideas always remain ideas, that is, unproductive, sterile; this is the realm of the bourgeois, of the pharmacist.

Even the weakest minds can grasp some idea of the whole. Collecting—no, running through—vast amounts of individual ideas requires the greatest mental powers. There is the admirable saying: *The more things we know, the more we know God,*[22] should resound like music inside and out, on the streets, around us everywhere.

22. Spinoza. (Trans. note.)

176

Light bursts from the detail, not from the whole. Light shining from individual details creates the whole. Man does not create the whole.

177

—But no one measures these unspeakable exertions, he says. But the greatest among them, the world, measured them.

178

Everything ever created was a fragment.

179

Offering Proof

All proof is relative. To prove simply means to place a thing in (proper!) relation with more things. Offering the best proof means bringing the most things into proper relation with each other.

Instead of "proving," one could also say "demonstrating connections." There is no other proof than demonstrating connections.

—So then is proving something an endless process? Indeed, it is; in the end, if we had no quantitative limitations, we would have to use everything to prove any one thing. (Absolute proof, as geometricians conceive of it—or more exactly, those who have a false idea of what geometry is and believe they can apply it to life—is a childish conception.—For what happens in geometry when something is proven? The proof becomes absolute to the extent that it elucidates the relation between one thing and the next.—This is not possible in life because each thing borders other things *all around* and all these things shift each other.)

What, then, is "common sense"? Having very limited horizons and not knowing it.

Am I saying this is bad in every way?—Sometimes, to some degree, it's a blessing!

180

Stupidity is a primary concept; evil a derivative one.

181

It is understandable that the common man worships authority and power above all else. Those who cannot see the infinite number of threads (the dynamic connections) adhere to what at least a *few* threads represent in their (provisional) union.

There is an antidote (infallible, acting of its own accord): knowledge.

Power is universal, omnipresent but also appears to us in the temporary and clearly discernable form of a person. Such a ruler *is* an embodiment of power (reality) and it is therefore legitimate for those who see no other embodiment, no other visible form of power (reality) of similar proportion to revere him. Those who advance in knowledge also advance in the recognition of power's manifestations. Power becomes visible within an ever-increasing circle: for them there are no more such figures of authority. For the knowledgeable, the powerful have already become like boulders but they, the knowledgeable, own the earth; the rulers may possess a piece of rope (the union of *several* threads) but the knowledgeable possess nature itself (through knowledge), which constantly produces billions of threads that can be twisted into a million pieces of rope. *One* piece of rope against nature's billions of threads: when a ruler moves his rope, dogs and cats that happen to be in his presence revere him. (Reverence and partial dependence are two different things.)

182

Always be suspicious of a teaching that aims to restore the past (a past about which little is known).

(Whether it be the teaching of the aged Tolstoy who wanted to revive the conditions of the earliest Christians or of powerful political movements like Fascism.)

183

As long as the awareness of something is lacking, it cannot be a sin—though it can certainly be an impediment. Once one is conscious of the impeding thing, it is a sin.

184

"Rest will fix it." No, rest does not fix anything, but (beneficial) movement does.

185

Whether Galileo said "and yet it moves" or not, or whether someone else said it doesn't interest me and hasn't for a long time. Nor does the question of whether "this" or "that" should move. All that matters is whether one can say *". . . and yet it moves"* or not.

186

Do not believe what people say! Do not believe that once evil sets in, it continues of its own accord and expands until . . . That is pure nonsense and unnecessary. Evil can be studied once it has appeared and a means of protection be created against a similar evil, against its expansion. What people say is true only for the lazy, that what has begun must continue to grow, feeding on itself like cancer.

For the lazy: those who do not intervene. It all continues, feeds, expands according to its nature; evil, good. The good? *Only that good which is none at all*, like the Salvation Army.

187

That morality which runs counter to a higher morality no longer has an ethical basis.

188

The spiritual man (or productive man, which is the same) can only hate *one* thing: stupidity (or laziness, which is the same).

Depending on the circumstances—according to the kind of relation, the way by which we approach the matter—we say "laziness" or "stupidity." That Goethe preferred to say "stupidity" allows us to pinpoint his time and place. Today we place more emphasis on the possibility of change and on circumstances and say "laziness."

189

Spirit is measured by the strength of its resistance to what is commonly called spirit.

190

Consistency. Many boast that they have thought the same thing for twenty years—one should crown their work by specifying: "in other words, nothing at all."

191

The bourgeois judges people negatively—those with no bad qualities are good—; the man of intellect and spirit judges people positively—those with no good qualities are bad.

192

While making progress. He who measures himself against those behind (under) him is lost. (What prevents him, when he has slipped backward, from comparing himself to those behind him and so on to point zero? That, indeed, is the likelier progression.)

193

They say: "He is the newly born man of the future." No, he is only predominantly the man of the future and must daily extinguish the man of the past within himself. (Those who do not live in continuous change are null and void.)

194

Those who have no self-discipline—to me this seems certain—are incapable of intellectual or spiritual achievement.

They are no doubt perfectly suited for the usual occupations: the office director or the house rules, etc. provide the discipline. But for spiritual and intellectual undertakings, where can one find systems with bosses and rules and requirements to help them be realized?

I am, of course, speaking of discipline exerted on those powers that make works of the mind possible, not the kinds of discipline that would appeal to a pharmacist; I mean, for example, a painter's discipline over his pictorial abilities, not over his clothing, his mealtimes, his sexual behavior—or only to the extent that these things (clothing, social conventions) make the other (artistic processes) possible or impossible; a completely personal matter.

195

There is no system (for life or any part of it) that renders intelligence superfluous.

196

When lifting a heavy weight: if you give it your all, the result will depend on external circumstances. But if you don't, then it will depend on you.

When you give your utmost, you do not need to make a *superhuman effort*; if you don't, you will reach exactly your level.

"He put in a superhuman effort." I certainly believe it—from the negligible results I concluded that he wanted to force things above and outside himself instead of engaging, investing himself completely.

197

There are no preparations! Only work, i.e. execution; admittedly, execution of many different kinds.

Some devote all their time to preparations, others are overly hasty, wanting to skip stages in their work.

198

You see it every day: people do not help each other because they do not want to.

"The only purpose in man's life is to promote his own well-being and that of his fellow men to the extent his powers and his station in life allow." Lichtenberg

—It's not a matter of being able to work magic; simply offering more help will work wonders.

199

If only everyone understood that they have but *one* homeland: that is work. Indeed, good work, true work.

200

Types of Knowledge

It is not a question of knowing an enormous amount but of knowing the right thing at the right time. André Gide is such a man; he always knew the right things. Others who seem very knowledgeable only have apparent knowledge. No one can know a great many things *concurrently.*

Knowing a great many things simultaneously is for libraries; we are not walking libraries.

> As for the "right thing at the right time": this is a capacity usually noticed later; in the moment, its depth is not recognized. That's just it, others do not know the right thing! That is also what makes Lenin such a gripping example. The walking library, always chattering, someone always talking of heaven and earth makes the biggest impression.

Thomas Mann is certainly not such a mind, and yet the slight danger of a great simultaneity of knowledge is perceptible at certain points in his work;[23] a danger in that it begins to create hindrances to the necessary profound deepening at any time. There is a certain grace in being able to choose. We usually think it a blessing when we can know many things in parallel; but there is a still higher, more luminous blessing in being able to select the right thing at the right time (even if against others, even to the others' detriment and with full responsibility!).[24]

Every instant has the potential to yield the superlative; one must simply be able to receive it. This receptivity is, in fact, the highest knowledge.

[. . .]

23. Written in 1933.
24. Cf. 10.

202

An idiot. He spent his life researching whether or not what was up to *him* to discover had already been discovered by others, so that he wouldn't have to bother discovering it.

He had delusions of grandeur: he took himself so seriously that he would have been ashamed to follow a path someone had trodden at some point before him.

203

Legacy

It is not easy to live according to the precepts of great thinkers, that is, to follow the precepts of great thinkers who are dead. Each of the two ways, the two possibilities of doing so conceals its particular dangers.

One can follow their precepts to the letter. The danger here: meaninglessness.

The other way is to recognize that their sentences must be altered, expanded, to keep from being bound to the exact wording, and one must dare to create new sentences from the totality of their thinking. The danger here is: the creation of something completely different (like gospels by Saint Paul).

What is the good way, the path of proper discipleship? It is only to be found in the difficult. — It is only possible when one undergoes a similar experience, when one *re*discovers the inexpressible in the sentences of the particular thinker; — when one can rebuild sentences from the entirety of his thought and, with the same effort, create something appropriately new. — Are these sentences ineffectual? No, but they are only effective when one has, through one's own powers, come very close to the original: then the spark is transmitted.

204

When did I have that incomprehensible dream about precious stones?—"You *produce* them, you don't find them. You produce them from the earth."—?

It was a tremendous intuition, the dream of a transition.

205

A new religion never declares on its arrival, "I am a new religion" (whatever calls itself religion should never be taken seriously), but instead declares, "the Truth is . . ."

> That is how one recognizes it.
> (For *they* too . . . "will only be saved through faith.")

206

Necessity, yes. But man makes manifest his great strengths only in what he performs "freely." The quotation marks are important. I know very well that freedom is a higher necessity (a necessity related to wider circles), one that does not appear to us as a necessity close up.

> All superior schools, in all eras, were voluntary (certain Greek philosophical schools, for example, or schools grouped around a particular master in the Renaissance): that is, attendance was not compulsory, rather, it was very difficult to gain admittance.—Almost all intellectual achievements originated "in idleness." Anyone who accomplished anything during his school years (here I mean in our schools) generally accomplished it outside of school, not in it. Why did Montaigne, Balzac, Goethe, or Lichtenberg not become prominent in the schools of their day or their equivalents, but outside the institutions they were encouraged, even expected, to attend? Why did Alexander, Napoleon, or Lenin not achieve greatness in the *existing* systems, faithfully fulfilling their obligations and potential in the places they had been assigned?

207

One's personality is formed through spiritual and intellectual experiences, in exactly the same way as the power of the papacy was formed by the crusades.

Few understand this; most assume that it takes shape "of its own accord," quietly, through "growth" (and other such obscure, meaningless terms).

A young man between twenty and twenty-five years old may have an experience in which the concept of "God" is central; afterward the *substance* falls away, that is, everything that seemed important in the intense experience at the time — just as the crusades did not achieve anything — and something barely noticed, if at all, remained: a hardness built through the struggles, the exposure, the summoning of strength to confront the world, through the first questioning of the world and the experience of isolation experienced. The young man later abandons everything he fought for and recognizes the contingency of the forces that had gripped him — yet he emerges from the experience as *a man*.

208

Christianity

It initially reigned over part of the world (a very small part compared to the whole) only to the extent that it changed people. Then it dominated *the* world through the esteem elicited by its actual impact. — A (relatively) small internal change gave rise to an enormous external expansion of power.

If you compare the Christian communities of the earliest centuries with the crusades and the global power of the popes, what comes to mind is the trajectory of a writer, who, driven by spiritual realities (necessity) creates a true work, but then, after he has achieved success through this work, his earthly existence becomes more powerful, gains priority, and he increasingly forgets his beginning (the extensions of his work become thinner and thinner until they disappear altogether) and not just his beginning, but all that made this powerful external existence possible.

A Balzac or a Goethe, however, remain noble and spiritually productive until the end. Why? Because from the very beginning, they never disowned anything, they did not "come out of the blue."

When did Christianity cease? By the time of the crusades, in any case, it was already distant history.

What, exactly, is the spiritual? It is the initial stage, the burgeoning consciousness of a power that can change the world. The opposite of warriors and the clergy.

We call creative those eras that had many of these initial stages, eras of continual revolutions: Greece (but not Sparta), the Italian Renaissance. In contrast we have the Middle Ages: enormous power held by the clergy, the military, knights, and the nobility. Uncreative to the highest degree;[25] a latent time for development that from a distance gives the impression of being "dark." Indeed, it truly was the dark ages.

209

With learning. And with developing the world:
It's not that simple! It's much simpler.

210

Instruction

Most difficulties, in fact, the great majority do not come from the fact that the material is hard to learn, but from the fact that the teacher says it is.

25. It left behind architecture and a bit more; but keep in mind that it was a period of a thousand years.

If it were difficult and the teacher said, "it's difficult," it would still not be as hard as it is when the teacher says that easy things are "hard." This completely confuses the (gifted) student.

When will it finally end? When will the pharmacists be thrown out of the educational system and banished to Devil's Island or some other penal colony? They who destroy precious goods through forced labor!

For the gifted student says "it can't be that simple" about the laws of elementary physics. "It can't be as simple as it seems at first glance, as it is on the page and as it sounds." And so he seeks out material to learn that is *external*, in the void—; he summons his energy for pointless approaches, he succumbs to the law of *false preparation* and no longer *sees*.

The worst is not that student does not learn, but *that he unlearns how to learn!* (A crust forms. Getting rid of it later in life will require enormous work in the best cases.) This is the effect of schooling. This is why I vote for the Devil's Island.

Proper language instruction is the one that does not allow for preparation, but immediately offers something definitive and *gives* it.—Even if it is just *one word*. If "columba" is said, you have Latin.

It's the same in all branches of knowledge.

New productivity comes from production. A leap must always be made from the preparation, the first, decisive leap—and it gets harder and harder.

Human dignity does not suffer these preparations and takes revenge with a kind of sclerosis: it wants to create at any price and if no good path toward creation is available, it will find a bad one.

That school declares: "Humble yourself! You will not understand anything for a long time yet (—once you have scaled the Olympian heights of a professorship, then you will surely understand the entire world). For now, bow your head in preparation."

[. . .]

214

I very rarely find what children say to be *droll.* I almost always find it to be serious.

215

The main effect of contemporary education is to make students immune to learning.

216

What has already been said a thousand times, can be repeated countless time more; but it should never be parroted; therein lies the difference.

217

Dangerous Intervals

There is a way of hindering accomplishment that is usually overlooked. It first became obvious to me in the "logical thinking" of schoolteachers.[26] Now I see it more broadly: in all that does not happen because *time* is taken for things that do not require it.

(One could say: he takes his time getting out of bed. As a result: he falls asleep.)

For almost every activity it is important *not to take a running start.* So many results are sacrificed for the run up!

26. Cf. 210.

218

When someone does nothing, he is also far from preparing anything.

There are no *necessary* preparations. Any preparations necessary to a planned creative project are themselves creative.

People spend most of their time in preparation, especially—and this is the crux of the matter—in unnecessary preparation.

(They generally spend what time remains building funerary monuments.)

219

Beautiful weather will lead you to great creativity, it will, not you yourself,—but only if you have exercised your powers in all weather.

You therefore do not need to wait for beautiful weather; no, you *do not have the right* to wait for it.

However, the use of your powers should proceed in a steady line, not in fervid fits and starts (because your progress will never be more than intermittent and you will miss good opportunities)—and then you will never believe that beginning is difficult!

220

We do good work, that is, we always use our strength for that which brings reward (and the highest reward!)—but not because of the reward.

221

One must do what is definitive, that which one *wants* to be definitive—not preparations that will *lead* to it.

As with writing, the primary rule is: the essential first! So, if one is aiming toward state B, one should not bring in the opposite state

A for it to lead to B. Our life is too short—in the meantime C and D could intervene unexpectedly and change everything and you will never finish your project.[27]

222

The artist. He never found the right shade of the color he had chosen (even though he had covered half the world in his search), and it was all extremely complicated:—there was no life in it. He only found the right color when he wrote with his own blood; then it all became very simple.

223

Haste . . .—should one never be in haste? Haste and urgency are appropriate for one thing: accomplishing the essential before dying.
[. . .]

225

Wastage is the highest (the quantitatively most important) law of nature.

226

And even if misunderstanding is ninety-nine times greater than understanding, it is still not misunderstanding that counts, but understanding, that 1 percent.

---

27. To show mercy to inadequate readers for once, I will include this (weaker) variant: ". . . in the meantime C and D could intervene unexpectedly, change everything for the worst, and we will still not have expressed what is most important to us."

227

Once again: when I climbed highest, I saw that genius and socialism were one and the same.

I don't see this every day. But in the mountains I also don't see a certain ridge in connection to another every day: only when I have climbed very high up the one mountain from which you can see it;—from that altitude you can see the single wave that created the entire range, that still flows through the range which, from the valley, looks like two peaks.

228

Again and again you hear "strong" and "weak." "Van Gogh was one of the strongest." "—was so weak."

But strong *in what?* In physical power, in patience—or in the *will to reality?*

229

All that exists is illness and healing. There are many other things as well, to be sure, but they have no value—just apparent existence.

230

Illness has no value, nor does restored health; healing is everything, healing is humanity.

231

"She will never be done with her symptoms": because she suffers much *too little* from them.

232

A miracle does not originate in external coincidence, but in the power of one's conduct.

233

Misfortune

"Misfortune alone is still not complete misfortune . . ."[28]

. . . and material privation becomes truly terrible when *this state of want provides reasons to cease all activity.*

> On the other hand (in a less definitive sense), the greatest degree of material distress is reached when it begins to isolate us from others.
>
> (Those who avoid the indigent are not particularly gifted intellectually or spiritually—but they are legion.)

One need not invoke the reasons for abandoning activity in indigence: they come in droves with exceptional intensity; just a fraction of them would suffice.—One *must not* accept them.

Even if our activity becomes ever more restricted (in external terms), it must persist time and again!

Circle after circle will collapse but your activity will flourish in the next (inner) circle—otherwise you are truly lost.

In the end, the violin player played on his bones after his last instrument was destroyed—that is, the last thing that served him as an instrument since he had been reduced to using random devices!

(Once his audience had disappeared, he could still write for eternity. Then they took away his notepad. He could still play for his four walls, then they took away his violin.)

28. Cf. 333, 52, 100.

234

The greater the losses, the more our inner light must shine. When affirmation is affirmed in all, negation merely disappears.

235

Of Good Minds and Bad

I would like to express the revulsion I feel for certain ways of thinking that serve the interests of the system and its powers of demonstration! Ways of thinking that create a structure of thought! No one can create a monument with their thought and yet imposing structures are built to impress the pharmacists; the hope is to reap fame for these elaborately constructed forms, more fame than is possible from modest things that are the truth: the eternal fragments, the shards that constantly reveal new gaps, slivers of rock broken off of mountains. Such fragments of truth, like those Heraclitus, Goethe, Lichtenberg, and others have brought to light, have made little impression on men in general who prefer a completely structured world, with precise divisions, God sitting on the very top and below him the pyramid with drawers for all odds and ends.

"Please don't come with any new facts, now that my system is complete . . ." Such is the attitude of many a famous philosopher, but none adopt it so thoroughly as theologians. However, another kind of mind delights in new elements, nutrition that will enrich and expand its ideas dramatically; eternal progenitors, their ideas multiply and become legion. While the former fear and fight against reality's every discovery, the latter welcome the new and call on everyone to work together. The former prefer to turn to unseeing minds—minds that think, of course, but only with their eyes closed—; they call precisely on the pharmacists; endlessly they call: "think logically!"

As if logical thought were not self-evident.

But this is how they capture others: by telling them that logical thought is difficult. While these good people struggle with a non-existent difficulty, they easily fall into the system; it never occurs to them to test the system with *realities* (since the system is as good as any other).—It is as if a philosopher or theologian were standing in front of a cabinet. "You cannot climb in," he tells the young and the pharmacists, "the step is tremendously difficult." Once people have climbed in, in their delight at having made such a difficult step, they do not notice that they have been locked in the cabinet.

[. . .]

237

"For we know in part": Saint Paul was right. But to me partial knowledge is preferable to his empty universe which must invent a God to fill the void and which would not subsist without God's guiding hand.

238

When you imagine God for a long period of time, He ultimately appears. You could also summon the devil and assorted spirits in a similar fashion. It's difficult to determine in which moments these spirits are all united. At least such spirits appear differently each time, which is why the religious have ordered: "You shall not make for yourself an image!" otherwise, if one were to compare all the *different* images: when there is but *one* God . . .

239

According to what we know of history, nothing has ever happened, not even the smallest event, that would indicate the existence of a god. Why, then, should I accept the existence of a god?

However, according to what we know of history, every time someone has spoken of God, called one of his projections God, we can explain why he has done so.

It is, therefore, utterly impossible not only to prove a god's existence in any way, but also to justify the assumption that one exists.

In order to justify the assumption that someone is sitting in a shed, must there not be some sign of his presence, however small? You must have heard a sound, however faint. Or you must have seen a shadow. Or footprints leading toward the shed. Found an open door that had been closed. Seen smoke rising from the chimney. Someone who had been in the area must have disappeared. Or you must have seen, heard, smelled, learned something.

Wanting to prove His existence (or even just to express one's assumptions about it) is as pointless as wanting to prove that there is a sewing machine next to my desk when no one can or ever did see, hear, or feel any sign of a sewing machine, nor did anyone ever have any evidence whatsoever on which to base such a claim. (The desire to prove the existence of an unknown civilization numbering a million people in deepest South America would be much less otiose.)

The cleverest of the theologians have understood this and have thus retreated behind the Revelation.

But the Revelation is exactly what we have already touched on. A skilled psychologist would be able to trace the Revelation in every single case back to known elements that have nothing to do with a divinity.

240

I believe that when someone *clearly knows* that there is no God it is, first of all, something important and, second, something rare — much rarer than one would think. Most have no opinion on the matter. It also seemed to me earlier that one could examine the question with indifference — God seemed so unimportant that one need not bother with the question of whether He exists or not. This changed as I met and observed more men and learned more about them.

241

Theory is the enemy. Observation is an ally.

"Won't that attitude lead to a complete muddle?"

You can bungle just as much through observation as in any other way! If you observe without kitsch, there's no confusion, no general collapse, instead you draw a line that leads toward the eternal, as close to the eternal as we can reach.

Who, and how many, truly observe?

242

What is observation? Love.

[. . .]

244

Man focuses on what has disappeared and easily forgets what he still *has*.

245

Decadence. In times when one hears much talk of decadence, there's good reason it is a frequent topic of discussion. Men have always been decadent—it is entirely a question of perspective. During the times in question, it is the point of view that is decadent: one that sees in all phenomena only the traces of decayed earlier forms, for example, on a tree in March, it sees only the dead leaves from the previous year.

246

Thrift, on the other hand and despite everything, contains an aspect that is part of the highest wisdom, a majority of it, in fact; the recognition of the importance of the small, of invisible beginnings, of apparently insubstantial things that, together, are a force capable of conquering the world.—Whereas the disdainfully superficial declare, "Nothing can be done with so little," and never change the world.

247

Almost all the great teachers contain every human possibility, but with varying emphases, that is, in different quantities.

It is History's task to bring them to fruition, one after the other.

248

Too much of this—too much of that; in other words, the good becomes bad, the bad good. What is to be done? Find the proper dose: *nourishment* is the absolute!

The young always seek their well-being in systems—not in nature.

249

What is most important is that *tension* be maintained in spiritual development, in agreement as in contradiction. There must be a locus of resistance. "Well, we made it!" the representatives of the *other* society call. "You've *gotten bogged down*," would be the response: what some call spiritual resistance.

250

When man invented (discovered?) planimetrics, they measured everything according to a grid: rigidity, for example, or the color of deep water, or electricity, or faith.

251

Idiots always try to relate one thing to another instead of differentiating them.

252

If only people were at least aware if they were guided by ignorance or judgment . . . !

("At least . . ."? No, it would be a great deal. — Perhaps inaccessible.)

253

The unfortunate state of affairs in our time comes from the fact that most specialists flatter themselves that they are universal, instead of acknowledging that they are specialists just like others are specialists. The politician imagines he is the world's savior rather than a politician. As a politician, he may well contribute to saving the world, but through political means. The artist, in turn, carries on as if the politician could not possibly contribute to saving the world. (— because they work in different ways; he is offended by the others' means — as if another profession did not require other means. The artist works within the absolute, but without time — the present —. The politician works in the relative and therefore has time.)

254

The deepest sorrow is always that which is connected to an accomplishment.

255

Two kinds of reproach are the most offensive: those that are completely false — unfounded, inapplicable — and those that are true (*this* one knows all too well!).

256

Fame.—The superior in spirit do not scorn fame despite recognizing its vainness. They accept it to a certain extent, quite simply because of the material necessities of existence. They accept the false construct because certain elements replace, at least in external effect, the simple and true thing they will never achieve: respect.

257

Creative Spirits and the World Around Them

A real insight must often be defended against the endless assaults of others who do not understand it by reinforcing it to such an extent that, simply as a result of the reinforcement, it *becomes* false. One must be on guard against this danger (consciousness is the best means). Stendhal had the ideal approach to this difficulty: he simply ignored the incomprehension of others. This requires exceptional strength. (If you're looking for a counter-example, Nietzsche is the most obvious.)

"He simply ignored": when his perceptions were right, he must have known, insofar as others were involved at all, that they could not understand him; if his prophecy that he would be understood in one hundred years was well-founded, then he could hardly be surprised that others had no wish to understand him, their incomprehension being equally well-founded.

Stendhal—or Spinoza. Their superiority provided others with the excuses they would have been unable to come up with on their own. "Indulgence for the victor must be entrusted to time. Otherwise all that is left us is suffering."[29]

29. Heinrich Mann, from an essay on Wedekind.

258

The secret to accessing the creative, intensified by the current state of accommodations and the world, is to cut oneself off; but how can you cut yourself off without money?

Those who have even modest amounts of money do not understand this; they do not know how an utter lack of resources *pushes one out.*

259

On the Lack of Money

Production does not come from *other* things but arises from one's own condition! . . . Yet how can one perceive that condition if it is *permanent?* Just as man can become conscious of himself only through action, that is, through his effect upon other things, so a condition can only be represented (in a chemical sense) through its borders with others. — And it is self-evident that a condition cannot become productive without the awareness of those in it.

It is exceptionally difficult for those who were never indigent to imagine what it is like. For people in general it is almost impossible. — It is entirely a matter of training oneself to this knowledge, to seek it artificially. There are two methods: first, precise knowledge of the difficulties strengthens the powers of imagination; second, by reading good writers.

The worst aspect of indigence is the most often overlooked: many of those who have themselves been penniless, but only for a short time, cannot understand its long-term effects! — The effects of this condition change dramatically through long duration.

Temporary poverty (like partial poverty), even when it occurs repeatedly, has an air of being voluntary and has, as is well known, almost none of the determinative psychological effects of complete and lasting poverty. Consider the self-imposed privations of the miserly — hunger pangs on a high-altitude ascent — fasting as sport — Tolstoy's voluntary poverty in old age (which may have been an authentic experience but was nonetheless something completely different from the condition he intended to emulate).

260

On a Carapace

They want to feed the hungry, they offer food—and expect the hungry to be happy.

Rapid change *is* possible—but not on command.

He sleepily contemplates the new society, he who was fast asleep during its long absence.

He had devised a system of sleep that saved him. He had to take great pains. He won new friends: elves and spirits—he was now suddenly required to give them up. What right did the new society have to demand this of him? Would it be happy if treated in such a manner (with such a rapid and easy breach of trust)?

> In secondary school, at about the age of seventeen, I was taught one or two subjects by a teacher with whom I could have had a productive relationship; that was not the case and for only one reason: I could not suddenly discard the thick armor I had built up to protect myself from school and all teachers—despite having had a *good* teacher when I was fourteen and fifteen, by then it was already too late. All the more so because this carapace was not created externally and simply strapped on but was created from my own substance.
>
> This kind of armor deserves more attention than it gets.

Next door lives a man whose entire weekly assistance consists of six guilders. Abandoned by all, he is old and half-mad. He can often, in fact, almost constantly be heard groaning, cursing, and raging in his shanty. I soon became convinced that things had become so terrible (he was perhaps "half-mad" but certainly intolerable) precisely because he had nothing: nothing to do, nothing to drink, but worst of all—since he is at least seventy and fragile—no human interaction.

But my error was soon very clearly pointed out to me: someone had tried to visit the man but had been rudely turned away, had the door slammed in his face.

There it is! Do you really think *the man would still be alive if he were in any condition to receive visitors?*

One adapts to every situation to bear it as much as possible.

> The man would have expired long ago if he had not abandoned any condition that made visiting him easy! If he had not acquired this armor and shield, the only possible condition for him since he has lacked external support for ten years, do you think he could have waited for you? Remaining accessible for ten years? At whose cost?
>
> Stifter understood this: ". . . and when, on an impulse of belated love and pity, the mother would take the small being in her arms and cover her with tears, the child showed no sign of joy, but began to cry and struggle to escape the hands that held her. The mother grew both more loving and embittered in response to this rejection, because she did not know that the tiny rootlets that had once sought the warm soil of motherly love in vain had had to counter and find a hold the stoniness of its own being."[30]

261

Very often, past offenses are not forgotten in a spirit of generosity but of mean-spiritedness.

Take misdeeds one has outgrown, for example, mistreatment one had to endure as a child. The currently vulnerable are powerless to defend themselves against it. But those who are no longer subject to this mistreatment and could defend the powerless—perhaps even better than they could defend themselves—but nonetheless choose to forget their past ordeals are people of no consequence. They lack imagination and a sense of responsibility.

To put it more bluntly: they are rogues. (They have betrayed the one light in their past darkness: the hope that they could one

30. "Brigitta."

day do their best to stop those who commit the offenses they once suffered. — No one is free of this responsibility until such abuses are ended. The fact that someone no longer suffers mistreatment does not absolve him of responsibility toward others.

To put it less bluntly: such people pass up their best opportunity to be productive.

[. . .]

263

Knowledge and Belief

Knowledge cannot be preserved for long. It eventually sinks back into the more durable form of belief. (This belief is, of course, founded on new knowledge. Nonetheless, one can speak of "regression"; the "regression" in this case is not horizontal, but vertical: — earthward.) (Note that I say "it sinks"; that is precisely what I mean.)

But faith, the more durable form, lacks nerves: it does not notice pain or illness, to its very ruin.

264

Fragments and Variations on the Central Issue

Action is not supreme but knowledge is; that is precisely why taking action is the right thing to do, for action alone brings us uninterrupted knowledge.

Knowledge kills itself when it remains isolated; first it becomes a system, then it perishes altogether.

What are action's limits, its opponent? Hopelessness.

Knowledge is action's hope. But the father and son of knowledge is action.

—We are not really saved by belief, no matter how much St. Paul and Luther and all Catholics up to . . . Hamsun assure us that we are.

(Perhaps belief justifies us before God—what is that to us? It does not justify us before ourselves.)

We will not redeem things through beatification but by passing at the right moment from action to knowledge and from knowledge to action.

. . . Just as, when it comes to doing good, one cannot say: "Good has been done."

And if someone has been wise for seventy years, he must still become wise in his seventy-first year in order to be so.

Who knows, perhaps trees recognize, in their spirit, but one kind of striving, to reach the sun (to touch it physically): whence their form; we finally see: a beautiful tree.

Good health is nothing; but striving for health creates a high luster.

One could almost claim that all talent consists in reducing the will to laziness.

I am beginning to get accustomed to the idea that most people cannot improve. (Is this what Goethe understood by "renunciation"?[31]— was daily consumed by the idea, and still am, that people who could help, do not *want* to help: and yet, *there is nothing they need more*, in other words, they would help themselves every bit as much as others. A few claim they don't have the time. This is not true.

A library does not suffice as knowledge.

This sentence is not as simple as it appears. (I do not need to specify that I'm not referring to a physical library.) A library does not suffice because knowledge dies in every moment. (It endures a bit longer only in the somewhat lazier form of belief; but then it is no

31. This would, at best, be only one aspect of that "renunciation."

longer pure knowledge, pure learning but a much more physical process: the pressing of a finger on certain nerves . . .)

That is why acquiring knowledge is more than acquired knowledge.

The general public imagines that you know what you know and you don't know what you don't know; this is absolutely false. — What you know is clear as day at first and then gradually sinks back into zones of darkness: it sinks endlessly, extensively, and everywhere back into zones of darkness (deeper and deeper); some of it re-emerges: that depends on the extent to which resurrection is allowed.

The sphere of human knowledge is not like a king's treasure chamber in which treasures are collected and safely stored behind secure walls and each new addition increases the accumulation.

I will never find a more exact illustration of human knowledge than I saw at the fair: behind a platform there was a vertical track on which a ball rose, lighting a series of bulbs as it ascended. But this ball did not rise on its own: someone had to hit the platform with a giant hammer and the harder the blow, the higher the ball rose, the more bulbs were lit. The ball fell and the lights went back out.

Is nothing preserved? Your exertion, your slowly increasing strength, the joyful memory.

(And one more thing I'd almost forgotten but which people set their hearts on! You are rewarded with a little star made of colorful cardboard and wire. Most important!)

[. . .]

267

Authentic action is itself protection against presumption.

268

Those we call egotists do not think of themselves more than of others. They are simply prey to an obsession.

269

You need not *also* think of others. Real (true) thought automatically leads toward others.

You live neither in yourself nor through others but through being productive. (Regardless of whether you appear to be here or there — it is a matter of deploying your strengths where they will have the greatest result.)

Once you are able to see yourself clearly, you can see others as well.

270

"You definitely speak too much about yourself."

"Is that right?" the wise man replied. "Then I should study myself a bit more thoroughly."

271

Going, going . . .

— but going *forward*, not taking the well-worn paths. "Well-worn paths," that is, paths that are pointless, that do not lead forward but in a circle, always the same circle.

If you have no choice, then follow the circle; it's the best alternative, still better than nothing. Every prisoner in his cell knows this. — Only then does that little law of physiological limits begin, step by step, to become evident . . .

272

Ridiculous course of action. Using the examples of Hebbel, Beethoven, Spinoza, Schiller, and several others, all of them ultimately triumphant and famous despite wretched conditions, they want to prove that man is independent of his circumstances, that those who follow their calling can work their way up to a manifest historical achievement against all obstacles.

The others . . . somehow never come up as counter-examples.

273

Again on *fame*.[32] — The half-sage disdains fame because it is not true recognition (that the common man reveres fame is self-evident). The sage, on the other hand, welcomes fame gratefully, not because he sees any less clearly that recognition and fame are two different things but because he needs the latter, delusory one as protection against the world — roughly in the same way he needs money.

And who should become famous (that is, powerful)? Which should be more expansive in life, sense (the real) or nonsense? (It must be one or the other.)

Accordingly, the sage is glad that Spinoza and Hölderlin attained fame; he is delighted that they appeared famous until they actually were. Hamann and Lichtenberg never became fashionable, so I was never able to read the former's books and I read the latter's only in part and late simply because the editions were not large, or cheap or easy to find, and no doubt because for a long time I simply wasn't made aware of them. (And this is only one line of reasoning.)

The other line of reasoning: if Michelangelo had not become famous, he would not have been able to execute his architectural work or many of his other endeavors; we would have at most only half of Balzac's *Comédie Humaine*, because the miserable conditions he lived in would have killed him at forty instead of fifty; Goethe would not have been able to write either the second part of *Faust* or his *West-Eastern Divan* because he never would have reached an advanced age or if he had, he would not have been in the *state* required to write them. There are countless such examples.

32. Cf. 256.

The main cause of the artist's dependence is[33] that sheer spiritual or intellectual excellence is never a consequence of conditions but *form* in the most comprehensive sense; form in the sense in which great epic works are a different form than aphorisms; the Socratic dialogue is a form, as is Alexander's feat, and Heraclitus's adages: all these forms arose completely dependent on external circumstances. Heraclitus was not allowed to hold conversations (to realize his thought) in Ephesus; if Socrates had not found his ideal Athens for at least a few years or decades, he would have had to become a writer or would have remained completely unknown; without the popes and princes of the Renaissance, Michelangelo would have made only small sculptures at best.

274

You can shout "Give us a miracle!" for a long time—your call will fade away into nonsense.

"Give us food!" is the only justified cry.

[. . .]

276

Lorenzo the Magnificent lacked nothing to become a great writer, except the suitable sphere of life.

277

. . . He finally settled in completely comfortably for the night: dawn broke.

[. . .]

280

There are not so many tragedies. Faust is one, the other is that of the hero who struggles against clothes that are too tight. The latter, to be sure, makes less of an impression.

33. Cf. 100, 223, and *Nuancen und Details* III, 14.

The former, Faust, struggles against his immoderateness at the *end*, after he succeeded on every front. The other kind of hero (who would be Spinoza, not Goethe) lives in such terrible conditions that he constantly fears collapse (which Spinoza resisted most nobly); all minor Spinozas meet a tragic end.

Whispered objections sound: the hero absolutely must meet a tragic end. No, not absolutely. After all, Faust does not, does he? (Some meet their end at the end, others meet a financial end.)

281

The Gilding of Distance

Who does not like to hear the story of the man who, unshakable in his faith, sailed onward, unceasingly, across the ocean, where none had sailed before him until he reached land, America? But what appeal remains to this story if one knows he was under threat of assassination at every moment?

The worst was: his venture did not face one big obstacle; a hundred small ones opposed it, such as being stabbed or disappearing in darkest hour.

If the glory of our actions does not support us, if our actions are not at once their own reward and real enjoyment—what will save us?

It is not *the* Columbus who reached his goal who is most important, but the hundred other Columbuses of whom we know nothing because they *were* murdered.

For nature, in physical terms, wastes nothing, but organic nature (seen in terms of the line of its development) wastes a very great deal and human nature is perhaps the most wasteful of all.

282

If he can't even understand complicated things, how can he possibly understand simple ones?

283

Morality exists to release man from his duties.

Before he had to answer for each step he took, to take them in ac-cord with his purpose—now he only has to be in step, mechanically, with a ready-made schema and he is absolved of all guilt.

—but also from changing the world.

284

The Technique of Victory

They asked to what his unbelievable victory could be ascribed.

"It is due to the fact," he said, "that I never practiced winning."

The best technique for being victorious is not to have a technique for victory, but instead to have an objective and as a technique, an utterly devoted service to this object.

All those who fight for victory encounter lassitude sooner or later. From that point on, the advantage is decidedly on the side of those who are fighting for an objective because, whether they are tired or not, their objective will persist unwearyingly—whereas victory, merely an *exposed* goal, falls with the strength and desire of those struggling to achieve it.

285

"If you do not become as little children, you will not enter the realm of Heaven (or reality, or life)." Some adults have interpreted this great saying so literally that they fetch their pails to build sand-castles. The supreme example.

286

To understand human activity the most important force to observe is not the pursuit of money, but inactivity.

287

He who has much knowledge is good.
(But he who has not managed to become good, should not imagine that what knowledge he has is true, higher knowledge.)

288

I find those minds strange indeed who believe science will soon reveal everything to us. We already know their kind from *Faust*.

289

I have no love of mystery.
I do not deny mystery.

290

One often hears, "The dispute will last forever . . ." But the dispute is often *only the photograph of a* thing; and fools take the dispute seriously.

Does the artist develop what he produces or is it granted to him? Is his mind or his circumstances the decisive factor? This dispute will last forever.

These perennial questions are fundamentally badly formulated questions and that is why they will never be resolved.

291

On Pascal

There is a kind of madness, called precisely that, which obscures all thought with a thick, impenetrable veil so that it cannot reach others, cutting off all communication. But there is another kind of madness, not called by that name, that leaves intellectual faculties intact or even sharpens them and only affects the *soul of thought* (Pascal, Tolstoy in old age).

292

Believing and Knowing

Belief and knowledge are not opposites but very similar. They differ only in nuance; yet this is difficult to recognize due to the terrible misuse of the former word.

When someone says "I know" there is no doubt about what he has said; but when someone ways "I believe . . ." what is he saying?

Either that he does *not* believe; or that he neither knows nor believes; or that he assumes!

First case: The judge thunders at the witness: "You must have known that the accused . . . ?" and the alarmed witness replies: "I *believed* . . ."

Second case: Same situation, but with a less thundering judge; the less alarmed witness begins his response: "I *believed* . . ."

Third case: "He just passed by. I *believe* he's at the barbershop."

No one can deny that this is not a matter of connotation or figurative meaning, but of a perfectly vicious misuse.—Only in the fourth case does the word appear in its own meaning: "Simon Peter, do you believe in me?"—"Your faith has saved you."

Subjectively, complete faith and complete knowledge have exactly the same value. Their differences are only made manifest in their relationship to the external world. Full knowledge means having reached a place via visible paths: others can follow, they can head in the same direction, one can show them the way; belief means having reached the same place on nocturnal paths: this way cannot be shown to anyone else except through cries, gestures, and promises (using things that are not *here*); and this method is effective only with those who are already very close.

293

Individuals who have brushed aside or overcome every obstacle and climbed very high can never free themselves from this one sorrow, perhaps the last and greatest:

That others do not want to accept what they have recognized, without objection, as important and salutary: that these individuals, even though they know of a simple detour, cannot stop others from endlessly beating their heads against a wall, against a cliff-face which they themselves can see but others cannot; that these individuals must watch others squirm in the dust like worms even though they know the method, the secret of metamorphosis. The others, however, will not accept it. They refuse to transform themselves.

Having to watch this is perhaps the most profound suffering: but that is the view from all elevations; and it brings a most bitter isolation because there is no guilt involved: one sees only bare eternity. Guilt brings warmth in the frigidness of isolation, guilt binds.

294

The Tragic

It is the same with "tragic" as it is with "belief";[34] like "belief," "tragic" has only one strict meaning.

34. Cf. 292.

("But can't every word be used figuratively?" Every word can be used figuratively — by those who have the ability. Every mountain can be climbed — when you climb it.)

The tragic is always a temporal shift (time lag) between an individual's development and that of a community, the tension between an image of the world and history (the way of the world). But if Mr. Jones dies after sawing off the branch he was sitting on, that is not tragic, even if he leaves behind seven children, or even twenty, who will now no longer be fed: because there was no misfortune caused by a discrepancy between his personal development and that of society. In fact, there was no personal development at all; Mr. Jones had been regressing for some time. The death of hundreds of thousands in war is not tragic (it is, instead, a horrible calamity; war does indirectly cause situations that are tragic, but the tragedy is rooted in those who cause these indirect effects and are in that very location). For the casualties of war have let the horror happen (have gone along out of stupidity) and are therefore in sync with the course of history. The demise of the famous and all the anonymous revolutionaries, on the other hand, is tragic because it is caused by the collision of an image of the world with the (lazy, obstinate) course of world history. And if they did not perish, the tragedy is in their suffering. All suffering that is bound to an action is tragic.

295

He who must *seek out* an opportunity for heroism is either a child or completely unfit for heroism.

[. . .]

298

(When climbing mountains and on similar great ventures:)

Others must be able to keep pace or you need to detach yourself from them.

299

What is too bad is: those who have time don't see things; they are blind to powerful contrasts, to the tragic. But those who do see such things are caught up in them and have no time.

300

There is so much each of us can do! If only we each knew *what* we can do! If only we did not always want to do what others can do much better. Herein lies our misfortune.

The rich always want to give moral instruction instead of money. And the poor would like to do what only the rich can — that is, to give money — and they completely forget what riches *they* possess.

[. . .]

302

Stupidity and laziness may not be exactly the same thing; nevertheless they are intimately connected and by their example we see, more clearly than by any other pair, how when in harmony, things can make each other swell to enormous proportions.

303

Growing old is not a matter of graying hair, but of becoming brittle, of closing oneself off. Most Swiss are elderly at nineteen.

304

Apropos Faust, they talk of "unfathomable profundity"? No, instead: endlessly spreading influence.

305

(Certain enemies of truth—in questions of upbringing, say—
invoke Goethe:)

. . . always poor Goethe! Just because he understood ten times
more than other Germans, he is meant to have understood everything.

306

For something to be measurable, it is not enough that it be past;
it must not be the source of any life.

[. . .]

310

Seers have naturally *always* been half-blind.

(In a society of windows and eyeglasses, telescopes and microscopes are considered blind.)

311

Gothic cathedrals radiate colossal sparks of inspiration? But they
required the plinth of the Middle Ages that had none.

312

To belittle certain people, Hamsun said of them: "They want to
be faster than life." ("My son is fast as lightning. He'll go into business.")—They *should* be faster! But the damn thing is, they aren't.[35]

313

Universal consciousness should not see any limits to phenomena.
Limitless phenomena, however, are not visible.

35. Cf. 109.

314

I would like to be able to say:

"I, too, am capable of blindness; but not like everyone else. Less capable."

315

Only those who can offer proof of very positive states of mind should indulge in foul moods.

316

Few understand that formal creativity can also be part of relations with others.

317

On the Beneficial Power of the Church

> They have offered all their goodness to the Savior
> They themselves no longer have any.

I do not know whether bad men join the Church or whether the Church makes them bad, but it is certain that most of the bad men one meets in civilian life are also men of the Church. This does not mean you cannot find a thoroughly evil person outside the clergy (a wizened, green-faced farmer, banker, or police officer) nor that — what is rarer — one day a clergyman might not appear with a heart not made of cement or plaster.

318

When we are near the end of a stage of development and are fighting for the best results of that stage, we find the highest achievements of the preceding stage more congenial than the beginnings of our own. (We view these beginnings with disdain.)

That is why Rilke preferred things to confused people, why artists prefer animals to people, and why Stefan George could talk with simple people but not with the well-educated.

[. . .]

328

When someone speaks the truth and does so in a larger context, the result will inevitably be a great work.

This phenomenon is as rare as a great work. — For even those of honest character begin to plagiarize as soon as they say more than a brief sentence.

329

It is important not to forget this about the piano: when you make a sound through certain movements near it, the instrument resounds. The universal — seen from the bottom up — is just such a musical organization; when you make the *proper* movements, whether large or small, this organization will resound.

[. . .]

333

Misfortune alone is still not complete misfortune; the question is how one endures it. Only when it is badly endured is misfortune complete.

Good fortune alone is still not complete good fortune.

III

TALKING, CHATTERING, KEEPING SILENT

You're *not* correct!" That may well be true;
But it's not much of a claim for you;
Be *more* correct than I! Then there'll be much
ado.

Goethe

1

"Work is always an internal process; and it must always be directed outward.
Activity that is not directed outward is not work; activity that is not an internal process is not work.

All work must be directed outward: but what if internal matters, internal zones
of work are involved? Then the activity must be directed outward relative to the internal: this interior becomes exterior again. (Thus is clarity an exteriorization of the
unclear, thought an exteriorization of presentiment, the spoken word an exteriorization of thought, the written an exteriorization of the spoken.)"[1]

From this it is almost self-evident that speaking sometimes qualifies as work—that is, affirming and affirmative, valuable—and sometimes not; and the same kind of speaking is work for *some* people, but
not for others. It qualifies as work in those cases where it fosters life,
turns obscurity into clarity; it is worthless and objectionable in those
cases when clarity has already been achieved and therefore speech
represents nothing other than a *deferral of action*—or of new action:
when it is not a preparation, a necessary preparation for action and

1. *Nuancen und Details* II, 51.

therefore itself an act, but instead falls in that category of superfluous, crippling, deadening preparation.[2] One can hardly warn others
strongly enough about these little-known dangers. (Think of a high
jumper who, every time he nears the pole at full speed, turns back at
the last moment only to execute the approach one more time.)

We can call the former *talking*, the latter *chattering*.

2

One of the greatest misfortunes is that men no longer want to
talk.

— only to chatter or keep silent.

3

Who does not need to talk? First and foremost, those who write
well. (They skip that stage in the fullest sense in that they are on a
higher level, their current position contains the former.) Others have
the duty to talk —: otherwise how could man progress? At the same
time, a powerful stricture must always remain active to annihilate all
the bad things they say.

I see an extraordinary significance for the human race in writing and, looking backward, an extraordinary significance in talking. From one recorded thought, don't ten spoken ones follow? And
doesn't one spoken thought give rise to ten obscure intuitions? And
this process goes further: thus, on the whole, from the darkness of the
universe spring differentiation, knowledge, and act; man takes part,
progresses, becomes powerful.

Is it possible for both talking and writing to be completely replaced by action? This is certainly possible in theory — but how far
is it possible in practice? It is already extremely rare for writing to replace talking (as rare as great writers are reclusive).

2. Cf. II, 118, 197, 216–223.

It is almost impossible to skip two or more stages—to leap from intuition to act (to an act that is not a chance event, but true, meaningful work). That is how animals proceed and how far has it brought them? The question is badly phrased (—because animals, too, in millions of years . . .). How far will *mankind* advance using the animals' method?

4

There may be several reasons why we so often hear talk of bad situations and so seldom of good ones (or so often of the bad aspects of a situation and so seldom of the good aspects), but one of them is important and profound:

A bad situation needs to be changed; a good situation should endure. *Talk brings change.*

An additional reason: we often do not at all realize when a situation or one aspect of a situation has improved.

5

While many are very preoccupied with the unconscious, subconscious, and similar areas, in short the varieties of less than full consciousness, there has long been an inadequate awareness of the many, yes, almost infinite number of degrees of full consciousness, *degrees of intensity of knowledge.* The simple man is still of the opinion today that one either knows a thing or one does not. He could not be more mistaken! The strength of knowledge varies from person to person, from day to day; it's no less variable than the state of a drop of water in a current, in a fountain even! (Hence the fact that one cannot preserve one's knowledge and retrieval of what is known must always have occurred quite recently.) As a result, reciting a well-known quote can, through a change in emphasis, become a significant accomplishment.—Another way of grasping the importance of talking.

6

Not talking, when it would be possible to do so, when there is an opportunity to talk, is a luxury that only the very rich can allow themselves without disastrous damage.

7

Keeping silent acquires meaning only from the surrounding talk; it is like a punctuation mark, it cannot stand on its own. Like an em dash that binds two ideas.

Punctuation marks are important; does this mean that those who have written poetry using only punctuation marks have written poems?—To be precise then, punctuation marks are more than simply keeping silent, because they allow for variations while just staying silent does not (there's the period's crude, earthy silence and the semi-colon's higher, more transparent silence, the comma's clear, plain, merely postponing silence, the deep, forceful, extensive silence of the ellipsis or the em dash's silence like an arrow shooting into the distance, among others); ordinary silence is equivalent to *one* punctuation mark repeated ad infinitum.

This is not to say that you should talk all the time. If your silence will emphasize something that you have said or are about to say, then keep silent if you wish. Silence alone is nothing.

8

. . . Silence, they say, is golden. How far below zero must their talk be if its lack is like gold.

9

A man whose qualities are exclusively negative—he doesn't smoke, he doesn't drink, he's not intemperate, he doesn't intrude in others' business, he doesn't hurt others.

10

"A significant silence." Moderation—the lack of immoderation; and all that is creative, all that is valuable appears immoderate—only has meaning insofar as it is the foundation (*le fond*), the connection, the connecting element that makes the unusual and the excessive possible. In itself, it is not significant. It is exactly in this way that silence becomes significant, insofar as it allows, as a framework, the meaning of the spoken to be enhanced. No silence is significant in itself.

11

"Nonetheless, were there not some who ensconced themselves in their enjoyment of silence?" Yes, but only by means of their thoughts, the precursors of talk, which are dependent on talk and which deliver snippets of talk to you. Those who enjoy, enjoy *something*; the enjoyment of nothingness is not enjoyment.

12

I would like to sing the praises of eternal silence—but, to be precise, by this I mean Bach's music, Montaigne's talk, and other things that make a wonderful sound.

13

Go ahead, praise silence, for all I care—but talk well and at length about it.

14

Who is permitted to remain silent?

The military and most especially the higher command. Napoleon! Because the dynamism of the words he flung out expands to colossal dimensions. And Goethe, Hölderlin—because they have spoken a million times.

> Those who keep their peace need have little fear;
> Man remains hidden under his tongue for many a year.[3]

One could charge these words of Goethe—the second sentence—with optimism. Is man truly hidden there? In the cases mentioned, the answer is clear.

15

Would I ever advise someone to be silent? Never. Instead: talk and talk! And whenever he starts chattering, he should get one right in the kisser!

16

There are two kinds of chatter. The first: stringing together many meaningless words about a meaningful topic. The second: wasting few words on many topics, but on topics that are completely insignificant.

The second is the worse kind of garrulousness. One could call the first rhetorical chattering, the second is merely common. For the inferior, silence is golden. To talk at length without chattering is the most difficult.

17

Chattering is always an avoidance of work.

The first, common chattering, is that of the busybody, who has adopted techniques of the epics: avoidance of external work. ("Lizzie ordered furniture yesterday, don't you know. And the people in the

3. Goethe, *West-Eastern Divan.*

apartment next to her said: Well—. Mr. Jones also wants to move soon, in which case, he'll leave his furniture in the old apartment. Mr. Andrews just got a raise. The cook's a divorcée.")

The second, rhetorical chattering, the chatter of the pharmacist, which has adopted techniques from philosophy, science, and elevated prose, as well as from poetry: avoidance of higher work. (Think of all those middling lawyers and all the middling politicians in the world; the pubescent; young girls; almost all women who write; most writers.) Avoidance of higher work: of scientific discovery; of constructing their own sentences.

18

A third kind of chatter should also be mentioned, the one that is least well known:

I would like to call it *laconic* or *rustic* chatter. In public opinion and in most books, peasants have the reputation of being taciturn. They are certainly often speechless. But once they start speaking, we would, in most cases, have to call them chatterers (which might offer some insight into the circumstances of their usual speechlessness) but in a different way than those mentioned above. Theirs is neither the chatter of the fishwife nor of the poetasters and lawyers: it consists in the five or even ten and twentyfold repetition of a single, short often maxim-like sentence that is completely meaningless from the very beginning or at the latest by the second repetition ("That's life."—"Yes, yes, that's how it is"). This chatter is perhaps the hardest to bear.

[. . .]

21

Still, for those starting out from silence, chatter is also the first station on the way toward talk. Thus, even though chatter is aesthetically inferior to silence — it certainly is more disagreeable — chatter is nonetheless superior to it.

In other words: chatter, unlike silence, can be subjected to criticism and thus indirectly productive.

Chatter is superior to silence for the same reason a babbling child is superior to mute flesh.

The old question — which is worse: chattering or keeping silent? — is thus decided. Two examples that illustrate well the value that chattering can have are an adult learning a foreign language and a babbling child. The child is the more important of the two; it is clear in his case that chatter is the first stage in emerging from silence, from a chaos in which everything is objective and nothing human. Because creating forms is not *one* of man's qualities, it is the very essence of being human.

22

In general, we can expect more from those public speakers who begin uncertainly, or at least seem uncertain, without striking verbal embellishments, than from those who begin with a flourish, whose source is not the spirit, but the conservatory, the theater, the market.

23

If appearing before a large audience were not usually associated with nervous excitement, I expect speaking would be in an even worse state. For then, in my opinion, even more of the best speakers would risk lapsing into pleasant conversation ("since we are all so cozy here together") and becoming slightly heady from the agreeable company. As a result, they would fail to maintain the inner tension that leads to the dark gravity that is indispensable to a *legitimate* presence in such a place; a gravity that is probably sustained by the nervous excitement.

— this excitement, sparked initially by external circumstance, is suddenly transformed into a related excitement through the *magnitude* of the circumstances, helping keep the speaker focused on his essential task and keeping him from falling prey to dangerous delusions.

24

For the public speaker, it is especially important to *avoid a complete connection* with the audience . . .

Friendly conversation, an open exchange, the audience's pleasurable excitement and the speaker's pleasure in eliciting that excitement, this mutual reinforcement presents a danger. — A division between the speaker and the audience must be maintained; the speaker must stick to his topic, go into unfamiliar territory; he must always hover at a slight remove or what he says would be worthless — and he a haranguer, a performer, a declaimer.

[. . .]

27

Competition. — Were he to return to Athens, i.e. Montparnasse, now, after having spent three years in solitude, whereas you have spent the last three years talking: how would a debate, pitting your strengths as orators against each other, conclude?

You have talked nonstop in Montparnasse. You were constantly practicing your skill and you defeated everyone there in debate. He, in his solitude, never spoke with any visible men, but only with the greatest men of the past, with Montaigne and Spinoza and Goethe — with trees and birds and other absolute things — and he was defeated:

As a result . . . he will defeat you.

IV

> Not everyone who receives a pregnant
> thought becomes productive; he probably
> thinks of something already well-known.
>
> *Goethe*

1

When children like a book, they immediately want to read more
by the same author. They read every book they can find by that author,
one after the other, from beginning to end. And as soon as they've
used that author up, they regret it. Many adults read this way, too.

And what does a *reader* do, when a book pleases him? Without
exception: he rereads it. The second reading never merely confirms
the first reading but surpasses or deepens it.

No real reader has ever used up a true work of art.

The real reader will always discover new aspects of well-written
works. Each reading will have new effects. When he knows a work
"by heart," he carries it within, it becomes a part of him. It is as in-
exhaustible and creative as life, because it is itself life, a real part of
things and unpredictable in its workings.

Lichtenberg wrote: "A sure sign of a good book is that the older
one grows, the more one likes it . . . presuming one grows wiser with

age . . . A book is a mirror. If an ape looks into it, an apostle is not going to look out."

It's possible that reading is not as difficult as writing. There are many reasons that might explain this—yet at this point I have no empirical evidence, which would be the only real proof. Until I myself can count more people who can read than people can write, you won't convince me.

It's better not to speak with anyone who considers reading a passive exercise. Who knows, perhaps they will also consider listening a passive exercise and your speech will either put them to sleep or do them in.

2

Test:

Require a reader to understand Proust and Lawrence, Lawrence *and* Proust. These two writers are contrary in many *expressible* ways; but only those who recognize what these two have in common can perceive what is essential to literature and this is inexpressible.

These two names could be replaced with others. Here, they serve merely as examples and are suitable because they are names of two genuine writers (albeit of unequal stature; yet Lawrence, too, is essential. He had something to say, in the highest sense of the term) who appear to have nothing in common as long as one remains on the surface, looking at the movements they represent and their "opinions."

Lawrence railed against Proust and denigrated his significance whenever possible—which is understandable when one knows how restrictive a path to redemption D. H. Lawrence preached at the end of his life . . . (Voltaire's words come to mind: *Let us forget the dreams of great men and remember the truths they have taught us.* In this case the "truths" are the marvels of artistic intensity that Lawrence achieves incidentally or while developing his absurd doctrine.) Furthermore, Proust no longer saw any possibility for human fulfillment in sexual relations or in friendship, at least not for the sophisticated.

The reader who condemns the one writer and swears only by the other has not turned his inner eye toward that which, both despite and through their peculiarities, can be found in both (who, as noted above, are admittedly not of the same stature). He is unable to apprehend any brush with the inexpressible or what I will call the REAL.[1] Instead, he is trapped in the expressible, the programmatic, mere subject matter—for *everything that is easily named belongs to the subject matter.* He does not perceive the essential in art, but only what is dispensable, what served this or that writer as a stepping-stone.

3

Subject Matter, Content, Form

"Everything that can be named easily belongs to the subject matter." This may refer to subject matter in the narrower, usual sense or to something that is usually described differently: everything in a work of art that is easy to name or distinguish with the usual means, with familiar methods at hand, all this remains at the level of subject matter; it is unimportant, not indispensable to art.

For years I have found the various classifications in the verbal arts—novel, novella, story, essay, etc.—along with the associated investigations and valuations, to be of less and less interest. Their possible fruitfulness, their intellectual consequence, seemed more and more doubtful to me. These erudite investigations and distinctions may, at certain times and in certain places, have merely had a purely practical significance and perhaps still do: but what is their depth

1. And so it's possible for such a reader to consider Jules Romains, who wants to be our century's Balzac, as Balzac's equal or at least close, or to deem Jakob Schaffner's novellas of central importance even though a novella like *The Laughing Captain* is as devoid of the inexpressible, of the REAL as can possibly be imagined.

compared to the vital reality of Goethe's differentiation between these three elements of a work of art: *Subject matter, content, form!*

Where there is form, there is always content and always subject matter. The poet, therefore, need not worry about subject matter or even content; his only worry is form. *Through the form he has achieved, he achieves everything.* This may sound paradoxical. There was a time when I myself refused to accept it, but through experience and by looking at it more closely, it becomes apparent that this is completely different from what it first appears to be. Form does not bring about a reduction of the spirit, of value, of actual *life*—on the contrary. The artist need not worry about content; if anyone need worry about it, that is nature. In any case, nature, in it, behind it, must deliver the entire content—woe to the artist who pursues content or who wishes to increase what content he has! As for subject matter—this cannot be said too often—it is the most insignificant element. There is always enough subject matter, everywhere and always; nature need not deliver it. Anyone may avail themselves of it wherever they are, in whatever amounts they wish. It is there for us just as space around is; nature need not give us space, we are in it; where there is no space, we cannot be. Subject matter is nothing, content is a blessing, form is achieved through utmost work and grace. There is no virtue inherent in subject matter. What can be confusing is that *this* subject matter allows *that* artist to unleash his virtues, but not *this other* artist. If subject matter were a virtue, then all artists would be equally blessed through it.

With regard to painting, almost the whole world has become aware of the insignificance of subject matter. With regard to the verbal arts, however, we are still at the level of children. Who could claim, without appearing ridiculous, that a painting "only represents" apples when apples have been depicted so many times? Who could demand that a Cézanne depict a less common fruit, one from somewhere near the source of the Amazon, say, in order to increase the value of his paintings? We now know that efforts to increase artwork's value take an entirely different *direction.*—Some of the greatest writers have taken their subject matter from others' writing without this fact causing the value of their work to suffer any detriment.

The following maxim of Goethe's, this fundamental saying, should be the starting point for any artistic training:

The subject matter is clear to everyone, the content is evident only to those who have something to contribute and the form remains a mystery to most.[2]

This maxim is itself a mystery to most.

4

Genuine writers are few and far between, but are there more genuine readers?—At any rate, nothing is closer to writing than genuine reading.

I will clarify and prove this statement. More than once, in the flood of what is published today I've had the experience of coming upon a good, a satisfying sentence that drew my attention to an author: afterward, on closer inspection, I realized that I'd misread the sentence and it was, in fact, just a banality. It became clear, in other words, that the writer who had sparked my interest was myself. Without noticing and without changing my habitual way of reading, I had constructed a good sentence (at least one that I considered good). Is there a clearer demonstration of how close reading and writing are?

On occasion, as I reflected on a thought that had become clear to me, I thought I remembered having discovered it long ago, just as clearly expressed, in some book or other. Then, after looking in vain for the passage in Spinoza or perhaps Montaigne—whether in order to quote or compare it and certainly to marvel at its acuity—I realized it did not exist! Instead, I found only passages touching on the question at hand or, although superficially very different, in profound

2. *Maxims and Reflections* ("Art and Antiquity").

agreement, like structures rising from the same foundation. Does this not illustrate the work of reading? How one thing overlaps another when we read? Or: how reading and writing are just two expressions—admittedly different in potential—of *work* in its highest form?

Another observation must be made here: sometimes phrases that are truly profound can be found even in *humorous corners* of the newspapers. These deep thoughts were certainly not *formulated* by the writers who contribute to these sections: chance brought these words together through their pens in combinations bound to resonate with this or that reader above and beyond their banal meanings, resonances to which the writers themselves may be deaf. (It goes without saying that this applies only to short phrases. The same is true in the mountains where the outlines of tremendous sculptures are sometimes evident in cliff faces—visible only to eyes that have sculptural aptitude. "And that's the difference," someone will say. "With finished sculptures, the artwork is visible to *every* eye, not only to the sculpturally gifted . . ." But that is not true.)—One of the most compelling examples: "Papa, what does the wind do when it's not blowing?" Is this not a child's naïve question that seems comical and, at the same time, the seed of a marvelous satire of human limitations, very close to Heraclitus's essential teaching?

[. . .]

6

Our eyes should be able, like our hands, to leave marks on things in proportion to their power to leave traces in books proportional to our understanding.

To reread books—*Faust*, Montaigne, Pascal—after they have been read by such and such . . . and by such and such . . .

Reading a book one time slowly is not enough for true readers. They must read it two or three times. For pharmacists *one* quick read is enough.

He has read *Faust.* He has read Spinoza. He has also read Edgar Wallace and understood him as well.

In most cases, when someone says of true works, "I understand *this* part, but not *that*," he has understood nothing at all.

7

Human Dignity and the Dignity of Books

Many people think books are there for us to take care of.

One person tore a cheap paperback edition of *Faust II* into sections so that he could always have one with him. Another began decrying the destruction of the book. Better that books remain attractive than be read.

This was a respectable man: rich, tidy, always well-dressed who owns many beautiful books without a single ruffled page.

"Conserving cultural goods." That's all very nice. But it's better to create new ones by putting the old to use. And what exactly is he conserving (the manuscripts of important unknown, that is unpublished, authors?) in an age when books are published in editions of thousands and a new edition of thousands more can easily be printed when needed? Is he conserving the *work?*—the smoothness of the pages!

Let no one touch your books, not even with their eyes! That's why it is best not to lend them to anyone. Don't let them lose any of their value. There is value in them: that you can believe!

Maintaining a book's value so that it will benefit others is a Christian thing to do.

His forehead shone brightly like the covers of his books. Every day he oiled and polished the former and took a dusting brush to the latter, handling them so carefully that he never lost a page or even a word. He wanted to preserve both in pristine condition for future generations. He kept both, brain and books, in the same condition in

which he had received them. They shared the same fate: their value
was contained; it was never made evident.

    [. . .]

9

    Dogs and inferior men devour what pleases them very quickly;
but what they don't like they consume slowly, assuming they do,
in fact, eat it. Lowly men read (albeit dogs do not) *through* what
pleases them at a most rapid rate (they speed *through* it and believe
they've read it *thoroughly!*)—on the other hand, they slowly, ever
more slowly, read what doesn't please them, assuming they will, in
fact, read it or wish to.

    (—whereas a *reader* will spend ten days on a volume of Proust
but will dispose of ten average contemporary books in a single day—it
is, after all, a question of elimination.)

    When reading Proust, you must truly *read* him. (If you skip a
few pages, those pages are missing; the writing in front of you does
not force you or enable you to reconstruct the passage you skipped
because this passage has its own life. It, too, is by Proust and cannot
have been written by anyone else.) Everyone agrees that there's no
need to read the majority of contemporary books, especially not those
that general opinion would have us take seriously; you can look them
over, leaf through them, read a number of pages and skip the rest;
you can get an idea of the author's "opinion" and, more or less, of his
style. What has been lost?

    But I believe the books that need not be read at the time they are
published (more precisely: not by readers like us) will not be considered the most important later on and may perhaps not be considered
at all important. (In the future, when the chatter about them—how
they express the "spirit of the age" and so on; as if the task of litera-

ture were to compete with the radio, film, and newspapers—will have died away.)

10

One way to determine whether or not you will want to frequent someone (this test, however, is only valid for people with a certain level of education) is to ask: "What have you read?" When someone begins his list with Homer, Pindar, . . . and gets to Shakespeare only in the hundredth place and Goethe in the two-hundredth (or simply begins in a tone that makes it clear such a list is coming; there's no need to listen for long), then you know there is no speaking with him. If someone responds with the question "what do you mean by *read?*" there is hope.

If the person asked gives you a look that indicates that he answered that question for himself long ago and says, for example, "Spinoza, Gide, Proust" (I repeat: these three names are merely examples), then you know this is very likely someone with whom you can have a real conversation.

If someone answers with twenty modern writers, this is not someone you will want to frequent.

11

Those who have not read anything and have no concept of literature are not so bad, but Lord protect me from those who have read a great deal and have no concept of literature!

12

Definition: When asked what the essence of poetry is, someone answered: Poetry is the exact opposite of what most people think poetry is.

13

How does one best disguise a message? Through very close proximity to the truth.

[...]

15

Personal experience:

For many years, the only proof I had that my books were being read was an occasional grease stain here or there. Then came my first success, unexpected and disappointing. A woman into whose hands one of my works had fallen said the book was very beautiful. She was talking about the cover.

Later, I realized that the few readers I had could be divided into two main groups: those who said I'd become obscure and incomprehensible and those who found me not only easy to understand, but downright banal. (To be precise, they didn't say this in so many words, but it was clear on the one hand from their claims that they'd often read this kind of thing before and on the other hand from the baffling speed with which they finished the text and set it aside, jaws moving like cows chewing their cud or with the expression of a waiter at the end of a long shift.) The second kind are the hopeless ones.

To use a comparison that some may find pretentious insofar as it concerns an aspect of the matter that doesn't interest me in the slightest: if the first group of readers have gotten lost in a mountain gorge, they can still be led out of it; the second simply declare that there is no mountain and therefore no need or even chance to attempt an ascent. They can cover it with one hand on their own doorstep—and they do.

The terrible thought that others won't understand paralyzes us as we write. What experiences, obscure to the entire world and long obscure even to ourselves, we are trying to convey! This can occur even when writing a letter: you improve a passage and yet you know that you've made it less comprehensible to your correspondent . . . (What to do? Should you restore the passage's previous version, a version you know to be *lazy*—conventional: therefore in large part moribund: therefore false: inadequate, sign language?)

What to do?—It's simply a matter of loving your *reader* enough not to betray him for the merely visible . . .

16

If someone can't read, may he at least be learned.

> This may seem to contradict one of my previous statements: "God save us from those who have read widely and don't have the slightest idea what literature is!" This is not to say that a learned man has no understanding of literature. A learned man may have several good insights and have mastered many scholarly concepts, and yet still be a long way from deep, authentic reading. A learned man, armed with an education and some insight, can still be of service.

17

And you, when you read, what happens? Perhaps this: take Proust or Pascal (I give these two names merely as examples and prefer the second because there's so little danger of getting caught up in his subject matter). You feel like someone who has suddenly entered a dark room, leaving behind the previous tolerable level of light: semi-darkness. Your eyes gradually get used to the dark and scan the room (the darkness begins to recede, to dissipate). Who is watching you? A crowd of pale ancestors—you hadn't noticed them when they were quietly observing you. Here and there, a piece of jewelry flashes, a candle glows. Gems smolder, dark red and serene. And through a window that gradually comes into view you look out into the most remarkable exterior, a world (none other than the old world, your own mundane world) so layered, so painted, so much *richer* than all you had known . . . and at the same time delicate, fleeting and almost blurred, like the view through a pane of glass on a rainy day or the shapes that appear on a piece of white blotting paper, no clearer or more distinct. What is it that you see? The old, day-to-day world, where you just were.

18

But on close examination, we must acknowledge that a good reading cannot last, that as soon as one engages fully in reading, it almost immediately shifts ground. Even when we seem to still be reading, we are in fact no longer truly reading. (I believe I remember Lichtenberg having said something to this effect.)—No matter how captivated we are by "dramatic tension" when reading good and the very best authors, this *captivation* is not an engagement in truly superior reading.

The best reading impels us to write, to speak and think or, at least, to read again what we've just read—not just to keep on reading. (Which we naturally also continue doing, but it represents a new start, placing a new bet.)

[. . .]

21

What won't a writer do for his readers! (Even those writers who seem indifferent to them.) That is the question. The greatest writers are those who give no thought to the reader, being supremely confident they will, in fact, have one. Such were Montaigne, Hölderlin, the late (greatest) Goethe.

I later found this confirmation in Goethe's writing:

"The greatest respect an author can have for his public is never to produce what is expected of him but only what he himself finds right and useful at the intellectual stage he and others have reached at any particular time."[3] There are variations in the "Tame Xenias":

3. Goethe, *Maxims and Reflections.*

> "Why do you wish to distance yourself from us
> And our opinions?"
> I don't write to please you,
> but so you may learn something!

and again

> He who lives in world history,
> Should he follow the moment?
> He who observes and strives through time
> Is the only one fit to speak and write.

No matter how loud and forcefully some affirm it: a writer's worth is not measured by the extent to which he is in step with the times—that is opportunism, not literature—but instead, if his relationship to the times can or must be measured, by his opposition to the times.

More and more, I have had to convince myself that a writer's importance is proportional to his ability to disregard the reader, *to possess an unshakable confidence—since nothing exists without the social context—that he will nonetheless have a reader and a wonderful one at that.*

V

ART

Of all things human the most precarious and
transitory
is power which has no strong support of its own.
Tacitus as quoted by Goethe[1]

The closed circle is pure.
Kafka

1

Art and life. In ever new ways one sees: in art, one need not worry
if what is being created is old or new, only whether it is right. (And:
"Beauty can never understand itself."[2]) It is always new—and old.

But does this also apply to life?

(To be more precise: the new in any creation is manifest in the
visible, it is what the eye first perceives and is crucial for development;
the old is found in a deeper, more lasting level and is almost always
overlooked at first.)

From this we can compose a response to the inevitable objec-

---

1. Hohl misquotes Tacitus Ann. XIII, 19 "as cited by Goethe." The actual
source reads: *Of all things human the most precarious and transitory is a reputation
for power which has no strong support of its own.* Translation by Alfred John Church
(1876) (Trans. note.)

2. Goethe, *Maxims and Reflections.*

tion: what good is this constant talk of artists and creative intellectuals?

(One must be of flesh and blood, the thin and reedy schoolmasters call. Let them go to a butcher shop.)

Even when art or creative intellectual works do not strike us as being of paramount importance: decisive questions for the artist are decisive for everyone. (For everyone who matters: for all those struggling toward life—and therefore already alive.) The artist is not essentially different from others; he is only different insofar as he represents a higher potency of the same elements and the same processes. He is a *typical* specimen of the human race—an especially distinguishable one.

This could be an artist's response when he is told the only question is whether others come to him or he goes to others: Are you sure that this is the question—? Wherever I go, you will follow one day.

In the world there burned a fire, somewhere off the beaten track. But when it grew cold, everyone gathered around the fire. Then it was the center of the world.

2

Art and nature. The artist should aspire to the imitation of nature (aspire, I repeat); yet if he should perfectly achieve this imitation, his achievement would not be art.

I once saw a landscape of canals, not a particularly beautiful one. I had known it for years and always found it rather gloomy and dull: but on that morning, it was suddenly significant. What spread out before me was no longer nature, but art, nothing other than a painting, the work of a master. How did this change come about? I was able to determine it: an unusual atmosphere, the hour's particular light severed the connection between the upper and the lower levels, a piece of the world was rent, the hills seemed to tremble on their pedestals. In a word: nature had been exploded.

But then, wouldn't art also be nature? The secret: art certainly is nature, but a new one.

3

Art is not to be found where people think it is, but always somewhere else. *Always elsewhere* than people think.

4

They are always arguing about the relationship between art and life. Either they claim that art and life have nothing to do with each other or that art and life have a great deal to do with each other; but art and life are one and the same.

5

What is art? Flame. What does the artist do, does he produce flames? Not at all. For that is something man cannot do and even if he could, what purpose would it serve? Such flames would be immediately extinguished. — Instead, the artist provides the elements that will inevitably spark a flame as soon as another element is added (reader, listener, viewer).

These elements always spark a flame but without being consumed themselves. Accordingly, it would perhaps be better to speak of canalization, of a *system* of canals that allow the eternal elements to flow in proper proportions — here this means: so that highest existence is attained. (In other words, the flame appears when someone introduces life into one of the raw, primordial elements, the eternally circling streams, by connecting his own vitality to it.)

6

In art there is no interior nor exterior. Art is purely externalized interior.

Yes, one can probably define art as the place where things are such that one cannot define them as internal or external.

[. . .]

11

Words are not vessels for the inexpressible but *bodies.* They do not hold something or bring something. Before inexpressible meaning they are as mute mimes (the Trojan war or the voyage of the Argonauts are similarly mute mimes); they bow and bend, self-contained bodies; they are like marionettes—: yet the dance these silent mimes lead will offer you, at best, a fleeting, anticipatory view of the inexpressible and you will gain life. "Everything transitory / is but symbol."[3] Words are transitory.

12

Now the inexpressible is in the act, now in the mind, now in the word—and always in the same amount.

13

Material

In a broader sense, every artwork is but a letter. (One writes the correspondent to whom one would like to be bound. With Spinoza, with Rilke, there are letters in the usual sense, which, although ostensibly addressed to a pseudonym, are intended for the most remote horizons, for near eternity. The recipient of Mrs. Jones's letters is just Mrs. Smith and perhaps not even she.) Van Gogh's letters, the best of them, are not an extension or an "explanation" of his "works," but they are on a par with his paintings. Hebbel's diary is of no less value

3. *Faust II*, lines 12, 102–103. (Trans. note.)

than his plays; this is also true of Gide's "open" forms compared to his writings in "closed" forms. Lichtenberg's observations, in which he so often speaks "only of himself," are certainly of much greater value than Klopstock's "Messiah." One can achieve the same high level in all forms. The hard part is reaching those heights.

Yet whether one finds these altitudes more in the ceiling of the Sistine Chapel or a simple letter depends on personal circumstances and not on significance. One could even write a critique of the critique and a letter about the letter and say just as much in the second as in the first. If what the word designates is insufficient, then sufficiency will lie in the declension of the word and on and on. If not in these blocks of wood, then in rubbing them together—then in the warmth and in the colors engendered by the warmth, then in the colors' tones, and from these tones everything emerges again, becoming once again a world (with blocks of wood). The mind *always* has enough material.

14

Art has no subject. It is itself.

15

This man actually could have written (or painted) very beautifully; but every time he had an impetus, he had no ideas. At other times he had wonderful ideas, but not enough impetus to express them. How much they suffer, those one meets so often, who lament the greatness of their minds, who lack only this or that in order to . . .

Montaigne did not have that much pity. He seems to have known such people; they are not just creatures of the present day. "I sometimes hear those who apologize for not being able to express themselves and maintain that their heads full of fine things, but they cannot communicate them for want of eloquence: this is bunk."

He can write; he just lacks *material!*—The weather was finally clear; all that was missing now were trees, fields, a landscape—heaven and earth.

It was a river of great power and marvelous vitality but unfortunately had no water and no bed.

[. . .]

22

When judging writers, I've always valued spirit over form, insofar as it's possible to distinguish between the two (which, in truth, is not possible . . .); I've valued spiritual significance over simple "artistic" aptitude. And it's good that I did! The spirit will always be master— we cannot perceive the proportions clearly by daylight. The forms— when the day is done—won't be measured against other forms as they are during the day! Instead, everything the spirit leaves behind will be called form. (And what is called form during the day will become a secondary product—if it is not forgotten.)

23

In distress even the most insignificant of beings can access the power of words; then he can hear, he can speak. Great artists are continuously in a state of distress.

[. . .]

25

Dimension. When will art no longer be judged by dimensions? Some claim that the epic poem of several thousand verses, the long novel, etc. are the "great forms" and that Lichtenberg, Pascal, and Valéry, by contrast, did not achieve a great form. A blind and illiterate goatherd who has forced his way into a library and feels his way along the shelves will come to the same judgment on literary dimensions as a many a man of letters—and on the same grounds.

The true dimension of art is not size *but courage.*

[. . .]

28

Craftmanship. This is not easy to understand: that one must master all artistic techniques and that technique is no use; that one must perfect one's craftmanship as much as possible in order to see that craftmanship is nothing (—when it is not a constant nuisance).

All learning in art—as important and at the same time worthless as it is—is less a matter learning than *unlearning,* of freeing oneself.

Those who, on the third level, recover the integrity of a child (i.e., the integrity of the first level) are true artists, creators—and very few in number.

For almost all founders at the second level: they get lost in the mastery of technique (the sum of contemporary knowledge about their special areas); they never emerge from the seething crowd alive.

29

The model does not instruct the painter. What does then? One artist says that his experiences appear before a screen of fire. (Not his early or past experience, in a second edition, so to speak, but those he has just undergone.) He is not observing the model here but is perhaps observing his observation of the model; in any case that is closer to the heart of the matter.

30

There are perhaps only two fundamental elements in art: gentleness (not tenderness, which is flaccid), which Goethe had, as did

Katherine Mansfield; and forcefulness, which Hölderlin, Michelangelo, Dostoyevsky, and Goethe had.

(Anyone who does not attain one or the other—is nothing.)

31

Those who claim that Katherine Mansfield is imitation Chekhov (would have been nothing without Chekhov, etc.) must be answered with: you are right. And Chekhov in turn would have been nothing without Tolstoy (for it was reading the novella *The Death of Ivan Ilyich* that awakened Chekhov to his true life). Tolstoy himself is easily connected to a few forerunners and these did not create anything not already prefigured in Adam.—Did we not descend from a father, we would admittedly be nothing. We would not have existed.

Let the eye linger on those who descend from a father and yet are still nothing.

32

The author of *Faust II*, Valéry, Proust, Thomas Mann, or Karl Kraus are not what I call *pretentious artists*, but Beethoven, Schiller, and Victor Hugo are. Because attention given to each detail in the work of the former is rewarded, while in the work of the latter, that attention comes at a price. The work of the latter demands that one first get drunk in order to oversee their mistakes and weaknesses. One must cover immense distances to finally be in a position to contemplate *their* higher spirit, their pure will, and their actual contact with the inexpressible, which had been hidden so long behind floods of rhetoric; a position from which one must declare oneself *for* these fundamentally powerful, affirming spirits. Are *these* not pretensions?

—But, a few will object, with *Valéry*, too, they had to cover immense distances and make an enormous effort until they found the living core of his work.

If you cannot see because you are blind, that is your fault; if the artist makes you cross the Sahara to reach what he offers, then the fault is his.

[...]

35

It would be important to describe a firework display in great detail—even more, to describe the spectators' sensations, their experience when watching this primitive and edifying display—because it corresponds exactly to the wrong conception of art.

("There goes another one."—"Let's go home. Show's done.")

—whereas art, for those who understand it, is one occurrence after another, a series that keeps extending, keeps branching out.

[...]

38

No, art is not a sum of things painstakingly held together. Expressing yourself, from wherever place you happen to be (—which, admittedly, requires origins of many facets . . .)—is enough.

To purify yourself to the point where you offer *only* what is necessary;—by necessary I mean what you have seen (experienced), better yet, what exists right now—without adding *anything at all*, that is without the slightest trace of form created through something previously seen (experienced) or in existence: this is art in full.

(From this point of view Goethe's poetry is subject to criticism here and there and Hölderlin, of all the German poets, is least subject to criticism.)

What we think separates the most is what connects. And what is added in order to create connections saps life, weakens—separates.

[...]

40

Someone said that art arose from joy, that it is a luxury; art's complete opposite, he posited, is the terrible gravity of the mind and spirit, what he called "the prophetic." According to him, the great artist Shakespeare was, in reality, a mere scamp, a frivolous person, etc., and I need to clarify my understanding of art's essence.

I found his view of art disagreeable. — Many years have passed since then. Finally I found refuge again in Goethe, who wrote: "Art is concerned with the difficult and the good." And elsewhere: "Art is based on . . . a profound, unshakable seriousness."

I also thought that it's not difficult to call Shakespeare frivolous, a man we know so little about that arguments over his identity are still being conducted today. To be sure, insouciance occasionally comes to the fore in the work of artists we know better (Molière, perhaps, or Mozart). Yet we must not forget that they are far removed from us: distance gilds so beautifully. It is clear that great artists about whom we have more information offer very different pictures of their temperaments, whether their names are Gide, Rilke, Katherine Mansfield, Rodin, Cézanne, or Balzac.

I have never forgotten Burckhardt's observation that in Archaic Greece, singers and seers were one.

[. . .]

VI

ON WRITING

> The poet should live more? He does live more.
>
> *Karl Kraus*

1

Painting has been able to develop in a purer fashion and with fewer restraints than the verbal arts. This is because there's a great difference in the material conditions of these two arts and their ways into the world. (The circumstances of their entry into the world work reflexively on the activity of the creators for art cannot arise in circumstances *completely* cut off from society—if it ever does, then only in very brief and isolated cases or only apparently.)

The verbal arts are dependent on the crowd, on the size of the audience (a book needs a thousand readers or it won't be printed), painting on only a few connoisseurs (a half dozen may be enough).

And it's not even necessary that these connoisseurs (critics, art dealers, collectors) truly understand the work; it's enough if they are interested in it, for *any* reason at all. They let the prices rise, they "launch" the artist, open a worldly existence to him, solidify the ground under his feet so that he can stride forward, and they alone— show me the crowd that supports a Cézanne, a Picasso, and whose judgment plays a decisive role (even more, *played* a decisive role) in their rise. (That crowds end up following, not leading, is not important here; what is important is how the artist can begin his way into the world.)

Thus it is, in a certain sense, easier to paint than to write. Even if many who begin as painters end up as conventional decorators, the writer faces even greater danger of slipping from the real to the pleasant due to the aforementioned circumstances.

2

With regard to a report on a congress of Soviet writers: that a few representatives of the people describe the impressions that artworks have made on them, express what they feel is missing in them, what they would have demanded or wished otherwise, is certainly an excellent exercise. This, like every natural and sincere reaction, can encourage art.

For art is not independent of its readers (listeners, viewers); there is no denying it: we require a reader . . . An artwork requires a reader: and yet—this must be emphasized no less clearly—it is only dependent on *its* reader: and this reader is in no way identical to the crowds of readers that can be found bustling about in any era. Parts of the particular reader may be represented in those toing and froing: but his center is elsewhere.

It would therefore be absurd to conclude from this report that the people could offer conscious directives for new art forms! That is utterly impossible. Here a strict law of priorities is in force. Art is in advance (insofar as it is art—), not the people! Art may be rejoined in the future by the best that stirs amidst the contemporary masses and develops out of them, but it will first follow a much *greater arc* than many imagine—just as Montaigne was once a marginal figure until humanity integrated him as it developed over time.

I later found this most beautifully expressed by François Mauriac:[1] "The truth is that the impact of a Montaigne is not immediately obvious. On a political or social level, it is easy to follow a man's traces: the furrow dug by Karl Marx can be seen with

1. *Le Temps*, 4/9/1937.

the naked eye. But the ramblings of Montaigne, of Pascal or Proust, the very secret alterations worked on the human elite through Mozart and through Cézanne, are of a completely different order and elude our grasp."

I could cite a more exact, more extensive passage by Proust if it were not too long, in which he maintains that each work must create its own posterity; "If the work were held in reserve, were known only by posterity, then this same posterity would in fact be none for this particular work, but would instead be a group of contemporaries who simply lived fifty years later. *And so, if the artist wishes for his work to follow its own course, it is necessary for him—and this is what Vinteuil had done—to launch it where there is enough depth, into the full and distant future."*[2]

Not once has a new art form been created by the masses—not any more than scientific discoveries are made by the masses—but instead by Gide, Proust, Karl Kraus, the true experimenters, the true bearers of substance (which is the same thing).

[. . .]

4

Next to the press, film, radio, the novels of Edgar Wallace, every attempt to write significant prose is a delusion as long as it must compete with these things (that is: to want to operate as Balzac did). It is delusional to try to write prose that pleases readers and, at the same time, is of high value. If it is to be of high value, prose must recognize its own domain, a domain in which it will not be subject to competition from the cinema, radio, or Wallace's novels, nor to competition from the press or any other bawlers or industries (competition against which it will, of course, *always* lose). It must be able, with a serene smile, to let these pass and embark on paths traced by a Rilke,[3] a Valéry, a Mallarmé.

2. From Proust's À *l'Ombre des Jeunes Filles en Fleurs*, Pléiades 1st ed. (Paris: Gallimard, 1987), p. 532; emphasis is Hohl's. (Trans. note)

3. I am thinking here exclusively of the late Rilke, and even so, I was surely overestimating him at the time I wrote this note.

5

Now and then one hears the objection that *material* is necessary; no matter how elevated the writer's spirit, it works through his material; it cannot be presented stripped bare of the material (they may try to use this as an argument in defense of the novel, etc.). Have I ever denied what is correct in this proposition—that what is most elevated cannot been presented completely bare? I am obliged to quote myself: "All significant world-systems, even the most splendid, can be more or less summed up in *one* sentence. And this sentence is almost nothing. The significance of the creators is revealed by the fact that they were *not* able or were only barely able to utter this sentence—a sentence which any pharmacist's apprentice can say with ease—but instead struggled for most of their lives to formulate it."[4] I could cite other passages but this one should suffice as proof of how clear it was to me even then that the one idea or the few ideas one has cannot and should not be present nakedly, but must work through myriad aspects of the current era. Those who raised the objection above should also understand: *these myriad aspects of the present can no longer be external events* (as in times when the press had not yet developed) but only internal events—thoughts. Having a good architectural idea does not exempt one from knowing which are the proper building blocks. In earlier days, a writer communicated his ideas through varied external events (even the best can't do this anymore). Now they are told through individual thoughts, levels of thoughts, and events within thoughts. For the most part in any case; such profound change does not happen suddenly and naturally. This change began earlier (most clearly in *Faust* and yet a writer like Julien Green, a work like *Adrienne Mesurat*) is still possible today. Péguy, Proust, Karl Kraus, Valéry, Gide, Rilke: a list of writers that is not meant to be complete but to show the direction which many of the most spiritual and intellectual acts of our time have taken. (Nietz-

4. *Nuancen und Details* II, 27.

sche should be named as well. And in particular Hebbel, who developed his gifts most in his journal. I would not hesitate to add Thomas Mann, despite appearances, to this list.)

We can be certain: if all the forests were to be used up, many people would inevitably begin to claim that only wood construction is possible and they would never admit that one could build quite well with new materials that had since been discovered (or *created*).

6

It is not at all important for a writer to have a "good subject" (a subject one can objectively deem good), or "sound, solid material" (as Balzac and Hebbel surely did; as did Zola, Bourget, Jules Romains, and many others), but it is important that the subject matter, whatever it is, be *charged* for that writer with deep internal meaning, out of reach of any control. What was the subject matter of many of Katherine Mansfield's stories that attain extreme poetic heights? It means nothing if a writer today has the same subject matter as Balzac, nor would it mean anything if Balzac had never existed. Furthermore, if his treatment of that subject matter were better than Balzac's it would not be relevant. An inexpressible difference remains, a difference in nuance that cannot be articulated or learned, which, following Curtius, one could perhaps call — to give it some kind of name — "composition" (worlds away from "construction"! which can be explained, named, learned). There are a number of words one could use instead of "composition" since it is a vague designation, which does not compel us to see what it describes. It is, in any case, very difficult to see. It only becomes clear through examples. Curtius discusses it by comparing Balzac with Zola. Zola has the same formula as his predecessor: enormous subjects, pivotal themes: but the "composition" (however many "compositions" he created) in his works is generally inferior, lacking the level of vitality we almost always find in Balzac (except, that is, for *Germinal*).

[. . .]

9

The "plots" of most modern novels—that is, the element that makes these works novels and not just books, notations, essays, or simply prose—are:

A way of capturing the reader! Bad readers, that is. And yet they do have significance because, first, they help spread the work so that it is more likely to fall into the hands of a good reader; second, they may enable the scrap of a good reader hiding inside a bad one and unable to manage a proper reading on his own. (Admittedly, the question of whether or not this kind of facilitation makes sense is grist for a long discussion.)

10

To capture readers, one must write novels. To lose them, one must write well.

On this:[5] "More and more, I have had to convince myself that a writer's importance is proportional to his ability to disregard the reader, to possess an unshakable confidence—since nothing exists without the social context—that he will *nonetheless* have a reader and a wonderful one at that."

11

The novelistic form has yet another advantage: novels are an excellent resource to learn foreign languages (summarily).

12

In a newspaper, I read that François Mauriac said the following in an interview: "All my books have a secret part I treasure. And yet, in not one of them do I find exactly what I would have liked to

5. Cf. IV, 21.

put in. I believe this is true of all novelists. When Valéry rereads 'La Jeune Parque,' he surely has the sense of having created something, of having accomplished what he wanted."[6]

"I believe this is true of all novelists." I believe it too! But it *wasn't* always this way. This wasn't the case back when one could still write novels because one had to write them: legitimately write them. (It still was at the time of *Madame Bovary*.)

[. . .]

15

Where does the density of literary writing come from? Where is the thematic breadth found with so many acts are piled onto, compressed into each page without preambles or prolixity?

It's not a question of content but presentation.

For many years I didn't know the secret to formal capacity is simply finding the proper distance (a matter of focal points)! The focal point in which a thing or one's words ignite is miniscule. (The lens, the eye is mobile in relation to the object: its power to burn is limited to a single point.)

16

I suddenly realized that I had only ever considered the art of narrative in relation to *quantity*, to the quantity of material, of material that was already at hand, material that had to be dealt with. (—the way a farmer must *master* the grass on his field when it has grown high: he must find a way to reap it all and bring it home!)—whereas the art of narrative has almost nothing to do with such material quantity, as little, indeed, as the style of a swimmer crossing a lake has anything to do with the amount of water in the lake basin! (Is there a book richer in material, of greater epic amplitude, than *War and*

6. "Nouvelles Littéraires," 2.23.1935.

Peace? And yet, even *its* author had to admit that he could only use
a minute fraction of the vast wealth of material available to him.)
We don't speak of the swimmer as encompassing the water, instead
he crosses it, draws a *line*. Similarly, countless other lines could be
drawn through the writer's wealth of material; each of them would
be just as *masterly* as long as the writer's mind . . . Art is not an act of
encompassing but of making gestures, of conjuring with magical gestures—or it is a line, an evocative line.

17

That's why it's completely impossible for someone to write well
and, at the same time, to write too much about himself.[7]

For the difficulty of finding a thing's focal point, the point of incandescence
that calls art to life—or: of finding the conjuring gesture—or: of drawing an evocative
line through it—this difficulty is so great that the question of whether the material
is great or small becomes moot.

18

"Please explain." What is well-written can't be explained; that
is, in fact, the very definition of good writing. Good writing can't be
explained for the simple reason that it is itself a superior kind of clarification. The only possibility would be to speak similarly or better,
even. But those who are inquiring are surely not asking for that, are
they? No, they simply want to be served up a few cheap banalities on
the side: what they actually want is for that piece of good writing to
be defiled.

7. Writers of the first rank, like Lichtenberg, Proust, and Karl Kraus, were
constantly being reproached for this by people who were merely displaying their
utter ignorance about art.

19

There are writers who are easily understood and writers who are difficult. Karl Kraus, for example, is one who is easy to read; Maupassant is difficult. We will never, therefore, recommend Maupassant to the ignorant but Karl Kraus instead.

For what is easily seen in Maupassant is worthless: his work is a pitfall. There is no such ease in Karl Kraus's writing (apart from the sensationalism of his polemics, which are now dated). His writing is difficult to approach, hence easily understood.

20

All forms change . . . Happy are those who can find deliverance from academic theories of art! The secret is simply this: writers are explorers who express themselves (and constantly suit their forms of expression more closely to the results of their research).

Such were Katherine Mansfield and Heraclitus, Gryphius and Balzac, Hölderlin and Thomas Mann, and everyone in between.

—They will obviously not write things like "the early bird catches the worm!" or that coots "mask their inborn wildfowl pride with a beggarly air"!⁸

21

About a writer (who has many brothers): Does he have a lot of material?

—A lot of spittle, rather.

[. . .]

8. This sentence (by Adolf Koelsch in the *Neue Zürcher Zeitung*) is a typical example of a construction that most people will find downright "poetic" but in reality is simply bloated inanity because it expresses neither inner tension nor external perception. Not one of the three elements that make up the phrase is *true*: in connection with these waterfowl there can be no discussion of masking, of wildfowl pride, or of a beggarly air.

26

Poets do not ponder differently than others, just more.

They apprehend.

We are immersed in things as fish are in water, but poets apprehend them.

("It's all right here, but where to start, / how to get ahold of it, that's the art.")[9]

27

True poetry is the opposite of fiction.

Nietzsche said, "the poets lie too much." Hölderlin "yet what remains, the poets provide." Do these two serious ideas contradict each other?

28

In sculpture, the material must be everything, if I can put it this way: marble must become marble *again* after all the changes have been wrought; what emerges in the new form must be marble again, marble as it was when still in the mountain. There is no place for anything that is not marble: consider Rodin's Balzac and compare it to the memorials in those so-called final resting places. But in writing, to take ink as the starting point is a big mistake. Many people make this assumption but it's still wrong.

You must write with that corrosive liquid that etches stone and metal, that takes life and transforms it.

The substance of writing is the word, not ink, nor sound.

9. Johann Wolfgang von Goethe, *Faust: Part Two*, trans. Martin Greenberg (New Haven, CT: Yale University Press, 1998), lines 4929–30. (Trans. note.)

29

Words that do not perpetrate violence are words only if you are dimwitted. (Or if they are plagiarism.)

30

On Plagiarism

If someone were to transcribe *Faust* exactly, down to the last syllable, but put his name on the title page instead of Goethe's, would that be so terrible? One could imagine that in doing so he had thought extensively.

But the others, their case is much worse. They have taken only parts of it and mixed in a great deal of . . . "their own stuff": but from their own stuff it is clear that they didn't think at all.

If I were ever to encounter one of these great plagiarists, a paragon of plagiarism, as Lichtenberg described them! But today it seems that great plagiarists are as rare as great writers:

"The reason plagiarists are so contemptible is that they only plagiarize meagerly and in secret. They should do so like conquerors who are now considered honest folk. They should blatantly have others' works published in their name and if anyone objects then beat him about the head and shoulders until blood spurts from his nose and mouth."

Yet Lichtenberg must have been a great optimist. "The reason they are so contemptible . . .": for how many of them are truly held in contempt? Aren't they actually, on the contrary, given prizes and honored as authors and poets? Would they cease to be honored, even in these times, if their plagiarism were proven? Does the difference lie in the fact that in Lichtenberg's day, the finer methods of plagiarism had not yet been discovered?—How do they do it today? They appropriate things from other plagiarists and subject it to a game of mirrors; they combine things of various origins—how is one to prove plagiarism in this method? So they believe with justification that they will escape detection—even from their own consciences.

Now we have a new means of detection at hand: we approach from the other side. "We will not show that you have stolen the ring: it is proof enough of theft if you cannot show us *how you acquired it.*"

But what are we talking about here?—Don't words belong to everyone, like the air, and therefore there can be no talk of theft?— Each word speaks for itself, speaks through its particular structure. It is a living, organic process. And if we cannot recognize today whether the tree grew on your ground or whether you went and felled it elsewhere, then we will tomorrow. If your first sentence does not make it clear to us, the following ones will.

There is no part that is neither our own nor stolen. *Everything that is not our own has been stolen.*

What is our own? What we can account for in full and in every single part.

For words and even phrases do not at all belong to everyone as the air does; they have been fashioned by someone and they belong to that person alone until someone else buys them. The ransom is sheer necessity. If you have used these words without paying that price, you have stolen them.

He who sees something and puts it into words, says what is right and *true.* But because most plagiarists, to their misfortune, do not copy a saying from *one* who sees, but bits of sayings expressed by several, they end up with a saying that has been spoken from multiple places and does not correspond to any reality. What happens, to give a very crude and obvious example, is this: someone looking down into a valley from high on a mountain wrote, "A train crept past like a caterpillar." In a train station another wrote, "The express train roared by." A third, who did not *see,* composed this sentence: "The train roared by like a caterpillar." This example is only a schema (just as the laws of geometry schematize land surveying and the laws of physics schematize natural processes): the same procedure of compiling a poem would be much more complicated because one is faced with a multifaceted structure. It's not only matter of external vision, but also of inner vision; one must consider not just logical and grammatical connections, but also the connections between *this* sound and *this* vision, *this* sensation and *this* thought. It would be necessary to show that the writer, had he truly possessed *this* thought (grasped it, achieved it through his life) would never have written in that tone, etc.

Someone is yelling in the garden. A heavy stone fell on his foot: he justifies his yelling. Someone begs, "Stay with me. I'm dying." You look at him and his pallor, his tone of voice, and a hundred other tiny details you cannot name all compel you to acknowledge — as all would be compelled — that these are *his* words. This is how it must go with all you writers.

As I've written elsewhere: "In dire need, inferior beings access the power of the word. Great artists are always in a state of dire need."

In a time like ours with its *fiction industry* pushing the young to write novels . . .

There are two things one would wish for the novel: first that novel writing be forbidden, punishable by law; second, that some magical power remove any and all possibilities for a novel to have the slightest measure of success. Then a work like *À la Recherche du temps perdu* or the works of Gide or Kafka would doubtless still have been written. But what of the majority of books by Wassermann? Or all those by Jules Romains? And most of the famous American novels, those floods of drivel? — What would the world have lost? [. . .]

In art there is plagiarism or non-plagiarism (what we call "the creative") and nothing else. What is not plagiarism has meaning: what is meaningless is plagiarism.

The whole art of writing consists in not using a single word without complete responsibility.

31

On Quoting

Every time he quotes someone else, Mr. X apologizes for not offering his own words. That is very suspicious, indeed . . .

Is writing really that different from quoting? The words, after all, are already there!

Because the creative process and that of making a serious judgment are so similar, one can not only experience the same uncertainty when judging something as when considering one's own creations, but, in fact, occasionally one might even confuse the two—since the two activities differ only in degree of intensity. Thus the art of quoting, seen with a certain remove, can be just as difficult as writing. The mere juxtaposition of two quotations creates a construct.

One brilliant quotation lies within everyone's grasp. (One need only take one of Goethe's sayings, almost all of which are good.) The difficulty begins with the second.—Books found at the flea market were full of marks in pencil: as a rule, one pencil marking tells me nothing about my predecessor as a person since the books are good; but with the second or third, a dark suspicion sets in about the previous reader's understanding of things, about what kind of constructs might have arisen in *his* mind . . . ; a suspicion that begins to harden into certainty even before I find a "how's that?" here or a "bravo!" there.

He who has nothing of his own to say, must struggle to offer something of his own. He who is without means does well not to borrow from anyone.

But the quotations included in Montaigne's writing could make for a thick book; and it never occurred to him to apologize.

He reads with such force (as Lichtenberg did), that he no longer knows if the work is his or someone else's.

—Don't laugh too soon. He climbs. "Only because of the mountain," you say. But where the mountain ends, he continues to climb along the same trajectory, above and beyond. He has begun to write and doesn't notice.

He who feels a difference when moving from quoting to writing, as if switching from a heavy load to a light one, from effort to receptivity, from (toilsome) climbing to effortless rolling—he is most certainly neither able to quote nor to write.

"The article is done," the editor cried happily. "I've just marked in red ten or so passages that need a fitting quotation. The secretary should preferably choose them from Goethe."

"Make sure they are fitting!" he called out again. And then: "Choose predominantly from *Faust II*, the part that hasn't yet been thoroughly *picked over*."

A mere change of emphasis in otherwise similar notions creates various effects, meanings, values. Yes, even a slight change in emphasis can signify a great deal [. . .]—To change the status of something in the realm of culture, in literature, can be *productive*, even creative, if done meaningfully (the young do not understand this).

Ideas are already present. The *ability to foreground* one is no easy thing.

Once one understands the importance of this and understands that there are *degrees* of knowledge, degrees of intensity, that one neither "knows" nor "doesn't know" in elevated realms, then one understands the danger that one kind of knowledge, nominal or formal knowledge, represents for mankind and always has. (The principle of inoculation, of immunization.—The pharmacist. The disastrous effects of schooling.—Why is it that a laborer is likely to understand *Faust* better than a pharmacist?)

"The water is warm." And this water is warmer. This iron is a great deal hotter. This red-hot iron—. And a few thousand degrees is enough heat to melt a celestial body.

[. . .]

33

Political and social writers have almost never created art because their works are not constructed from primary, but from secondary material; their primary experience was elsewhere; yet art arises only directly from primary experience, or more exactly, *as* primary experience. Because the place of their most immediate involvement, the authentic experiences of these writers is in social transformations and political developments, their writing, from an artistic point of view, is wan, without a truly independent existence (which does not exclude educational value—quite the contrary; art is a very unsuitable instrument of education: it assumes a high level of education).—Art is a pinnacle of experience and not connected to external events. It is not transmission, not the preservation of a scent, not a means of harvesting fruit ripening elsewhere. Art itself is the real fruit.

34

Proverbial expressions—like "Home is where the heart is"— should only be used in rare cases. When? Exclusively when the context makes it clear that it has been used with complete awareness, which is almost never the case—unless one has altered it slightly, even simply by changing the word order to unseal it, to reanimate the words and allow them to breathe again.

35

Above all, nothing dreamy! Not even what you can record at night and bring into daylight. Even your most elevated and most difficult passages must be as clear as the most ordinary ones—even your hallucinations, even your transitions to strange hues of rarely seen landscapes.

[. . .]

46

The melodious. When someone finally came my way and read something I had written, he uttered the following judgment: "What I like about your manner of writing is its musical quality." That this should be said to me of all people after I worked for years to strip any musicality from my prose!

Melodious prose—for "melodious" is the precise word: "musical" could cause some confusion: one could understand that the prose described resembles music insofar as it can do without any explicit subject matter, which is high praise, to be sure. Melodious prose, on the other hand, can be heard from countless pulpits, if not from all. To evoke melodies in the reader's mind using silent means is more difficult.

47

The writer, as I envision him, does not deliver succulent roasts, nor does his prose ring melodiously. But some of the sentences in the pages of writing he completed through infinite exertion have the dark, glassy gleam of metal.

48

Your sentences should be like metal, not paper. Have you engraved them well? (No? That is risible.) They are of paper.

Not just *sound* like metal.—What you are peddling are sounds that drifted in from the street, people speak in all sorts of tongues now. And there are a thousand devices that multiply sounds. The air is filled with them. Must you avail yourself of one of these?

The best part of a bell is the metal, not the sound. Lichtenberg says: "What the pealing of bells may bring to the rest of the dead, I cannot say, but for the living it is dreadful." And in *Faust* we read:

> . . . That dinging, donging
> Grates on every man of feeling,
> Spoils the quiet of the evening
> With its bimming and its bamming,
> Mixes into everything
> From christening to burying,
> As if between the bam and bim
> Life were a mere interim.[10]

"Your sentences should be like metal": and not silver, that soft, milky-black material, but gold or one of the more noble metals, if an alloy, then brass; or ore. And if not metal, then stone. Sculpted rock is the most divine.

Have you heard tell of the marvelous, secret, viridescent boulders? They stand along the mountain lake, alone and isolate, you think. You cannot hear their life or see their movements; you pass them with your wisp of a newspaper, good only for the smallest concerns of your brief days; you need millennial-eyes in order to see how the boulders live and speak, how they are connected to everything around them.

49

An alteration is visible when you come to the end of a text you are writing, an ending that is usually external—perhaps it can only occur with an external ending—a publication deadline, for example. The alteration may seem positive or negative. (The positive effect is limited to the exterior, the physical, so to speak, the animating aspect.) Most often, though, the alteration seems negative. Best is to write a work without an end, like Pascal's *Pensées*.

10. Ibid., p. 217. (Trans. note.)

VII

VARIA

> . . . Some writers all too often write what any-
> one could write and leave behind what only they
> could have said and what would have immortal-
> ized them.
>
> *Lichtenberg*

1

He chalked this or that failure up to love. Some became suspicious and asked around. Love said she knew nothing about it.

2

In that country is a small town in which there is no other profession than night watchman. All the men there are night watchmen.

3

He was given a surface that stretched from here to . . . (an im-
measurable expanse) and told to paint a picture on it—.

4

I showed a child the stars and he saw them at night. But when he
looked for them the next day he couldn't see them. He complained
that I'd shown him something that didn't exist. "I know because now
I can see more clearly than before—all the way to tops of the trees!"

5

One night, a man dreamt of two things: a very pretty young woman who snuggled up against him and a disturbing encounter with the police who confused him with a burglar and threatened to lock him in jail. The two dreams had the scorching clarity that keeps them vivid throughout the day. The man roamed far and wide all day, convinced he would find the young woman. The day passed and the chill of disappointment enveloped him: the young woman had not come. Neither had the misfortune, of course. But he hadn't expected it to.

6

It took him a very long time to go into the water and yet, the moment he was in, he began shouting obscenities at those still on shore.

7

The alteration of an object observed by the observer is also very marked when the object of study is the state a *human being* is in. When a visit is paid to the unhappy, the sad, or the lonely: they are changed by the visit.—The deep-sea diver brings an immensely powerful light nine hundred meters below sea level in order to *surprise* life. But the light only scares away the creatures that were there and attracts others that weren't. (Nevertheless, in those depths physical eyes have seen splendors barely surpassed by sights our inner eyes see in poetry or dreams.)

8

When everyone says that some potent thing (eating, drinking, smoking; but also taking an afternoon nap, sleeping in, taking cold or hot baths, going to the seaside, to a cold climate, any kind of travel;

sexual relations or abstinence, etc.) is demoralizing, then it is demoralizing. Because the average person feels some powerful effect (the nature of which is still undecided) and categorizes it as demoralizing of his own accord. That explains why, in countries where drinking alcohol is considered harmful and disreputable, those who drink alcohol soon become wrecks; only the strong in spirit can resist. In other countries like France, however, those who drink just as much or more maintain all their faculties. Similarly, in those countries where smoking is considered demoralizing, it demoralizes; in Holland, however, people smoke like chimneys and need not atone for it (they have an excess of tobacco and that is why general opinion does not find it demoralizing). Hebbel noted long ago that some people only become good because they were always considered so and that others, who were always seen as bad, became so. — Only the strong in spirit can resist.

9

He thought the window was open and so he fell back asleep (fresh air always made him tired).

But the window wasn't open.

10

Story

Three men had a terrible argument; each argued with the other two. They were arguing about what makes up a house.

The first said: "A house consists of: a cellar, a ground floor, a first floor, a second . . ." and so on.

The second cried: "A house is made of wood, stone, mortar, metal (etc.)!"

The third, furious with the first two, calls them liars and scoundrels, exactly as they were insulting each other and him, and announces that a house can be divided into lines and showed them a floor plan and an elevation on which were designated the length and width of every wall, and the length, width, and height of every room; only these drawings show the exact parts of a house, everything else is rubbish.

Is it necessary to add that the three men argued until their dying days, because not one relented, given each was correct? They died one after the other, each one an idiot and a hero.

11

Short Story

First, they asked why the frozen man was in such a terrible state. "He lacks heat," the wise man said (isn't it astonishing that they needed a wise man to make this observation?). "He was without warmth for too long." Then they brought him something hot, warmed him up a bit, and, when his condition still didn't improve much, they called out: "Look here: does he jump, does he hop as we do? He didn't lack for warmth after all!"

12

Storylet

Fine little ladies and little gentlemen: the gentlemen in their shiny, black, narrow, pointy shoes, the women gleaming in silks, jewels, and décolletés, all indulging in dancing and diversion in a room filled with glittering of chandeliers high among the rock and ice walls of the Himalayas, that is, in a room of a hotel built into the ground, where they lead their pampered lives. They all *laughed* at the sight of two rough primordial figures who suddenly appeared cloaked in wool and leather with ice picks and hobnail boots and coated with ice. — The fine ladies and gentlemen danced and played in the glittering room. They gave no thought to the hazards and difficulties of the climb. They had come up on the train (a more advanced kind of Jungfrau Railway) and lived in the hotel. *There is no more train*, the new arrivals said.

13

Little Story of a King

This little story comes from a time when there were still kings — that is, when you could still tell a king from a doorman because they had functions: internally different and externally, too. If I don't transpose my story, it's only because the word king, although dated, still has a nice ring to it. (You may come up with some alternative.)

The sovereign was meant to travel personally to some region in his realm or some important occasion or other — I don't remember what exactly. No expenses or efforts were spared in preparing a worthy reception, a broad road was built across an empty field.

"I'm preparing the road for the king. Get out of my way!" the roadworker said to a man walking toward him.

But the man walking toward him was none other than the king himself. He had left his retinue and traveled ahead alone.

But he was not in disguise! *He was not dressed as a poor beggar* — disregard those lying tales! — he appeared just as he was. He looked exactly like a king and no different. They did not recognize him.

"Even if a low-ranking member of the king's retinue came along, adorned in silver and braids came, we would no doubt also not let him disturb us. — We are busy here with the preparations that will serve other preparations that will in turn lead to the greatest, the final goal. — The envoy of the high commission who gives the orders is very strict and has seven medals. And one day a member of the commission itself came — we were all afraid. A minister at that . . . he must have a thousand medals!"

The king walked on, across the field, on foot, and was gone —.

His lackeys arrived after him at full gallop and the road worker prostrated himself immediately before them. The rest of the story is of no interest to those who interest me.

[. . .]

15

Two Brief Stories

1. On those who want to give others what they themselves want to give and not what others want. A starving man was given an expensive cigarette holder. — For a long time a noblewoman had promised to give a poor woman a Christmas present. The poor woman expected a sum of money (the gift was meant to be a handsome one) or perhaps some provisions: ham, cheese, a goose? She was given a clothing storage unit, the latest model, a marvelous invention that automatically turns toward the shade, its price was high (of course, it cannot be resold).

2. Something in this house is not in order, more accurately, it is filled with a *terrible* disorder, screaming, yelling, a bit of smoke now and again. — Title: *Education.* The end: . . . we hear a loud shout: "Fire!"

And they shot at the house.

[. . .]

17

Tavern on Kasernenstraße. Some say this tavern is bad. I don't think it's so bad, in fact it seems better than the average tavern hereabouts. I like to sit at the window; the long wall of the barracks is the only thing facing the window. It's dreadful, to be sure, but I find it very symbolic.

In between — along the street — a constant stream of people flows by (and a bit of the sky is visible above).

People think the owner is a bad man because he has such a low forehead. I know he's a bit mad, but it could be worse. Besides what publican is not mad?

[...]

20

Moon Forest, Hedgehog Forest

I went out and into the forest because I was worn out from working on a project I was determined to finish that day without making any progress. I wanted to refresh myself for a new bout of work. I harbored a dark apprehension—I didn't want it to become more definite—that I wouldn't reach my desired goal this way but would instead find myself even further from it. How had it gone in many previous similar cases? How had it always gone when, my mind dulled from protracted efforts, I forced myself outdoors for half an hour (I went out at any time of day and most often at night, without letting any encounters, any external factors intrude on my extended solitude) to force the situation, to acquire on a short walk through the municipal forest a new keenness of being by striving to *relax, to clear my mind of all thoughts*—before suddenly turning back and hurling myself again upon the passage that had become hollow and bogged down? How had things gone on each and every one of those occasions? The passage became even more rigid, even harder to grasp and my impotence greater.—That is what had always happened in the municipal forest that I called the hedgehog forest (because I once came upon a hedgehog in it). But this time I didn't head into that forest but into one of the two other nearby municipal forests which I called the moon forest (because on my first walk through it an enormous moon had shone down on it).

Not much happened on that walk—nothing external—and yet it was the decisive experience that formed the root stock or the foundation from which the most essential elements developed over the following years.—An internal experience with unforeseeable conse-quences; a long-prepared realization that crystallized into consum-mate clarity.

—Thus I reached the moon forest with the dark apprehension, fed with memories, that for all my efforts I would not reach my goal. But things turned out differently.

For some reason I didn't try to relax, to clear my mind of thought. On the contrary, I examined my apprehension (the dark one I carried within), I studied what had happened in all similar cases, I reflected (and did not rest), yet it must be noted that I was applying my mind to a completely different object than the one I had left at home, this was *a different mental activity.* I reflected and noted some of it down on paper and—

—achieved two things at once. First, the desired refreshment and a new ability to return to the work I had left at home; second, the results of the just completed examination already written down in part.

Furthermore, these two things reinforced, overlapped each other in a kind a spiral or in the form of a fugue—in that the first was proof of the second, the second a miniature repetition of the whole, the whole a magnificent illustration of the second—all this became clear to me in a flash.

The discovery was: *we grow through producing, not through rest.* (Or: *production strengthens, not rest.*)

This sudden illumination of the world brought proof from all sides of the law: rest kills. What is sleep? Perhaps the spirit's rest, its refreshment? No, sleep is a turn toward another, an even more power-ful production: through this new activity the spirit gains access to new sources so that (on awakening) it can resume the previous activity "refreshed" as they say. And it's therefore, in truth, precisely *not* rest that refreshes the spirit, but another intense activity. The spirit gains new strength from unsuspected directions. There is no such thing as rest. Rest is simply death.

Some may speak of "dreamless" nights; the spirit was so far away, busy on such an elevated plane one cannot remember, elevations one cannot look up to.

—"But is the opposite—that rest strengthens—still true for the body?" Just a little, as a closer examination will show. "And for external, vegetable nature? Doesn't one speak of winter rest?"

That so-called winter rest!—I looked at the smooth, apparently lifeless trunks of the, for the most part, leafless trees. No, it cannot apply here either, I am most powerfully convinced! (Biologists will be able to explain it in detail and no doubt already have.) Nature simply turns to another form of productivity in this state of "rest," which is rest only from one perspective, it only *appears* as rest because of our faulty vision. Neither trees, animals, humans, nor spirit can live at rest: life cannot remain immobile at one level. Life is *only* ever productivity and ascent—and then comes death.

This, then, is what I understand: my discovery applies not only to artists but must be a general law. And I could formulate it thus:

Contrary to what the ancients taught, nature is not conceived of as motion and rest, but only as motion.

21

When sleep is an end in itself, it is good—good in itself and good for other ends—; insofar as it's meant to create a path to something, it's not good, not in itself, not for other ends.

This can no doubt be applied to everything, to all our concerns and activities, formerly called our productivity; again this strikes me as a bit doubtful: can we call it all productivity? And our legitimate pleasures as well?—Certainly. It must be so; and it's all one: our specific impact. *Work* is something altogether different than what one usually means, *here* lies the flaw in our thinking and the cause of further difficulties.[1]

22

A *word of warning.*—This does not mean that one can turn to any *random* activity to refresh oneself (as certain people like to claim, especially those who stand to gain by the recommended activity). Not at all!

All activity must be legitimate, this is a strict rule. The greatest and only genuine misfortune lies in engaging in an illegitimate activity—and the fight against this is the single greatest and most honorable battle of mankind.

23

What answer should one give when asked to what extent a legitimate activity can be hindered through external circumstances?

(It's a matter of that hindrance of legitimate activity which, next to the hindrance of laziness, affects a vast number of people:)

It's difficult to speak about in general, almost impossible—one must consider each situation, each case. Perhaps in this general anecdotal form: there is a hindrance, you are the hindrance. Good. Made aware, your ire is raised, you fight against it (against the hindrance): you are no longer the problem. Your struggle against the circumstances that are hindering the legitimate activity *is* itself a legitimate activity.

—What, after all, is spirit but the constant variation of its field of activity in order to elevate life to a level appropriate to the inexpressible, always something different: the founding of a state, this or that discovery? A simile of Döblin's is compelling here, at least it keeps

1. Cf. all of Part I as well as the notes on the preparation for death: II, 118, 216–223.

springing to mind when I try to discuss the spirit, the struggle and true activity (the individual's and mankind's): Döblin takes the rolling of a stone up the same hill again and again after the stone rolls back down each time: man must roll it up to the top of the hill again and again, that was his life and that is life. You could also talk of swimming in the current—against the current.—This is a comparison seen from a great elevation: the stone is life, the life of the spirit—"eternal life"—that we must achieve. The stone does *not* represent external results! Those will be achieved. Everything external changes: today we can fly and cross the ocean with ease; tomorrow we will irrigate the Sahara and harness the power of the moon—with time man achieves what he desires, achieves the most unimaginable goals. Man's nature, his project and thought will also undergo changes, his knowledge and abilities will change drastically—there is only one thing, I believe, we will never be able to change, never be able to achieve: that man will be able to rest.

The possibility of the spirit, of legitimate activity, is always there; but the external (visible) results will be to a great extent variable. They will vary greatly in their *dimensions:* from the works of Shakespeare and Napoleon to the struggles of all the unknown, the anonymous, materially oppressed prisoners.

24

What does the *Tale of the Three Tasks'* storyline offer other than this proposition, set down in my experience of the moon forest and the hedgehog forest: that one type of productivity engenders the other?

The birds—the elephants: part of nature or symbols of nature's power. Yet the titans—men perhaps? But men are also a natural force, if one considers them as a whole instead of counting them up individually.

25

The Tale of the Three Tasks

I hesitated to include this story: what is the point of repeating a well-known tale, moreover repeating it inaccurately—given that I read it when I was a young child and not again since (I don't even know who the author is)—with all the changes that creep in over time, especially under the influence of my internal experiences, and adorned, furthermore, with inevitable interpretive flourishes?—Can something written in one form not be related in another? And what if it's precisely those changes and flourishes that are central?

Once upon a time there was a king's son and in a country far away there was a king's daughter who was the fairest in the world (the entire world: all possibilities). The most beautiful princess, in other words, the greatest significance, the object of the greatest significance.

"The prince was inflamed with love": that is, he felt an almost overpowering urge, he felt he possessed the strength to reach her and wed her; to reach the object of greatest significance: to fulfill his destiny.

But one must set out for such a goal.

And rightly, he did want to set out. But his country's sages counseled him against it, the elderly ones most of all, of course. Those sages he listened to—whose clarity of vision on certain matters, after all, had been proven by later events—said that many had set out already and none had obtained the king's daughter. Not a one had returned and he, too, would perish . . . When he listened to them, he became hesitant because, as has been said, they were wise men. When he listened to the voice of his inner certainties, known only to him, his decision to leave became compelling again and he forgot the sages. Finally, defying all obstacles, he set out. Defying the obstacles was not difficult, he needed only ignore them. Anyone else could have done it as well as long as he felt or perceived the same certainties, the same object within.

Initially, his journey was very long and tedious. Tedious when one compares all his encounters along the way, diverting as they were, to his ultimate goal. These encounters didn't alter his goal in the slightest and didn't seem to bring him any nearer to it. The journey was tedious (for all its external diversions). It was tedious, alarming even, because it left the prince always alone with ponderous thoughts of the goal he was striving to reach, that ominous kingdom which never appeared any closer, a perpetually distant goal known only to him. But that was only one segment of the journey; the next one led through the desert and was no longer as barren.

First, he came across great flocks of birds caught in nets, pitiful, helplessly trapped, near death. Nothing but the eternal desert and the nets full of birds awaiting death; only the birds of the sky, caught in nets (those who would turn them to profit were not nearby). He freed the birds and they soared away in great flocks. They didn't even thank him, but he hadn't expected any thanks. Their soaring flight into eternity was thanks enough.

Second, he met elephants that were also victims of a terrible misfortune (several of them had fallen into a trap and been injured). He freed the elephants, an easy feat for him but also an unavoidable one. It was necessary: he could hardly have continued on *his* way without freeing them. That would have hampered his just conception of his inner meaning, his steadiness.

(And here I must insert a brief comment concerning those who preceded him. They had felt no such necessity in similar situations. They'd continued on single-mindedly. *Neither the power of the goal nor their love was great enough.* These were sufficient only to lead them rationally; but not to feed an obsession to prevail over everything and change the world. They headed toward the goal like rams.—Weaker men would have let themselves be distracted along the way.—)

Third, he heard a rumbling that shook the ground and saw a fiery glow in the sky throughout the night. As he approached, he saw titans forging monumental works. He did not even come up to the knees of these desert giants. With their highly developed arts, they created enormous works of all kinds. But then he heard a howl: one of the giants had been wounded and did not know what to do, nor did the others. They were skilled, prodigiously skilled, but could apply those skills only to the creation of their monumental works . . . but in the perfecting of those skills, they had lost the ability to do any other kind of work, such as the gentle treating of wounds. It was easy for the prince to help. He cleaned and bandaged the wound and did so in the same spirit, for the same reasons as he had helped the animals earlier. He stayed until the wound had healed or was certain to heal and left, this time showered with gifts and thanks as the titans were nearly human.

Finally, the prince saw the king's palace surrounded by spikes on which were impaled the heads of those who had tried to win the king's daughter. They had failed to complete the required tasks.

He was given a magnificent and friendly welcome. He was informed of the conditions: if he could complete the three tasks, he would win the princess's hand. (And now he *saw* her . . . she was more marvelous than he had imagined — no, there was no one more marvelous. As marvelous as in his wildest dreams: there she was *again!* A complete marvel — her image had faded a bit during the long journey.) — But if he failed to complete even one of the tasks, he would lose his life and his head would be mounted on a spike in the long row of his predecessors. It was the old king who spoke thus, a gray, icy monarch, glacial beneath the splendor and courtesy; and underneath his expression one could detect scornful laughter. His daughter, whom he displayed only once under heavy guard, was kept imprisoned.

On the first evening the prince was locked in a room filled with millions and millions of grains of various kinds piled into a single enormous mound. He had until dawn to sort the grains perfectly and if he did not finish by daybreak, he would be lost.

At midnight he sat and wept. He gave himself up for lost. He had not begun his task. Even if there were twelve of him, there would be no point.

Hark! What comes whirring in on him in his profound dejection, one foot already in the grave since he had abandoned all hope and almost expired. At first, he had no idea what was happening. There were dozens, hundreds of little birds—flown in through the grate—picking at the grains. The grains were soon properly sorted into mounds.

The king could not hide his pallor when he saw the task completed at dawn. "And now," he cried, gray-faced, "your second task. Come and look!" He led the prince to a small lake in the park behind the castle. "You must drain this lake tonight. At dawn the bed must be dry—."

(Whether or not the prince felt the same despair again at the impossibility of the task, I don't know.)

The elephants arrived in a long, ghostly procession at the night. They pumped the lake dry, spraying the last drops of water at the palace windows at dawn, and disappeared. At least *one* voice cried jubilantly in the palace: "Come and look!"

"And now," said the king, his face a veritable mask of scorn (as can be seen on the faces of those no longer sure of themselves), "you must build a palace on the dry lake bed more beautiful, more intricate and larger than the old palace. You have one night."

In the darkness, the titans strode forth from the desert bearing shovels, levers, and hammers on their shoulders and carrying blocks of marble, wood, and sacks of cement and sand. A rumbling set in and the ground began to shake; from time to time, silence fell for a half an hour as they busied themselves with the fine work. In the morning, the palace was finished, higher, more intricate, shining brighter than the old one and the sun sparkled off the windows, its towers, topped with white gold, glittered at the king when he emerged, gray and extinguished.

And now there was no possibility that *anyone, in any fashion,* could resist the prince. He had achieved everything and won the hand of the king's daughter. Together, they moved far away.

26

No, it's not true that our spiritual and intellectual sides do not have meaning or importance! They will atrophy and suffocate if they don't take themselves seriously.

(There are those who preach a false humility—the product of a poorly understood socialism. Hypocrisy, the diminishment of life! I want to emphasize the other side of socialism: the one that releases life.)

[. . .]

29

The Tale of the Churl

He reminds me of that rough and tumble young man I once met in a mountain village. He was the only chamois hunter in the area. He alone climbed to high elevations, where none of the other village inhabitants would dream of following him. In daily life he was a good worker, the best of all, but in a lowly position. He was the poorest in the village and everyone took advantage of him. He could never show his love for the angelic girl, as delicate as a lily. Others, more suave than he, pushed ahead of him (he was not fresh and so lacking in boldness that others always elbowed him aside). On Sunday afternoons, for example, he sat silent and alone on the shed roof. The more adroit pointed him out with a laugh. He was the only one to whom they would attribute the *basest* motives were he to venture into the realm of the lily . . . They surrounded the young girl, strutting, flattering and cosseting her, while the rough young man—whom they all considered uncouth simply because he was silent and they took no notice of his unusual gaze—sat, filled with bitterness, on the shed roof or a stump, he himself considered no better than a stump. Did he have the right to love? He no longer knew. The others had the right to love, triumphant as they were.

Life went on this way until a terrible misfortune struck, a conflagration. Everyone fled before this deadly menace: what had become of the easy flattery? Where were the protestations of love? The uncouth young man was suddenly transformed as well; he became like an arrow and like a lion. He rescued the girl when no one else even thought of rescue, when it seemed impossible. For him, there was no question whether he should act when all others hesitated. And he did not act *out of duty*; he had always been *waiting* for this moment. His fervor radiated like moonlight; hadn't every fiber of his being strained *toward this?* Yes, he had become a sun: the way he ran to the goal so decidedly—no one had *such* a labor of love in mind—; here he overtook them all without being pushy, he could go on alone. A life might have been lost but *his* love triumphed.

30

Clothing is one of those dilemmas that are simply unresolvable:

If we are badly dressed because of internal and external circumstances frequently connected to intellectual work, we are often badly treated by the police and louts (also by innkeepers, waiters and the like) and this impedes thought.

If we are well dressed, we have a pass, so to speak, and the pack will not harass us on our wanderings; but at the same time the nice outfit distances us from the lower classes, from those who do the heavy lifting—whether they are workers or simply poor—and there is much more hope for the world in them than in those who equate us with our clothing. This, too, impedes thought.

31

Those who are more perceptive of things that are not generally noticeable in daily life—although they do have an effect on the quotidian—can be seen as superstitious.

It cannot be denied and has often been observed that certain places regularly have this or that particular effect (without any discernable cause). How is it that so many good and coherent ideas have occurred to me in the moon forest, in direct contrast to the hedgehog forest, located only a few hundred meters away, on the other side of the canal? And why do I have so many sudden insights and strange revelations in this café but almost none in that café opposite, while in a third I tend to become melancholic? Are these things now beneath attention? There are places and houses that have a negative, even dangerous effect. There is a *total obscurity* at which a few may laugh, but the future will not. We do not believe in this obscurity out of fear, weakness, or some other emotion but because we have observed it. A Balzac, a Socrates believed in it; neither of them were dreamers.

32

In a café, I thought I recognized a fisherman I had not seen for months. I approached. It was not he.

A quarter of an hour later I entered a different café. The sole guest was the fisherman.

I can't draw any conclusions from it.—But I've had this experience at least ten times.

33

He said he was so strong that he——could break one of his arms with the other.

[. . .]

35

Why is most of the correspondence we receive so wretched? (I don't mean letters from those with whom I have a particular, personal bond, but those of the same general level of culture widely speaking.) Because they make no mention of the *little* things (of daily life).

And the letters from simple, naïve, or limited people are not insignificant because there is nothing in them about big (universal, intellectual) things, as one might easily assume, but because the little things appear only in corrupted guise.

36

The writer's unpractical nature.— He examines circumstances that hinder him more closely than others do, quickly determines the cause of the hindrance, generalizes from that, and follows all the threads. Because the results of his investigation become ever more extensive and significant, he begins to chronicle it all: at the same time, he has not eliminated the cause of the hindrance which would have been easy to eliminate: he has not shut the door of the oven that is radiating too much heat; he has not opened the window, he can be found sweating, half-suffocating, bent over his work which has become more important to him than everything else: it was more important for him to answer the question at an *essential* level (aiming for a more wide-ranging, more complete solution), to make progress in his inquiry and, when the results became clear, to record them without succumbing to the slightest distraction and so as not to forget a single detail, to record them in great haste.

37

People of an extraordinarily practical nature are most often those who have a reputation of being very unpractical.

(They're just incapable of working with others.)

38

Variation:

Not all those who have a reputation of being very unpractical are practical. But there are certainly some uncommonly practical people among them.

Why are they incapable of working with others? Because they criticize every way of working, bristle at the others' countless futile movements. In the meantime, the work does not progress (at least not for those who can't see beyond the next quarter of an hour).

Most of these people seek refuge in art (to have an effect using signs). Very few have managed to make a name for themselves in history (a Napoleon, a Lenin).

[. . .]

4¹

There are practical activities that the likes of us cannot master simply because they're too easy.

Intelligence (attention) is always aimed *beyond* (accustomed as it is to meeting resistance, difficulties), in search of what must *be done* and, as easy as it would be to take the middle path, our attention always fails to perceive it.—Or: we cannot take such easily trodden paths; our great ability in finding the more difficult paths forces us to abandon the easy one.

Too great a talent for being practical is not practical.

[. . .]

47

Do not interrupt a tired man! Don't offer him a short rest: he would just collapse as a result.

48

The greatness of the Romans: they revered the spirit that they themselves did not possess.

49

He has no trouble understanding difficult things, but simple things are another matter.[2]

50

Vast distances sometimes give the same impression as essential differences.

Will the fool standing on the bank of the Danube, which extends before him like a vast, shining lake, believe that it looks like a thin blue ribbon from a distance?—The earth and the planet in the heaven above like a glittering star.—Human and animal.

An incalculable wealth of insight could open up for us through the observation of the process of compression and relative densities (not to mention states of matter).

A very great distance separates us from animals but there is no gulf (no essential difference) between us.

If one of the professors on the pointless faculty (pointless as long as they are not confined to the historical) had ever looked at a cat, truly observed it . . . , then he would have had to realize that it is essentially the same as us. (—the poets, keen observers, have always known this. Consider the tales of animal metamorphoses, the tales and dreams of *talking* animals. In Spitteler's *Olympian Spring,* too, there is a passage on animals of great intensity: on how they wanted to raise their hands in supplication . . . but had only claws, hooves,

2. Cf. II, 282.

and paws.[3] But a theologian need not put himself to so much trouble because he can see everything internally and has glued his eyes shut from the very beginning because looking is pointless and so on.

As if, in this most grave sense, there were a difference between the internal and the external!

"All the more so, if everything's the same, why should I look outward?"

There are many things that we will only encounter, at least only encounter *clearly*, outside ourselves.

51

The child praying in an illuminated window one night: we were walking along the street at night and saw the silhouette of a praying child in the window. What a strange feeling! A voice inside me cried, "Oh, if I had only *half* the energy that is being wasted there!" (By there I mean in every similar such case scattered throughout the city and the world.) It is terrible — and so many complain of alcohol and how it saps the population's intelligence and strength!

What if, instead of praying for a quarter of an hour every day, people devoted a mere five minutes to *thinking about themselves?* Even just one minute! — if they would simply practice, slowly, gradually, *seeing* themselves and others?

52

"He who can help but does not . . ."[4]

It's almost never the case, or at least very rarely, that one cannot help in the slightest (assuming the other is *willing* to accept help) — it's just as rare that one can help a great deal.

3. Goethe also boldly resolved this question anti-theologically: "Yes, the faithful little dog may accompany its master." To paradise, that is.

4. Cf. II, 161.

53

He only ever focused on the intellectual deficiencies of certain types but never on the flip side: if they were smarter, they wouldn't be as amenable.

54

I've observed that people (in bars and such places) hit each other more often to show their own strength than in response to some injustice. (I once watched as an argument simmered between two men for some time, then when one of them happened to glance down at his own forearm, which was very muscular, he was suddenly filled with a powerful rage.)

[. . .]

68

"*One* look is enough"—; But it was a long look that has still not freed itself (from its object).

69

Trisexual. Aside from men and women, higher beings love. They most all.

70

Imagination: He had mastery over the distant. Accordingly, when he found what was nearby inopportune, he could find refuge in the distant *good.* (He had mastery over the distant: this also means that in peacetime war was dangerous for him.)

71

When writing: . . . and the stone the masons praised so highly, the one they chose as the keystone, never amounted to much in the end.

72

Writers of novels and novellas: they think: "you've got to get past the uninteresting parts as quickly as possible" and they hurry, they hurry . . . That's the great danger, a complete mistake. You must bring in what's interesting from the *very beginning.*

73

He has the terrible advantage of *always* being wrong. How can one fight against him?

[. . .]

75

. . . the notion of a *great form* and other mad ideas. As if there were great and small forms in art!

The pastry chef, yes, he will take down a large or a small form from its hook (according to the price of the tart to be made).

The difference is quantitative: "Great" as an attribute of form only ever has a quantitative meaning.

76

". . . This poem came to me in the moon forest": things occur to us; we do not build or construct them. Valéry says this and all those who observe closely must agree; we are all nothing more than a finely controlled receptive device.

More and more, the term "composition" repels me, even though it's difficult to replace it with another, more accurate term.

77

I must fish when the fish are biting—not when *you* give me time, when I allow myself time, etc.

78

"But it's all just pulled together, simply assembled," they say of the piece of Goethe's prose I admire most of all (the "certificate of apprenticeship" in Wilhelm Meister). Yes: art begins where all artfulness ends (where the expression is integral).

79

The writer. He sits in wait—as the fisher on the rocky shore sits on the lookout for fish—as the hunter waits, in a fetid gulch, leaning on a tree stump, his rifle cocked. From time to time something comes, passes by: the shot rings out, hits the mark, the prey is caught, bagged. So the writer sits in wait for excitement on this languid day, his condition brittle, weak, and suddenly it appears, vivid, unique, simply resplendent: he finds it, gathers it up, takes it.

Does it come from him? No, it does not. Who could claim to possess such a thing?! He stole it, took it with him. He is a writer.

80

Much that is considered ridiculous is preferable to many a successful murmur.

81

Diamonds have the reputation of being very beautiful; I won't deny that they're also extremely hard, valuable for technological uses, highly refractive, etc.

82

They laugh because I find the glass marbles children play with to be incredibly beautiful. The reason for their laughter: because the marbles are inexpensive! Did I claim they were expensive?

83

For a long time, I particularly liked the word "half-blind." It had the opposite effect on me than you'd expect and I didn't know why. Suddenly I realized: because I was thinking of seers! Visionaries have always been half-blind. Telescopes in obscurity . . .

In a society of windows and eyeglasses, telescopes and microscopes are considered half-blind.

84

They walked and found nothing. Then the bigger one picked something up—a rock or clump of dirt—and lifted it up with great interest. It was obvious he would use it in his construction—it was so clear, a blind man could have seen it; but his companion was neither blind nor could he see. "Why is it," he asked spitefully (insulted that his companion had turned his attention from him to an object), "that I, who am certainly the lesser, can't make anything of it, but you . . . ?"—"Because for this to have value, it needs me," the former replied.

85

An original. Each time he'd gone into the woods or along the streets or had been asleep or been elsewhere, he always had a story to tell. "It's amazing how much he sees!" they cried. But he was more amazed at how much the others did *not* see.

86

Pascal—Carnival, Eternity—Lethe and Grotto

First, the horses shied, then ran wild and fell into the water and then Pascal shied, became a great writer and entered eternity.

That he spoke so beautifully is surely more important than his fright?

Times are eternal—why then are you so sad at the thought that soon you will no longer exist?

He kept searching through the empty space, still found nothing, not a thing, until somewhere or other he found God. At some random spot, he crossed paths with God.

Carnival, carnival!—in my mind I saw the procession of masks, saw them with eyes closed. Saw them all outfitted in magnificent SHELLS. Shells like those of pumpkins or tortoises, but colorful and varied.

. . . LETHE and GROTTO: who communicated the internal color of the play of names that came to me in a dream . . . (the slight transposition of sounds in the names of two sisters, which has a certain charm, or at least one of them does: Greta and Lotte")?

Shrovetide carnival: the only religious festival I recognize.

(And to think that in this frivolous city, carnival, the one serious festival is proscribed.)

[. . .]

88

Almost every one of the twelve people he had treated to a drink over the course of the day eventually came up to him and told him he was a good guy—not because of the drink, no, they'd all thought much of him before.

No one else came up to him to tell him they thought he was a good guy. From this it's clear how to open people's eyes.

89

"And now," cried the thinker after pacing silently back and forth for hours, "finally, I want a look at the clock!" He looked at the thermometer. But then he immediately forgot the temperature, too.

[. . .]

91

Animals[5]

This woman has such an attitude toward animals that she believed the following story without hesitation:

> A man tossed a piece of apple he had pulled from his tobacco pouch to a raven; the raven pecked at it greedily, but when it sensed the lingering taste of tobacco, it flew at the man and started pecking at him, someone who had never done anyone any harm.

At most the woman may wonder: "Are they really so intelligent?"

She sees animals as humans with limited capacities. She believes that what connects them (what they share) is *inferior* human intelligence and not the superior intelligence of all creatures (the ability to be in accordance with necessity, to be in harmony with the greater environment); she believes that recent developments in specialized knowledge date from yesterday, rather than having their source in the hundreds of thousands or millions of years of fundamental knowledge that flare up now and again in superior individuals (Goethe, Spinoza). They flare up *consciously*; that is, they appear augmented by the most recent developments, they shine *through the newly acquired and specialized knowledge*.

Goethe connects more closely with animals than the inferior

5. Cf. 50.

man does—it wouldn't take much more for this woman to demand that animals be well-versed in literature.

It's the greatness of poetry that puts one on the same wavelength as animals, not knowledge of the genitive case.

The pharmacist looks down on animals with pity. Goethe admires them.

The attitude of Christians toward animals is also interesting. The dubious stance of these people can be seen most clearly in their attempt to present their relationship to animals to a wise man who knows nothing of Christianity.

Christians regard these soulless creatures with untold contempt (contempt that is more or less masked by equally arrogant gestures of piety, pity, and charity).

And what about Francis of Assisi?

Perhaps he was no Christian . . .

92

I see no *essential* difference between man and animal—only a quantitative one, which can certainly be called enormous: a bit like that between man and genius.[6]

[. . .]

94

"For whosoever exalteth himself will be humbled; and he that humbleth himself will be exalted . . ." But knowing this, one can calculate and in so doing humble oneself by exalting oneself: one is then exalted. One must simply know up to which precise link in the chain one should count in order to truly be exalted or humbled.

This Biblical saying, admittedly not one of the most interesting,

6. Cf. 50, 91.

gives rise to a sport that many have succumbed to and through which more than a few sly souls have hoped to profit handsomely. Lichtenberg commented on it: "I find the falsely modest far more insufferable then the self-important . . ."[7]—It is, in any case, better to judge others by their positive qualities than by their other characteristics. Whether they humble or exalt themselves should not be taken into consideration at all.

95

Every day he brushed and groomed his modesty and fed it so richly that it gleamed, that it . . . far outshone the pride of others.

In the literatis' café. They constantly put their modesty on display for each other—the progress they'd made. One was far more modest than the others, a heated competition! Countering inconspicuousness with discretion, they battled each other like titans wielding swords, shields, and spears, all as cunning as thorns—rising up to the very heavens.

[. . .]

97

Names—Which great thinker was it—Hebbel, maybe? If I remember correctly, he said he admired Elise because she could do something he could not: name a cat.

Whoever, in all seriousness, gives a cat a human name, reveals that he understands nothing of names. ("He even named his two slippers." Lichtenberg)

It's clear that Katherine Mansfield understood this difficulty (impossibility), when you consider that she named her two kittens April and Athenaeum.

7. Spinoza put it more bluntly: "Humility is not a virtue."

98

I suddenly realized: I hate circles. Spirals are not circles. —I believe a circle is a lie.

99

"That's a great weight off my chest!" And yet another, unnoticed at first, immediately takes its place.

100

Why should doctors have more say over the use of your body than you?

[. . .]

115

Decisions are made on three levels:

1) The level of the pharmacists (partiality).
2) The level of intellect and spirit (of those who know that others, that everyone, somehow, is right, who see the plurality of the world spread out before them. Only principles can be completely wrong—never things or people, never manifestations of reality).
3) The highest level (where one is nonetheless partial).[8]

116

Offering proof[9] is, in my eyes, something very important, yet I don't believe anything can be proven.

8. Cf. II, 10, 200.
9. Cf. II, 179.

(It's important the way talking is: because it brings more things into relation with each other. — In any case, one must talk.)

(I reread Spinoza and realized that I'd never paid attention to his proofs.)

117

He believes that through much copulation he can give meaning to his life. You may as well rub your quill for a good long time to give your meaning to your writing.

On the contrary: As meaning increases, the external manifestation of all such things decreases.[10] This can be seen most clearly in Marcel Proust.

118

Those able to draw a precise boundary between art and philosophy must either have minds I cannot even imagine or none at all.[11]

119

It has taken me years to figure out why I hold the blind in such high esteem. Because I esteem vision so highly: blindness enhances vision.

Anyone who has seen a blind person will understand me. Such faces are not blind.

120

Infirmities. If I were hunchbacked, lame, a dwarf, etc., it would not matter much to me; essentially very little or not at all: it would

10. Cf. XII, 29, 70, 71, 78, 101.
11. Cf. XII, 39.

mean having one less possession, I would have to adjust to this new footing. Even if I were blind—naturally a great loss at first, but then another kind of vision develops; other senses develop and replace the lost one. (If a blind man were a writer—rather than the many writers who have become blind—he could analyze the faces things have for us in the dark;[12] or nearly unimaginable domains of sound.) But there is *one* thing I would not be able to bear or only with great difficulty (only now that there is no danger of it, can I speak of it with ease): to be taller than one meter eighty (or one meter eighty-five, but that is the absolute limit):—or does it not matter to those who are tall?

Someone should make a list of what tall men have accomplished and perhaps next to it, a list of what short men have accomplished.

121

There is a power before which the intelligence is quite small: stupidity, especially when combined with a tall stature, beefy build, and a commanding net worth;—in short, the "royal" element.

The right and proper king (Pfefferkorn in Thomas Mann, Zeus in Spitteler) always has an aspect of (prime) beef cattle about him and is very tall; those of political or military *capacity* on the other hand, tend to be short.

122

They start trying to replace the plug once the water has reached 212 degrees and is spurting out. Before, at 140, 160 degrees, they were satisfied; the plug was set. Now they begin trying to fix the water, the receptacle, and the plug.

12. Cf. Not the passing darkness, from which one only translates, but perpetual darkness.

123

(He could have written beautifully; but every time he had an impetus, he had no ideas and when he had an idea, he had no impetus.[13]) — He finally found a solution by looking at what the others were doing; each time he wrote a bit worse than they did; but similarly.

[. . .]

125

Vocations. — Since I've known waiters, once they got to know me there always came a moment when they assured me they were good psychologists — or: keen observers — they had seen a lot after all — ! I don't doubt that they've seen a lot but if that were what's required, what good psychologists cinema operators or pilots who have seen an entire city from above would be! — Their profession offers so many opportunities . . . yes, but it also depends on what they observe. "That gentleman there is winking at the lady for the third time." — "Mr. Jones is spending less time with the newspaper than usual: he must be upset." — "This stranger is poorly dressed and seems uncertain: he must be short of money."

It's clear that when they have nothing to do, they gape at whatever is moving in the room, namely, the customers. Observers! There are different kinds of observers, as there are different kinds of readers. — their profession offers so many opportunities! What a shame that Lichtenberg was not a waiter.

126

"It's just a mood." A mood, fine. Why shouldn't it be a mood? Avalanches, too, are caused by moods.

13. Cf. V, 15.

127

Distillation or: on drinking.—Here we have a distiller with his grains or his grape pulp, from which he will extract spirits. And I distill alcohol to extract an even finer spirit.

128

. . . on his ascent, a mountain climber steps on a ledge that breaks off behind him but still enables him to reach all the next steps.

129

A telling title would be *New Accesses.*

"Maybe I don't offer any new ideas but I open new means of access to familiar ideas."

130

While writing.—I write one to four finished pages a day in four, six, or eight hours—if I manage to write at all; usually no more than two pages and rarely more than three. This cannot be of interest to anyone. But what is remarkable is this: I almost always have the sense of having written ten or twenty pages (and then, astonished, I have to confirm the count in order to dispell the illusion); yet this is easily explained: so vast are the expanses I cover while writing.

The writing, what is visible, is only the summit or the ridge—but I walked through the mountain range, climbed mountains, and descended into valleys, I have searched through the entire range.

131

"I am now writing my friend, mankind, a letter; and he will read it." That is all.

They ask me what I'm doing. They expect me to give details about my *curriculum vitae.* Etc.

Or they ask what I'm writing *about* . . .

132

Subject matter.—When I am asked, yet again, what I'm writing *about* (which doesn't happen at the moment since I no longer see anyone), I will answer:

"About the relationship between reality and the real."

I'm happy to have finally found an answer. (Before I would alternately answer: "agriculture" or "about the yellowish green color of old church spires" or with some lengthy compound foreign word.)—My answer is one the person who asked will not understand but I do. It is obscure and clear and fits every occasion.

[. . .]

134

On the moon forest and the hedgehog forest. (I later came to realize that the moon forest and the hedgehog forest were strangely proximate and formed a mysterious whole.—The hedgehog forest is small and sandy; in the moon forest a far greater number of plants grow and they are more impressive.)

At the age of thirty, I moved from the hedgehog forest into the moon forest, but I did return occasionally to the hedgehog forest and besides, how could I ever have reached the moon forest without it?

(The hedgehog is prickly, rolls itself into a ball, and does not advance.)

135

Today, abruptly and for the first time, I came up with the hypothesis that perhaps the mind achieves its greatest power when it returns from insanity; that it might bring back from the edge of insanity its most ardent clarity—instruments to extract the purest clarity from the most incandescent fervor. It may well refresh itself in insanity—to be exact, in the mere proximity to insanity, of course—as in a bath; in that fervor it may forge instruments it might never have otherwise acquired. Neither the common man nor scholars are able to shed any light on this. I should have asked Pascal.

Valéry, too, perhaps. I'd also be interested in what Proust thought about this. *Perhaps* Nietzsche knew about it. Van Gogh *must* have known about it, but I am not entirely confident that he did.

Katherine Mansfield did not. Hers is a different case; it's clear that she drew her greatest powers from her bodily illness (tuberculosis).—While instruments that allow us to grasp the most extreme realities are *annealed* by the proximity to insanity, with her, aesthetic clarity, blissful and weightless, trickles down from above; ultimately, in utter clarity, both sources are the same.

Variation

. . . perhaps the mind achieves its greatest power, might bring back instruments able to withstand the most ardent clarity, when it returns from insanity, that is, from the edge of insanity where it struggled, where it vanquished something among the rocks . . . ; when it returns, it possesses a fearlessness in face of light and a metallic apparatus that allows it to grasp and wield what is otherwise immovable and beyond our grasp.

Second Variation:

. . . a fearlessness in the face of incandescent light, an iron calm before the flames bursting from the night *"which all would like to steal away from"* (for everyone *could* see them—if they could summon the will).

136

He who has never faced the possibility of insanity is no great mind.

137

Certain intellectual and spiritual works also require physical strength, especially in certain circumstances. A child cannot understand this.

I hardly need to say that I don't mean the kind of physical strength a sculptor needs to wield a heavy hammer; that just distracts from the important point.

138

The story of the man who in a dream was carried off great distances — more exactly, it was just a half-dream, for he was moving, was actually walking.

The distances, the things, the works were colossal. He plowed eternity, boundless oceans; with armies, with all the powers of body and mind.

When he woke, he found himself still on the old shore: he stood in his field. This old, long-familiar field was small and arid;

but it was plowed.

VII. *continued*:

Autobiographical Appendix

Despite my aversion to anything resembling a journal intime, *to any kind of diary at all, in fact (Gide's Journals are not actually of that genre, but are much more), I felt it necessary to include the following pieces in the final edition of my work. I included them not for the sake of the pieces themselves, but simply because of a particular service they render to the rest of the work. What that service is can be found in this sentence by the secret philosopher Andreas Ronai:* "Most writers believe they can ensure the universality of their sentences and their writings by cutting all the threads that tie their books to their personal experience; this only makes their sentences and works abstract, not universal. Universality comes from* the transformation of life into knowledge."

—You must see not only the peaks and summits, but also the forests and gorges from which they emerge; you must not only hear the melody, but also the muffled voices of the background from which they emanate . . .

That said, I have cut almost all passages of the kind in the original manuscript; all the pieces, that is, that did not bear an immediate and clear relation to the work. — But don't we find, here and there, texts of an autobiographical nature scattered throughout the work? It only appears so. When a fragment of personal experience is placed at a sufficient distance and handled in such a way that a flash — an image, a thought — can burst from it, and when the image or thought becomes more important than the experience that gave rise to it (thus the latter could be altered without negative effect in that the seen *becomes more important than the experience, the* real *more important than the actual), then what is depicted has been objectified and can no longer be seen as autobiographical. I could, therefore, include pieces of this kind in my work according to their thematic affinity without harm to the unity of the whole. — Yet for this very reason: my intention not to jeopardize the unity of the work obliged me to collect the following truly autobiographical pieces and set them apart in an appendix.*

139

Theme of the Day

For long stretches of time, almost every day or every few days, I would be struck—in ways and means beyond my control—by a particular quotation, most often in verse, which would then resound continuously in my mind throughout my waking hours, louder or more softly (sometimes so softly I hardly noticed it for hours); indeed, it would occasionally survive my night's sleep and ring again unchanged the following day. In rare cases, the same quotation persisted for several days—only to disappear as inexplicably as it had come; sometimes it held sway only a few hours and then was suddenly superseded by another. These quotations, which had a markedly playful character (they sounded both playful and "thoughtless," playful and *manic*, too—like a Tibetan prayer wheel)—, these quotations always stood—as I gradually realized—in an obscure but powerful relation to the essential core of my inner life at any given time. Not to my conscious preoccupation of the moment, but to the hidden substrate, the deeper problem. Nor was its meaning immediately obvious; in order to perceive its meaning, some remove, a greater distance was necessary; for that is where the quotation stood, from there it approached me.

The quotation *always knew more than I.* (I hadn't the slightest doubt that this would have been perfectly clear to me even without Freud, i.e. even if I'd never heard of his doctrine or its derivatives.)— Such quotations—I called them *themes of the day*—can accordingly provide a kind of key to my respective inner states and I noted many of them down during the few years in which these notes first originated, years that were so terribly dark and yet so luminous in another respect; I will limit myself here to citing some of the most significant.

For a time, I could only be content when these verses, which came to me without my control, were of a certain level of quality in content and form. I didn't have the power to summon these quotations—but I was soon able to eliminate the ugly and intolerable, that is, each time one came hovering, I quickly brushed it away.[14]

From the first year:

God, in His greatness, gives us gifts so generously:
But the smallness of our hearts is our poverty!

(Angelus Silesius)

and

Become essential: the world shall pass and nought retain,
not even fortune; only essence will remain.

(Angelus Silesius)

I annotated the following quotation with "The poisonous damp of this climate (climate in every sense of the word) so concentrates its effect as to cause physical suffering; and has a paralyzing effect on all thought and action":

Give us wings to cross over
And, with truest hearts, return again.

(Hölderlin)

Yet some of the quotations were prose:

. . . and the honor of valor consists in combat, not in victory.

(Montaigne)

Occasionally, they were my own words:

. . . (we have already often observed) how the prophets' predictions proved true—only the dates were mistaken.

and the related

---

14. Most often I was plagued by bad verse from Rilke's *Book of Hours.*

. . . (in reality, as it were) occurrences are diluted in many other things.

(Nuancen und Details II, 20)

and

. . . (Only when it is badly endured is misfortune complete.)
Good fortune alone is still not complete good fortune.

From the following year, initially in a bleak winter:

. . . so that I not
illuminate my own path to damnation.

(Günther)

. . . and our dearest
Live nearby, languishing on
Distant peaks . . .

(Hölderlin)

God is near
And hard to grasp.
But where there is danger
Redemption grows as well.

(Hölderlin)

In spring:

. . . as I bend forward
this morning
my temples refuse to leave the earth . . .

(Eduard Zak)

In summer:

He who has acquired no name, nor noble end pursues
Belongs to the elements, so now begone!

.   .   .   .

Not only merit but fidelity, too, preserves our person.

(Goethe)

I, too, consider best
What pleases the courageous man,
When in his warm and quiet nest
He keeps the sacred alive and warm

(Goethe)

God is free of all suffering and is not moved by joy or sorrow.

(Spinoza)

From the final year (1936):

And now be this a sacred legacy,
Brethren, for you good-will and memory,
Daily fulfillment of hard services;
There needs no revelation saving this.[15]

(Goethe)

Wanderer! thy strength wouldst try
'Gainst what will be and must?
Whirlwind and filth that's dry
Let spin and mount in dust![16]

(Goethe)

Then it was this or that passage from the scene of *Faust II* which I considered *my* scene above all others, the true foreword to the *Notes*, and the truest, most profound emblem of those few years; this is the

15. *West-Eastern Divan*, "Book of the Parsees," translated by Edward Dowden (London: J.M. Dent & Sons, 1914).
16. Ibid., "Book of Reflections."

scene titled "Dark Gallery" which tells of the descent to the Mothers. ("Can you conceive of emptiness and solitude?"):

> . . . Flee the created universe
> For the realm of forms untethered and diverse!
>
> .   .   .   .
>
> So limited are you, upset by an unfamiliar word?
> That you only want to hear things heard before?

These words recurred several times, often, in fact:

> He who cannot work magic now is lost.
>
> *(L. H.)*

Then, from the last song of the *Divan*, the comforting lines

> May courteous Gabriel
> Tend the limbs of one sore spent . . .[17]

On rare occasions it was a phrase clearly related to an external incident:

> If my letters are condemned at Rome, then what I condemn in
> them is condemned in heaven.
>
> *(Pascal)*

(After exceptional effort, I'd finally written and sent a long letter to a Swiss literary institution, which had the potential to change my material situation.)

Another theme of the day from the same month was even more closely related to specific external circumstances: after eleven and a half months in the perpetual semi-darkness of my room (lit only by a feeble paraffin lamp), my wife had finally been able to get the elec-

---

17. Ibid., "Book of Paradise."

tricity repairs done;—suffering from a toothache, I returned home in the rain and in the window above I saw *light*—; this put me in a truly poetic mood:

> Fair is the world to view, go where we may;
> The poet's world fairer and lovelier seems;
> On the pranked fields, sun-bright or silver-grey,
> Morn, noon and night what lights! what wandering gleams![18]
>
> *(Goethe)*

In contrast, a few lines, also from Goethe's *Divan*, resounded for two days or more, which I was unable to connect to external events, even after some time had passed, even after more than five years. Next to it I'd written "—I have no idea who the 'you' might be; but in exploring it further, it seems to me that this 'you' is certainly not a person." (But it was surely this: "Ardent and pure, a unity lies *in the image*."):

> And Allah's hundred names if I should name,
> A name for thee with each would sound to me.[19]

There is another distinctive feature to note here: many of the numerous quotations in Part IX ("Literature") either were a "theme of the day" or nearly were or were related to one. This illuminates another aspect I tried to elucidate in that section's preface: namely, how this quoting must be understood (above all *not as a compendium of world literature*, nor as coming from a wish to present a flowery multiplicity!).—This applies especially to the many quotations of Spinoza, whom I have only cited once here; they can be read in Part IX. Almost every single one of them was at one point a theme of the day.

18. Ibid., "Book of Zuleika."
19. Ibid.

140

I set myself the following rule: do not speak in the morning.

This is why: the world is sluggish. The world I work in is the opposite. —A concealing veil.

I realized it was a matter of shame, nothing else. Because *real* shame is a mechanism to protect life and the development of it can be interrupted or upset through contact with certain environments, like sunlight: a darkroom is necessary to develop photographs.

141

Two maxims I established for myself:

1) To rise early even when it will not increase my productivity *in the slightest* in the mornings.
2) To commit to physical exercise with great exertion.

Both are aimed at the greatest danger that threatens a man in my situation: flaccidity (*At this point* flaccidity could not cause me much harm; the danger is that when circumstances once again demand an ability to compete, he who has grown flaccid is powerless and must rebuild all his strength from nothing).[20]

"The brain, to be sure, obeys its own laws . . . nevertheless there is no great talent without a strong will . . . The elite keep their brains in a productive condition, just as long ago valiant knights kept their weapons ready for battle." (Balzac, *The Muse of the Department*)

(Does this imply that I should forget the second part of the duality I found, after much searching,[21] to be true? Not at all, but it strengthens the former. Balzac himself writes explicitly of the duality on the same page: "These twin forces . . .")

20. Cf. I, 12.
21. Cf. *Nuancen und Details* III, 13.

142

It's hard to constantly turn away from the difficult and toward what is easy—toward the living.

[. . .]

144

A kind of happiness: to have seen that everything will come; the discovery of one's working methods; to have seen that you don't need to strike at things, just to connect to life and that's enough to access the spirit.

It's a process of constant transformation, with no need to apply pressure anywhere . . . My erstwhile discovery (from last year: my acceptance of the necessity of using artificial means to create stimulation) is proven to be correct and relevant more and more each month. These attempts brought difficulties and dangers in the *next* zone but that, of course, is the fate of all new things.

[. . .]

150

From now on I will no longer say that I have finished a work: *everything is work.*

"Everything": whether I underline a passage from another writer or copy it down, write a letter, jot something down, think something, take a position.

After my recent, powerful conclusion of the third part of *Nuances and Details,* I again had the same unpleasant feeling, the same unease—even though I'd wanted and had decided on this constrained conclusion and printing and there was a point to it—that I have felt when forced to end letters, leaving things unresolved, and in many similar cases. This kind of conclusion is *deadening.*[22]

22. Cf. VI, 49.

151

Correspondence. I write in pencil. My goal is the utmost precision and validity (whether I achieve it or not is another question). Hence the calamity of my correspondence. Can I still afford to engage in it? Is it worth the trouble? I take the same trouble to write my works—I mean, what is generally meant by works: as if letters were not also works!—To finish a letter or make progress in it, I have to unleash a storm and tear at the paper with my pen (instead of continuing to set it to paper with calm precision). Sending a letter written this way rends me, pains my soul and my body almost even more—; it's pathetic and leaves behind the most unpleasant feelings. Or else I have to revise it and to that there's no end.

152

Peculiar.—When people from certain sects read something I've written, they say: "But that's dialectical philosophy!"

But others—and to which sect might they belong?—say only one word: "Austere."

153

This recognition has become searing: when writing under pressure—that is, for an external goal—I have *always* delivered inferior work.

And even if the Schiller Foundation and others like it were to promise me piles of money[23] if, by the nth of some month, I were to write this and that, which I am unable to write, then I won't even try.

Others—the lightweights—may well be encouraged by external necessity; for those who are themselves weighty, an extra burden leads nowhere.

23. There was absolutely no danger of this.

154

The still of night fosters ideas, but in my case these ideas are not as certain as those of dawn or the morning. The former arouse suspicion and one must be much more circumspect in their regard.

It would be good to examine the difference between those ideas that are formed in the morning and those formed at night; perhaps all of literature can be divided into two groups. (Night: Dostoyevsky; Morning: Goethe.)

155

I don't know if this is unconditionally true, but it's certainly true to some extent: I can develop my methods only in resistance. (To that extent, this recognition is worrisome.) But when I speak with Z., it's the opposite: I'm also developing my methods but resistance would interfere. That resistance spurs my production applies—if it applies at all—only within certain constraints. It depends on the particular kind of resistance.

The world's latent resistance, the conditions that allow one to develop them . . . Perhaps resistance is not the primary element, but is a *sign*, and without it there is nothing more to do . . . These are attempts in a subtle matter.

Another attempt: why is it that when I'm speaking with Z. or R., despite their approval, I can still create something (only a hypothesis since both are long gone)? Maybe the world's approval is something else entirely, namely no authentic approval, but simply a lack of resistance from the pharmacists, the most hopeless track one can slide on.

[. . .]

162

(At the height of misunderstanding:)

I must *chisel* my sentences since I do not have time to write too many more.[24]

163

(The day's chronicle.) What weather! (55 degrees Fahrenheit in my room. They're moving house at Ernst Schmitt's with a horrible automobile. Went to walk in the forest.)

Frozen stiff, the nightingale fell like a rock from the tree.

164

I'm someone who is utterly incapable of waiting; but how often have I waited in my life . . .

165

What's more, you cannot transmit knowledge, cannot *give* it: the best you can do is accelerate, encourage others to achieve that state themselves. — Yes, knowledge is a state of being!

If she were still alive, there is no one with whom I'd rather have spoken than Katherine Mansfield! And it seemed to me that *one* conversation would have been enough to solve her problem, to give her what she called for so desperately ("I want to be *real!*"), to increase it, to show her; to *give* her what eluded her grasp but which I know (whereas in other areas, I . . .). — That is what I *thought*; — but do I know if she would have been *able* to accept, if she was in a *state that allowed her to* . . . ?

For: "There are two fundamental mistakes about knowledge: first, that one can transmit it . . ."

24. Cf. 175.

166

Thinking is, above all, courage.—At (about) the age of eighteen, I made a strong start in thinking. Then came years of interruption and not simply because I was considering whether or not others might be right after all in their teachings and their assurances; I wasn't bold enough to look beyond their assurances; but *that*, in fact, is thought.

> —neither keeping pace with the assurances nor resisting them, but looking past them entirely, even if they are underlined a thousand times—and still moving forward.
>
> I do not say one should ignore what others say or their *testimonies:* just their assurances.

After a few years' interruption, my thinking took a mystical turn (and was not therefore actual thinking), which had the aim (I'm not speaking of a *conscious* aim! but when looking back at this progression from a great distance, the line becomes visible) of strengthening my personality. Another kind of interval followed, not a proper one, but one gradually filled with thought that contained a guarantee of permanence and which attained its highest form for the first time in 1934 (my thirtieth year, naturally). This was not mystical, but *world* thought, expanding on all sides, encompassing an ever greater sum of objects (not encompassing their sum but their totality), *demanding* ever more, dynamic thought advancing with the world, thought that demands learning, thought ad infinitum—in short, true, lasting thought.

167

I need friends in this world, not in heaven; I have enough in heaven already.

168

That I will have readers, in the most serious sense of the word, is beyond question. What I don't know is how many and when.

169

The children said, the neighbor works so hard! In the morning and at midday you hear him going tap-tap, then again in the evening and late into the night—and he doesn't even have a boss!

That was at a time when I found myself unable to do any real work and so had begun mechanically typing up the notes written on countless slips of paper (in a subordinate position, so to speak, working for myself and so I did, in fact, have a boss).

So then, I have finally found my first recognition, admittedly only among children and only because I go tap-tap . . .

170

But what is *the real?*

(After disquisitions on war, politics, death, and the plague.)

The real consists of a room that must be closed, lit, not too small, provided with breakfast at five or six o'clock, heated in winter, supplied with drinks and water every day. (A table, not too small, paper etc., these are self-evident;—but the rest . . . perhaps not?)

This is the real.

171

In extensive desolation a short parenthetical statement by Ramuz once brought consolation: "(which is the important sign)."[25]

A tiny lantern.

25. From a portrait of Fernand Chavannes: ". . . incapable of any intrigue or utilitarian demarche . . . who finally passed away leaving behind a large number of unpublished pieces (in addition to many other documents) because he had always

172

For years I have not lived through *three* successive days in which one or more of our most primitive material conditions weren't lacking. I am not speaking of higher, elevating things. But of the most common, easily named, unchanging things that can be summarized on a sheet of paper at any time—like lighting, heating, breakfast—.

173

"Spiritual strength under all conditions":
Even under *these* conditions?
Even under these conditions.
However, one must know the conditions.

174

The power of meditation is like an ocean and keeps me from writing for hours. (But during these hours I have written much more than ten good writers could have—on the other hand, I am not speaking of *their* meditation—unfortunately, however, it is not visible. I must fight against it and that's harder than fighting against anything else because this meditation alone is worth more than all writing.)

175

This much has become clear to me: my work will never reach completion; all the more reason for me to aim for the definitive.

(By completion I naturally don't mean the higher one of humanity, it would be ridiculous to speak of that. I'm speaking only of my few pages. No, not of the majority of my pages. I mean this in the usual sense: how will I ever reach completion when, before I have

---

continued writing (which is the important sign), not needing any hope in order to undertake a project, nor success to persevere."

reasonably finished the older pages, I always write ten new ones?—
With "aim for the definitive" I mean the following: letting what I have
already written alone insofar as I could only reach the definitive at the
expense of new sparks and work *only* on reaching this final, highest,
most actual formulation.)

176

I am not here to appear immaculate—of what use would be our
clergy then—but to bear ever more perfect witness.

For later.—I imagined I would have to correct this or that. What I mean is: to
change my views; better: to perceive *more that is new*—as I have had to alter earlier
writings;—as ultimately, and this is precisely the same thing in a different domain,
I must constantly correct the form.

VIII

PHARMACISTS

(On Fools, Editorial Staff, Dogs, Sundays and Holidays, Stupidity, Ugliness, Laziness)

> That you do not love men is right and just,
> It's humanity that one must love in men.
>
> *Angelus Silesius*

> I "shock" them, but if they knew how they shock me.
>
> *Katherine Mansfield*

1

He does not understand *Faust.* Nor Spinoza. He doesn't understand a thing about Heraclitus, or about Lichtenberg either; neither Gide, nor Karl Kraus. About what, then, does he understand something?

"About life."

He doesn't understand the interpreter at the border who still, in part, speaks *his* language; and yet he claims that he will understand what is said in the foreign country much better.

He was so blind he couldn't see that star through the telescope. Full of rage, he exclaimed that he could see it—this damn thing's in the way!—with the naked eye.

Never did he travel anywhere in a boat; he was frightened to death of even boarding one. And yet he claimed he could swim anywhere he might want to go, casually adding: "to New York; to Borneo; to Madagascar."

[. . .]

7

Everyone is allowed to contradict what I say; — but on condition, at the very least, of knowing what it is I have said.[1]

8

A *further definition.* Pharmacists are those who conclude from the variety of ladders that lead men out of the dark crevasses in which they sit and up to vantage points from which they can survey the universe that there is no universe.

9

Someone came up to me and told me I shouldn't spend so much time talking about pharmacists, it's not worth it . . . (thus proving himself one). — Certainly, I answered, it's not at all worth it for those who are complete and utter pharmacists; they can no longer be helped. I do it only for the sake of the others, those who stand on the *threshold* and can still be alarmed.

Will the excited crowds not stone them? Strange, when has anyone ever been stoned on account of absolute stupidity, of utter nul-

---

1. And those who only read fragments, who see this book as a collection of aphorisms, who do not penetrate the meaning of this work as a whole, will never understand this. The most important statement about the present work can be found in a review Armin Mohler wrote of the first volume: ". . . Ludwig Hohl *does not write aphorisms . . .* He has been unjustly reproached for writing in an 'inferior form.' This is a misunderstanding of what Hohl aspires to . . . *One must not take particular fragments in isolation, the work must be read in context.*"

lity? Was ever one of those stoned to death thousands and thousands of years ago a zero? If so, then only by chance or by mistake.

[. . .]

11

The most frequent thought that occurs to me at the sight of another person: "How does it survive?"

[. . .]

23

The *tremendous* change in my way of thinking should never be forgotten: it only became clear to me in my thirtieth year that I had swallowed whole the bourgeois delusion that philosophers were good for——philosophy and that life, which rules itself, is good for life and completely so . . . ; and philosophy, an independent luxury fixed somewhere outside life, is life's *counterpart!* (As a result, of course, I wasn't yet able to understand anything of Spinoza's or of Goethe's.)[2]

24

I propose that from now on we call the pharmacists "tenant farmers of quintessence."

One must be a right idiot to have a fixed conception, an immutable idea of the all.

[. . .]

31

Theologians. "No one knows what he's talking about!" A young man exclaimed as he ran up, trying to conceal his fright.

—Don't worry; he doesn't either.

2. Cf. I, 8.

32

He says nothing and takes a long time to do it.

33

How thankful I am to Goethe for that "regrettably" in the third line of the first scene in the first act of the first part of *Faust*![3]
[. . .]

61

Anyone who asks "why?" more than three times in a row is either a Socrates or an idiot.
[. . .]

79

Dialect

When I say that I hate dialects, am I against all peculiarity?

Not at all. Here's the difference: in cultivated language, peculiarities are productive—your peculiarity, if you have one, must take on a productive form if it is to be expressed in a cultivated language, in short, in language; in dialect, such peculiarities are simply the dialect itself; you add nothing. Thousands of people delude themselves; they credit themselves with an achievement when they've done nothing at all—haven't changed a thing: they have created nothing.

Your peculiarities will stick to you until you're dead;
Cultivate your qualities instead![4]

---

3. "Alas, I have studied philosophy, / the law and medicine as well / and, regrettably, theology." (Trans. note.)
4. Goethe.

To speak a language spoken by many others and still be singular, now *that* is difficult.

Dialect is not the language of the many but of the few. Few understand it; the rest call it original. *That is why* such writers imagine they have accomplished something.

80

Dialect is gesticulation.

Clearly, for farmers in remote valleys dialect is not gesticulation but in literature, it is.

81

Dialect in literature is either a mania (Gotthelf, Multatuli) or gesturing. (Still a limitation? As soon as dialect attempts to move into another sphere, it becomes mere gesturing. — Gesturing as Goethe understood it: "He who only communicates through gestures is a dilettante and a bungler.")

It's necessary to distinguish between those who write only in dialect — Gotthelf, Multatuli (in Dutch!), Hebel — and those who introduce a few words or sentences in dialect into Standard High German; the latter are worse.

[. . .]

84

A professor reproached me for writing only in fragments. He himself is a member of the university and therefore universal.

If only nature would soon transform itself in order to achieve such professorial universality!

He's incapable of reading one of my sentences three times; for on the second reading, just as he begins to understand, he runs away.

[. . .]

90

Why

I made the observation that those who ask "why" most often—who, in fact, rarely make any other contribution to the conversation—and ask this question with a furrowed brow and severe look, are those who have put the least thought into the subject and circumstances. All these whys are just a cover for their emptiness. Go ahead and try to explain anything to them! These people will only immediately ask "why" again. There's no helping them and they need no help. They're convinced they have found a coin that is valid everywhere and always exchangeable (which is why they hand them out so carelessly): endless wealth!

91

The intelligent man says something. The pharmacists hear it; they are struck by it and say something similar that is completely different.

Variation: There he sits . . . and all of a sudden, even as you speak, an expression of understanding flits over his face and you rejoice (you are recompensed, even if belatedly; the effects become visible). When he then opens his mouth, as you wait in friendly anticipation, he says something that sounds very similar but is worlds away.

92

Much that is very close to the truth is terribly far from the truth.
[. . .]

104

On cleanliness: I would much rather wear dirty underclothes than talk constantly of laundry.
[. . .]

110

Notional

(Future, merely notional readers of *Nuances and Details:*)

They tell me I take my points too far. They're correct insofar as I do have points to make and the readers have taken notice after being pricked by them.

When pharmacists read it, they either notice pricks or nothing at all.

A late blossoming . . . (still notional). —I finally had my first success. I'd always feared I would only receive vain praise and no true recognition. That I have enraged Mr. Jones is for me true recognition.

[. . .]

112

Do I write things that are filled with rage? Exaggerations that come only from rage are lifeless; instead, exaggerate and attack where you can be productive: I'm not persecuting people on their account. Faced with certain phenomena—like editors and dogs (in principle)—rage is *objective*.

[. . .]

117

Shame and Culture

When some poor man, who has never done anyone any harm nor even intends to, shows chance passersby a small scrap of flesh one usually takes the trouble to conceal and which may well be, as Lichtenberg put it, the only manly thing he has, he is locked up. When some individual, addressing an assembly gathered under the pretext of celebrating the grandeur of some poet or other, reveals to everyone the emptiness of his brain, he is showered with respect.

[. . .]

130

In the Forest

When the forest is agreeable for a change: sun, rustling leaves, the distant sound of children's voices—one of those horrible characters never fails to appear with their endless, infernal whistling for their lost dog—instead of thanking divine providence for having rid him of the appalling beast.

[...]

132

He had read almost no books of any value. But to preserve a certain harmony, he didn't understand the few he did read.

133

With pharmacists, most things are true or false "to a certain degree." But for those who achieve true comprehension, things are true or false.

IX

Master your reading, do not let it master you.
Lichtenberg

Not everyone is gripped by the word.

I have often frankly admitted that I have read very little. Had I read more extensively, I would perhaps have modified my judgment of this or that writer. But this documentary deficiency remains a deficiency only as long as one persists in misunderstanding the meaning and purpose of these pages. I have not in the slightest attempted to create a compendium of literature or of sections of literature; rather, the only thing that was important to me was to highlight, among all that I came across in the outside world, whatever had a powerful relationship to my internal world. Therefore, it was not a matter for me of gathering a wealth of quotations; anyone, myself included with my relatively limited reading, could have quoted others more abundantly; but what I have quoted is, to greater or lesser extent, related to the theme of the day (about which I write in VII, 139), and is not intended to offer a rich and multifaceted idea of what literature holds or of what I have read.

This applies as much to the polemical quotations as to things I've quoted with a more positive intent. In some cases—especially in the "treasure chest"—neither the quotations nor the authors I attack are of any significance to me, but rather each individual case *is significant as a representative* case. *I had a single aim: to use quotation as a*

means of expression that would reinforce my way of seeing things and
make my direction clearer.

1

The Novelty of Intellectual Discoveries

Valéry:

—This is not absolutely new, my friend!
—I don't give a hoot about old or new as far as ideas are
     concerned!...

(L'Idée fixe)

To these we can add verses from a famous book:

What you inherit from your fathers
You must earn again to truly own
What you never use becomes a heavy burden;
But what the Moment may create, that you *can* use.

Goethe offered a great many variations of this idea in published and
unpublished speeches, as in the *Maxims and Reflections:*

All intelligent thoughts have been thought already, what is necessary is to try and
think them again for oneself.
The most foolish of all errors is for good young minds to think they have lost their
originality in recognizing a truth others have already recognized.
The most original authors of modern times are such not because they produce something new but simply because they are able to say the same things as if they had never
been said before.

   In the fifteenth book of *Poetry and Truth* we find a more developed reflection that sheds a different light on the idea.

   It is said that the path has been struck and yet a path can rarely be spoken of
in all earthly things; for just as water parted by a ship quickly closes again behind the

hull, so when excellent minds push error to the side and make room for themselves, error quickly flows in behind them.

When I wrote, "Beware of those who have long been saved! . . . A rescue must always be of recent date," I meant nothing other than that.

But of all the various ways I know in which this perception has been expressed (I could quote many more), none resonated for me so intimately and at the same time so wonderfully and sublimely as this quote from Pascal:

> There are those who would have an author never speak about things of which others have spoken; otherwise he is accused of not saying anything new. But if the matter he treats is not new, his disposition is. In a game of tennis, two men play with the same ball; but one places it better. The author might as well be accused of employing words that have been used before: as if the same thoughts did not create a different discourse through a different arrangement; just as the same words form new thoughts through different arrangements.

2

Schiller: Anyone can correct him; but no one can write him.

3

Balzac on pure love:

> They want emotion and placid happiness is not happiness for them. Those women who have the strength of soul to bring infinity into love are angelic exceptions; they are among women as striking geniuses are among men. Great passions are as rare as masterpieces. Except for this love, there are only accommodations and passing irritations, both as contemptible as everything that is petty.
> *(History of the Thirteen—Ferragus)*

4

Two particularly luminous passages from Stendhal's *Armance:*

What makes misery so cruel for tender souls is the glimmer of hope that sometimes lingers.

Octave had no hope. His decision was made, and for the firm of spirit a decision taken, however hard, relieves one from reflecting on one's destiny and requires instead only the courage to see it through scrupulously; and that is not much.

And this passage on *glory* (which touches exactly on what I've noted on this topic: advancing a false value to replace the true one, when the real value is not recognized[1])

. . . she had begun no longer hiding from herself the fact that his kind of distinction was too singular and was too rarely copied from the recognized kinds not to require the support of fashion's all-powerful influence. Without this assistance, it would have passed unnoticed.

5

There is no dignity, no real life possible for a man who works twelve hours a day without knowing why he works. This work would have to take on meaning, to become a homeland.
(Malraux, *La Condition Humaine*)

How very deeply that last word appeals to me: homeland.[2]

All men are mad, he thought then, but what is human destiny if not a life of efforts made to unite this madman with the universe . . .
(Ibid.)

1. Cf. II, 256, 273.
2. Cf. II, 199.

6

> The absolute doubt Descartes demands is no more
> possible in the brain of a man than a vacuum is
> in nature.
>
> *(Balzac, Une Ténèbreuse Affaire)*

> I would not presume to assert that names do not
> influence destiny.
>
> *(Balzac, Z. Marcas)*

[. . .]

8

Edgar Allan Poe:

The introduction to "The Murders in the Rue Morgue" is astonishing! And this from "The Purloined Letter":

> "If it is any point requiring reflection," observed Dupin, as he
> forbore to enkindle the wick, "we shall examine it to better purpose in the dark."
> . . . as a mere mathematician he could not have reasoned at all . . .[3]

He quotes Chamfort:

> It is safe to wager that every political idea, every accepted convention, is nonsense because it has suited the greatest number.

9

Hamsun

Posterity might call him a great writer but it will certainly call
him prolific.

3. Cf. II, 27 [VII, 39].

(One should not confuse art with agriculture.)

With regard to *voice*, he cannot be surpassed.

10

Switzerland suffers from premature reconciliation, which, to be precise, is nothing other than superficiality.

1) It's surprising how quickly people there, themselves not unproblematic, can offer harmonious solutions when confronted with spiritual or intellectual discord—how quickly and *effortlessly* they do so without experiencing discord themselves: from which we can conclude that they are well-versed in harmonious solutions; indeed that's what they are in Switzerland. ("Yes, but don't you think a time will come when you can be this *without* being that . . . because you could combine the two without the negative aspect . . . etc.")

2) Literary criticism in Switzerland sits squarely on the solid pedestal of a conviction they have adopted as an axiom: in order to be good, a written work must always combine the two following elements: a certain spiritual significance (which primarily consists of praising conditions in the homeland) and a simple, powerful, sweeping, and easily understood plot (as in Gottfried Keller)—: accordingly Spitteler was a lost cause in terms of public success (as was Robert Walser to a much greater degree; but where would recognition of Spitteler stand without the Nobel Prize?); accordingly, too, all shallowness is praised. Nowhere else is one *so far removed from the observation and measure of LIFE* in literary creation. One would think literature was a certain *contrivance*: like a table or armoire, made of real fir or oak, exactly to specification.

[. . .]

12

Dialect

Swiss dialects are highly figurative—but falsely so. The imagery is forced, smacks of adages, misses the point, appears superficially as a creative act but in reality is lifeless routine. (In the long-forgotten sources of pure dialects in past ages, much of the corresponding imagery may have been vibrant; what we have now is a mixture of dialect and German.)

If the diction were the same in dialect and in German and only *individual* words had to be translated, the difference and the difficulty wouldn't be great. But the dictions differ.

Without God knows what kind of superhuman abilities, it's impossible to learn German in a few hours a week if you are speaking dialect the rest of your waking hours. (Quite apart from the fact that the teachers themselves can't speak German.)

I can still remember: when, as a speaker of dialect, you transition to Standard High German, the impression is one of slipping from the real into something artificial, papery—*chalky* (rather than of wood, earth or stone). How can anyone achieve art—life at its most intimate—using a material *to which he has no intimate connection?*

[. . .]

14

Anatole France:

Only fools place their happiness outside their own power.

(Thaïs)

15

D. H. Lawrence

He believed (it's important to emphasize that he was sincere, which is not the case with most others who have plunged into a similarly fanatic turn of mind as he did near the end of his life. Tolstoy in old age certainly cannot be summarily taxed with insincerity; there was in him perhaps some mix of insanity, gravity, and coquetry) — he believed that salvation was possible only through powerful coitus that met certain conditions (anything else was not truly living).

There is only one question to ask: what, then, should the ill do, or children and the elderly? (I have no precise knowledge of Spinoza's physical condition, but at any rate one imagines him to have been very frail and impotent: could he not find salvation?)

Lawrence was a typical forerunner (one woman compared him with striking accuracy to John the Baptist). He formulated the question correctly. He saw the desolation of the world, the impossibility of improving it through external means, the loneliness of human beings, the insufficiency of churches and religions; he *sensed* the solution and expressed it through images. What he proposed fanatically at the end of his life must be understood as an *image*.

(... legitimate work, ceaseless production, is obscurely bound to communication or is one with it. Yes, it's the same as communication, but we usually cannot see it, as it's a higher level of communication.)

16

Lawrence, Lady Chatterley's Lover: a book one is only able to truly appreciate later, after the smoke and sparkle of the narrative's appeal have dissipated: for this book has treated one of the most elevated subjects but with a strange narrowness, a certain blindness.

... and yet it's not false and is very *demanding:* this is an achievement.

A person deprived of communication "is not alive": how true this is! Who could doubt that the kind of communication Lawrence portrayed is a real one (a sensual communication with a sensual woman)? But the claim that this kind of communication is the only possible one for the wider world comes close to ridiculousness.

One can communicate with a child as a *helper* and protector; with a friend in *friendship*; with those at great remove through *intellectual creations* (the embodiment of true socialism): all these can be just as true and just as redemptive.

It comes down to the communication's *degree of truth* (the kind of communication depends on the conditions). Because Lawrence understood this so profoundly, delineated it through his critique, and expressed it so intensively,[4] his book is a great book.

17

What Hamsun and Lawrence have in common is that both believed they were thinkers but as soon they ventured outside the narrow range of their particular expressive powers, they uttered nonsense. Within their ranges, Hamsun is purer, Lawrence more important.

[. . .]

20

Montaigne, Lichtenberg, Spinoza

Three great events in my reading life, indeed, the three greatest events in the last decade or more (except for Proust, whom I discovered a bit later) all occurred in the same year, more exactly, in a period of just a few months, little more than a quarter of a year. The first was

4. Katherine Mansfield, a writer completely different from Lawrence, could write of Lawrence in her notebooks that what made him a great writer was his passion, and that, despite disagreeing with him on some things, like his ideas on sexuality, she felt closer to Lawrence than to any other writer.

Montaigne. I immediately heard an eternal voice, which, in its freedom, its significance, its calm and distant confidence, seemed to me
comparable to J. S. Bach's. As Montaigne himself wrote:

> We should have wives, children, property and above all good health if we are
> able; but we should not become so attached to these that our happiness depends on
> them. We must reserve a small room at the back of the shop, entirely our own, in
> which we can establish our true liberty, our principal refuge and solitude.

I rarely quote Montaigne, for the same reason that I almost
never quote Proust: *what* should I select? No matter where I open
one of their books, I could cite a half or a whole page. The crucial, the
essential element is not to be found in isolated passages but is spread
throughout the work's entire flow; what is marvelous is the discourse.

In contrast, Lichtenberg—my second great reading event—is a
writer I have frequently quoted throughout this work. Spinoza—the
third—is the one I've quoted least. And yet, some of his sentences are
more intimately, more internally bound to this work than any others,
not in a literal sense, to be sure, but, I'll say it again: internally; more
like breath; or like a redemptive presence floating above and around
me; or like snow-covered peaks in the distance.

I once bought an anthology of Lichtenberg's writings, a volume
so small I could almost enclose it in one hand (the smallest book
I've ever owned, but at the same time one of the all-time greats), at a
flea market for just a few cents (because in Holland books are priced
according to size and weight;—still, this primitive level of culture
allowed me to elevate my own, that is, despite having no access to
libraries or money, I was able to transcend my personal Dark Ages
as far as the availability of literary works is concerned). I had at the
time a strong reaction against Lichtenberg's renowned contemporary, Jean Paul, whom I faulted primarily for two characteristics that
were making reading him unbearable: first, there was his Roman-
tic heritage, the frequent weeping, the rivers of tears—his characters
only ever see the moon through a teardrop (which gives it a double

aureole); second, there was a marked cowardice I believed I could discern in his *thought*. To be sure, he did not lack for the subtlest of instruments with which he forged his way far along the most diverse paths, but as soon as he saw he was heading toward some inevitable conclusion that would have brought him into open conflict with convention, he took fright, retreated, and concluded his exploration with sentimentalities. After this highly celebrated and certainly extremely talented writer, whom I reproached with effeminate cowardice,[5] I discovered in Lichtenberg a genuinely great writer who had never been in fashion. Lichtenberg did not lay his hand on his heart, but instead wrote:

"Do not trust anyone who lays his hand on his heart when he says, 'I swear.'"

It was the first sentence I read upon opening the tiny book and — as has happened with more than one author — it has remained the essential one. It seemed to me to be the key to Lichtenberg's oeuvre. It gave the defining color to all of his sentences and accompanied them all as a bass note.

Then, on May 27, 1935, I received a copy of Spinoza's *Ethics* and as a result it became the most important day of that year for me.

21

Spinoza's Ethics

When I first got hold of this book (on a spring day seven months after my experience of the moon forest and hedgehog forest[6]), something extraordinary occurred within a few minutes, almost immedi-

---

5. I have not read Jean Paul since that time, but my memory retains, after more than ten years, a particularly wonderful phrase of his: "Everything resides in the *true land*, I say, but love dreams." Jean Paul is not to be dismissed too lightly. Otherwise, the greatest, most demanding, most infallible judge of literature in the world would not have admired him.

6. Cf. VII, 20–23.

ately, in fact. I opened the book at random and——; — just as when a series of rooms too dark to see through are suddenly illuminated with the flip of a single switch controlling all the lightbulbs and you no longer have to shuffle carefully from one to the next but can clearly see the adjacent room and more, gaining a perspective of the whole. Such was my experience when I read this phrase among the opening sentences:

> [T]he activities of the mind follow solely from adequate ideas, and accordingly the mind is only passive insofar as it has inadequate ideas.[7]

Or this one:

> In proportion as each thing possesses more of perfection, so is it more active, and less passive; and, vice versa, in proportion as it is more active, so is it more perfect.[8]

—I read in the foreword that the book should not simply be read but must be studied (only by following each small, individual step exactly will the reader understand). Lo and behold. But for *me*, there was no question of reading. It all struck me as something long familiar; I did not have to pause and reflect over any item my eyes fell upon; my gaze jumped from each detail to the whole without the slightest effort. A *current* ran through the book and illuminated it in its entirety: an electric current, no other word suffices. I did not read out of a thirst for knowledge, nor with the eager anticipation of learning something new. I was simply curious—"how did he do it?"—eager for a new form, filled with joy at the encounter and with admiration for the abundance.

As something long familiar . . . as if it were — not my brother but

7. *Ethics* III, prop. 3, trans. R. H. M. Elwes (1887). This and all subsequent quotes from the *Ethics* are from R. H. M. Elwes's translation. (Trans. note.)
8. *Ethics* V, prop. 40 (Trans. note.)

myself who had written it—and at the same time as if I were looking up at soaring mountains towering over me. These mountains were *my* mountains: the range in which I'd always struggled, down in the gorges, in the darkness, climbing endless mountainsides, in the folds of primitive forests without any view: and suddenly the peaks were there in all their glory, before my eyes, icy and blue, rising into the sky—clearly visible.

Books IV and V constitute the ethics in the strictest sense. The preceding books, less close to me on the whole, offer some metaphysical foundation. Now and then I felt trepidation before the enormity of certain abstract concepts or, more precisely, before the abstract enormity; then again, no other man who has ventured through such terrain has filled me with such profound confidence—confidence that he erred as little as possible.

The last proposition in Book V is sublime: *Blessedness is not the reward of virtue, but virtue itself; neither do we rejoice therein, because we control our lusts, but, contrariwise, because we rejoice therein, we are able to control our lusts.*[9]

I saw then that earlier I had intuitively fostered the correct assumption with regard to his concept of "God": whenever Spinoza employs this word, it can be replaced with its definition without any loss. This "God" has nothing whatsoever to do with any religious conception of God: that personal God who is "wroth," "vengeful," who "has created the world," etc. Sentences like these make it clear: "No one can hate God."—"He, who loves God, cannot endeavor that God should love him in return."—"The more we understand particular things, the more we understand God." Spinoza is a complete atheist.[10]—He is the most confident and most admirable of all atheists.

9. *Ethics* V, prop. 42 (Trans. note.)
10. This view was later thoroughly confirmed when I was able to read Spinoza's correspondence: because the letters are addressed to private people, he openly repudiates Christianity and religion.

If he used the word "God," he did so because it didn't bother him, because it supplied him with many connected human strengths and because it spared him difficulties.

There is a treatise to be written on why *this is no longer possible today*.

I add a few more of the propositions that made the strongest impression on me:[11]

Nothing can be destroyed, except by a cause external to itself. (III, 4—This, exactly, is Pasteur's great discovery!)

There is nothing positive in ideas, which causes them to be false. (II, 33)

All ideas, in so far as they are referred to God, are true. (II, 32—It is important to constantly keep his definition of "God" in mind as one reads: "By God, I mean a being absolutely infinite—that is, a substance consisting in infinite attributes, of which each expresses eternal and infinite essentiality."[12] Propositions 14 and 15 of Book I are also part of this.

No virtue can be conceived as prior to this endeavor to preserve one's own being. (IV, 22)

On the good—distinguishing between two kinds of "good":[13]

Man, insofar as he is determined to a particular action because he has inadequate ideas, cannot be absolutely said to act in obedience to virtue; he can only be so described, insofar as he is determined for the action because he understands. (IV, 23)—To act absolutely in obedience to virtue is in us the same thing as to act, to live, or to preserve one's being (these three terms are identical in meaning) in accordance with the dictates of reason on the basis of seeking what is useful to one's self. (IV, 24)

On false humility and the difficulty of maintaining the only worthy stance: an accurate estimation of one's self.

The emotions of over-esteem and disparagement are always bad. (IV, 48)—Self-approval may arise from reason, and that which arises from reason is the highest

11. Cf. VII, 139, final paragraph.
12. *Ethics* I, definitions. (Trans. note.)
13. Cf. II, 77, 269, 287, [323]; XII, 57, [81], 98, 139, etc.

possible. (IV, 52)—Humility is not a virtue, or does not arise from reason. (IV, 53)—
Extreme pride or dejection indicates extreme ignorance of self. (IV, 55)—Extreme
pride or dejection indicates extreme infirmity of spirit. (IV, 56)

On death:

A free man thinks of death least of all things; and his wisdom is a meditation
not of death but of life. (IV, 67)

On pleasure:

Pleasure in itself is not bad but good: contrariwise, pain in itself is bad. (IV, 41)

What I meant by the sentence: "Stupidity is a primary concept; evil a derivative one":

If men were born free, they would, so long as they remained free, form no conception of good and evil. (IV, 68)

He, who has a true idea, simultaneously knows that he has a true idea, and cannot doubt of the truth of the thing perceived. (II, 43)

He who clearly and distinctly understands himself and his emotions loves God,
and so much the more in proportion as he more understands himself and his emotions. (V, 15)

In proportion as the mind is more capable of understanding things by the third
kind of knowledge, it desires more to understand things by that kind. (V, 26)

In note II to Proposition 40, we find information on the three
kinds of knowledge distinguished by Spinoza; these are exceedingly
interesting and immeasurably significant (as is what he says about
"general notions" in the preceding note). What Spinoza calls the third
kind of knowledge is nothing other than *pure vision* and—would he
have admitted it?—is *creative*.[14] (From this follows the identity of art

14. It would be impossible to point to all the notes in my work that relate to this,
as I would have to list dozens of them, especially from parts I and XII that address
"imagination" and true work.

and true life or of true life and art, which I have emphasized again and again.)

I could have quoted many more passages—always with the self-evident understanding that it would not be some general summary of the *Ethics*, but simply a compilation of those propositions that had the most profound effect on me and with which I had the strongest connection—but I'll add only this one proposition from the series of particularly marvelous propositions near the end of Book V:

> Whatsoever the mind understands under the form of eternity, it does not understand by virtue of conceiving the present actual existence of the body, but by virtue of conceiving the essence of the body under the form of eternity. (V, 29)

Finally—like the builder in times past who closed up the vault of his cathedral at a vertiginous height, all the while bound to the earth by broad, secure, and massive walls—the author sets down the final proposition that so resounds as to make almost everything ever said seem but mere stammering ("Blessedness is not the reward of virtue, but . . ."):

BEATITUDO NON EST VIRTUTIS PRAEMIUM, SED IPSA VIRTUS; NEC EADEM GAUDEMUS, QUIA LIBIDINES COERCEMUS, SED CONTRA, QUIA EADEM GAUDEMUS, IDEO LIBIDINES COERCERE POSSUMUS.

22

When Balzac undoes the knots in his novels, he does not go on to smooth out the strings in order to make the victory more complete; he knows anyone can smooth them out. As soon as a bit of air is let in and the solution is clear, he turns to something else: like Bach, he leaves us in the middle of the matter; he makes no entrance or exit as a passage to the emptiness of the human condition: he stands there like roughly-hewn granite. He shows the reader no deference in the form of garrulousness[15] or flattery . . .

15. One should never forget *how* we must regard Balzac, that is, from what distance or, to put it differently, with what speed we read him. Cf. 82.

That Thomas Mann does not always maintain this lack of deference is the only thing that occasionally irritates in his writing. The penultimate page of "Descent into Hell" is wonderful—there is nothing more compressed, more intelligent; why these final two or three flaccid sentences (flaccid *here*, at least)? Why does he not leave us in the heart of the matter, why not break off as soon as everything is said?—No doubt Thomas Mann himself does not know why. These are differences in writers' natures. He does it out of an obligingness that Montaigne and several others neither have nor understand.

23

Ehrenburg: a clever opposition, without the *depth* of an André Gide; a clever, entertaining opposition.[16]

[...]

25

"Democritus, who was always laughing, and Heraclitus, who was always weeping," I read and had to laugh, initially. But even dumber anecdotes have often been believed, which says one thing: that both were very similar.

26

You occasionally hear it said of this or that writer: "Yes; but now he's old hat." You look into it and realize: he was never young!

(Is Klopstock old hat? Then why aren't Andreas Gryphius or Johann Christian Günther outdated?)

16. Written in March 1935.

27

Do not say "its poetic aspect," but instead "seen from another angle."

28

One should not poeticize when writing poetry. That's the secret.

29

It's not easy to pay your share; do not concern yourself with whether the others gather up all they can.

30

At some point you must leave philosophy behind.

All pure speculation taken to its end necessarily leads to nothingness. —We need a point of departure (not something speculative, but an axiom, that is, a blind assumption: therefore, there can be no talk of speculation that is pure from beginning to end): a piece of reality we wish to serve, something our conceptions will serve. If we start from nothingness, we will inevitably end up in nothingness again.[17] There must be an affiliation, similar to that which some seek or hope to find in nationalism: what we are speaking of here is truly necessary "nationality." This nationality is that of human life: we have accorded a priori a *value* to this life and what it seeks to achieve in its development. I find this correct. It's not lost on me that this is where (pure) philosophy ends (for it is and always will be impossible to prove the assumption valid that non-being is not as good as being—or that evil is inferior to good) and I find this correct.

---

17. Besides, nature protects us from this: "The absolute doubt Descartes demands is no more possible in the human brain than a void in nature." (Balzac)

31

Nietzsche's statement "The old god is dead" is a bad image or a very unfortunate turn of phrase. (Because some will mourn his death and worship him even more and others won't believe it.)

For being an atheist is no easy thing. In any case, Nietzsche could not manage it. I repeat what I've said about Spinoza: "He was the most confident and most admirable of all atheists."

32

Nietzsche. Main proposition: he was a much more profound thinker—*much closer to the heart of things*—and a much nobler human being (better, more benevolent, perhaps also: simpler) but as a writer he was less great, less brilliant than is generally accepted.

"Much closer to the heart of things": time will tell.—He had lost his way on his ascent, but he was on the right mountain; and not near the base, he had climbed high.

[. . .]

41

Established Critics

They are like beauty queens: not too tall, not too short; not too plump, not too thin; not too sturdy, not too slight; their busts are neither overly or meagerly endowed; as for curves, they have neither too many nor too few. All they're missing is beauty.

What established critics write is neither too bold, nor too conservative; neither too long, nor too short; neither too personal, nor impersonal; neither too easy, nor too hard; neither copied from others, nor their own.

They do not have too much imagination or too much imagery; their style is neither too ornamented nor too natural; neither too readable nor too impenetrable. They manage to please everyone. They are unassailable.

— neither open, nor close-minded; neither obliging, nor dismissive. You ask about their writing? It can only be described through these contraries.

They're always ready to defend the new: as long as they've had the chance to assess the odds of success by collecting the opinions of others — a process they call research; otherwise they stick to the tried and true.

They can even be bold — once they've been assured by one of their minions that the majority will follow them; then boldly, they stride ahead alone.

42

The Art Critic

One winter evening at six o'clock, a young artist went to pay a visit to a famous expert, the celebrated critic of a local cultural journal. The famous critic was at home alone and he invited the young man to bring his many paintings in. "A frugal man," the artist thought to himself since the lights were not lit. They talked. The great critic inquired about many things: the artist's origins, his financial situation, his relationships, how this person had acted, what that person had said. Finally, he asked to see the paintings. The shy young man didn't dare comment on the lighting, that is, the lack of lighting, and handed a painting to the critic in the now complete darkness, assuming the master of the house would turn on the lights. Instead, the critic began to talk. "Your painting is still a bit clumsy, uncertain; your style still somewhat undetermined. But there are promising elements, hints of something quite your own. Some nuance in your use of color is remarkable; delicate tones create atmosphere, yes, atmosphere! You must work, work constantly! Atmosphere, emotion, and supple painterly *élan*—lush and luxuriant application of color, melting forms, compositional confidence, and serenity! Promising, very promising. The road to art is a long one, but you have grounds for great hopes. It all comes down to intention—the *condition sine qua non* of art—as Goethe, who understood so much about our difficult and thankless field, well knew. This intention must emerge in the confident style of mastery."

Alarmed, the young man was speechless. "And what is this a painting of?"—"A garden with a windmill in the background, a garden of yellow roses in the morning light . . ."—"That's not what I'm asking," the critic interrupted him *for the first time*. "What is the idea? Where, in the world of art, did you find—I don't want to say influences—inspiration, rapport?" The young man explained and handed more paintings to the critic, who held each one only briefly. The audience came to an end. "Well," the great critic announced briskly, "a careful appreciation of your paintings will appear in the cultural journal soon." He held out his hand, which the young man did not take since he couldn't see it. "Excuse me," he stammered, "I can't . . . find my pictures."

"I beg your pardon?"

"My paintings . . . I don't know where they are . . . in the dark, I can't . . ."

"Good Lord!" the older man thundered. "Were the lights not on? Didn't the housekeeper . . ."

"It was a joke," he then blurted out in a hoarse groan, which did not convince the young man.

It had recently been rumored that he was suffering from a severe case of gout and only seldom went to exhibitions, through which he walked tentatively with a companion, his eyes always hidden behind dark glasses.

43

Why is it necessary to highlight so clearly the mistakes of certain great men — like Nietzsche? In order to not hinder the effects of their important positive qualities. When flaws are too closely tied to their strengths, they are often the weight which sinks the whole.

Nietzsche made at least two mistakes: 1. He made concessions to the reader (at least in *Zarathustra*. There is a quip that says Nietzsche also wanted to write an opera out of rivalry with Wagner). 2. Conceptual excess. His mania for aiming higher and hitting harder than the intended goal required (which always leads to self-destruction or to the undermining of his position). — Both mistakes come from the same source: his enormous, unbearable sense of isolation.

Some readers come upon these mistakes and stop reading: they had heard *only* good things about Nietzsche. However, those who are prepared for these flaws continue reading.

44

Differences. The journalist goes to *certain* places to catch sight of this or that; the writer observes things everywhere. The journalist does this for "work"; the writer always does it, he has no choice. — That said, a journalist is worth more than the average scholar (who can't survive without talent). The latter, however, is the servant, the last disciple of one great thing: knowledge; the journalist, on the other hand, serves an abject, maleficent thing: the press.

In *art*, personal worth is primary. Worthy art cannot be created by someone lacking personal worth. Knowledge can, within certain limits, be served by miserable people. This is not possible in art, which requires good (complete) servants.
. . . What they do have in common — complete devotion, incandescence, insight into the world (*pure vision*), which a Pasteur might also occasionally achieve in his scientific work — *is precisely art.*

45

Jacob Burckhardt, no doubt the greatest scholar with whose work I am familiar, was actually not a scholar, but a true writer (much more a writer, that is, an artist, than hundreds of those novelists and poets in Switzerland); a Goethean spirit. A writer for whom fields of knowledge were style and subject and who channeled his substance through the conduits of knowledge.

[. . .]

51

"All you ever talk about is art." Just the other day I read in Karl Kraus that it doesn't matter *what* we talk about; and that is most certainly true.

If you elevate yourself, then what you say will also be more elevated. "The better we know things, the better we will know God."

— everything you say will be more elevated: whether you speak of how you slept, of your morning grooming, of a leaf, of other people, of the accusative case; indeed, of other people, even business, even politics.

— You'd like, you say, to finally hear something about *life*. I don't understand. What would you like? LIFE? (Is it my fault that you fail at it? You should read me more carefully.)

52

. . . It's called the *fruits of reading*. A sweet pleasantry. From now on I will categorize my thoughts: fruits of the forest (the moon forest, in particular, has been conducive to thinking); fruits of the street; fruits of the cafés; fruits of the sea, and many more. *Fruits of the trees* when an idea occurs to me at the sight of a tree.

[. . .]

55

Who are the writers of all eras to whom I am most grateful? Do I even need to stop and think? Goethe and Spinoza.

There are others, too, like Heraclitus,[18] of whom I only know a little. My thinking has served as a conduit to him more than learning from him.

There is also the respect bordering on veneration that I feel for those who have achieved the most sublime reaches of what we call art in the strictest sense: Hölderlin, Bach;[19] and my great love: Montaigne. And so on and so on.

I almost forgot to mention Lichtenberg, the most marvelous of all.

56

When the novel reached its end, a form like Proust's appeared: real novels had become unreal and reality appeared in a form that was not a real novel. *In general, posterity decides who the true creators of form are.* This much is certain: those who are considered by their contemporaries to be the great creators of form are almost always imitators.

[. . .]

18. Heraclitus, certainly one of the greatest minds of Antiquity (by which I don't mean to say anything against Plato, Aristotle, and another, Pythagoras: they solved particular problems that Heraclitus did not solve). Plato, Aristotle, the author of the New Testament (and Socrates, too, is one of the forerunners in this line) "reigned" for two thousand years or, let's say, were emblems of the two millennia. Just as Heraclitus has for ten thousand years.

19. I hadn't yet encountered Proust's work when I wrote this.

60

The expression "to master one's subject" is completely meaning-less. A writer is no more able to master his subject than an ocean liner is able to master the water.[20]

[. . .]

63

"Essays that observe and interpret more than analyze": is what Hermann Hesse can write (*Neue Rundschau*, 1933). How can one interpret without analysis? How can one analyze without interpreting? I find this mode of expression completely obscure, if you can even call it expression.

What some find annoying in Hesse's writing is, aside from his rustic side, his deliberate soulfulness, his endless commentary—precisely the *interpretative* aspect; I would have been satisfied with analysis. There is a great deal in this Hesse-matter that reminds me of a towering plaster statue of Christ with a hand raised in blessing, as one sees everywhere.

[. . .]

67

On Plagiarism[21]

Almost everything written today is plagiarism—99 percent would be an underestimate—however, and this is the problem, it's *difficult to show* that it is plagiarism, since it has been taken from many sources and furthermore from sources that are themselves plagiarism combined in a complicated way.

20. Cf. VI, 16.
21. Cf. VI, 30.

It's much more pleasant when something is clearly and neatly taken from Goethe, Rilke, and other well-known writers.

The difference is that in such situations, the writer knows what he's doing. However, in the earlier situation, the writer — that is, scribblers the world over — usually does not know. — Or perhaps he is aware, deep down? But he won't admit to himself that he hasn't done any work. For that is the opposite of plagiarizing: work. In art, to work means to free one's gaze, to catch something, capture it, bring it back: this process is never plagiarism even if the wording has something in common with another passage (which, admittedly, is only possible with very short sentences).

The scoundrel who has stolen his "views" from others and cleverly reworked them, cobbling them into a new form with external methods, is alarmed when he comes upon similar forms elsewhere. A Gide, on the other hand, rejoiced when he found views he had elaborated (and was responsible for) in the work of earlier writers.

Why am I confident that this work is plagiarism — even though I completely lack the means, the knowledge that would enable me to trace it to earlier books? My confidence arises from this fact: it is not right.

However, not all acts of plagiarism are wrong. It does occasionally happen that someone is honest enough to copy passages, word for word, from a true writer. — Do I mean to claim that all falseness is plagiarism? Yes, I do.

[. . .]

69

Those who have nothing to say can talk about the entire world. Those who do have something to say will always write more or less the same thing, like Goethe for example.

Yes, even Lichtenberg, who knew better than anyone how to look in all directions! It's never *easy* to identify a writer's fundamental tone, but it may well be most difficult to describe Lichtenberg's. In this we can see the great difference between Lichtenberg and La Rochefoucauld, to whom he is compared now and again.

70

With each literary work, consider if it has an acquired radiance or a *hardness* that shines.

71

Who, in the past thousands of years, has seen clearly if not Lichtenberg?

72

The essence of art is not representation, as is always claimed, but (to express myself provisionally): making evident (bringing to light, to awareness) internal angles of tension.

73

What is good writing? *Speaking in your own words.*
This doesn't seem like much, yet it's essential and difficult to achieve. All other differences are secondary.

Yes, but doesn't it sometimes happen that a child——? That a child speaks true poetry? Yes, it does happen, we know (even though a child can hardly put together more than three or four words of its own). We must add that a complete sentence of just a few words can almost never be identified as poetry. To be certain about such sentences, context is necessary. The context may be other sentences (which need not themselves be poetry) or knowledge, acquired in one way or another, about the writer. Karl Kraus speaks of "the air my sentences breathe." It's extremely important for sentences to be breathing entities and not like gems (to which sentences should only be compared in another respect). The most devastating sentence I read in Balzac is (at the end of "La Grenadière"): "He was now a father." — For this reason, a text you believe contemporary suddenly appears completely different when you learn it was written in the 18th century. Whoever denies this fact doesn't understand a thing about literature.

[. . .]

75

On Heart-Warming Literature

I read somewhere that "light and warmth" are the two counter-vailing elements in poetry and the example given was: *Hölderlin* with the most light and no warmth; with almost exclusively warmth — Mörike.

So then, Hölderlin has no warmth. All the better! (In the margin I drew a blue and red heart tied with a red ribbon and pierced by an arrow.)

Around the same time, I came across this statement by a theologian: ". . . the thoughts of a true aphorist win our admiration but *they leave our hearts cold.*" On my life. I immediately thought of Lichtenberg, then late Goethe, and a few more. On my life——

If there's no crooning and courting — how else to express it adequately? — their hearts remain cold.

[. . .]

80

It is extraordinarily difficult to judge a contemporary style, i.e., one that has only just been created: because you do not yet know from what *distance* you must consider it.

81

He who has never been able to say, "Death, where is thy sting?" has no say. — Yet neither does a man who has never recognized that he will die one day. (XI, 13)

—and if a man has realized this, it is apparent in his *style*. This is no doubt.—People say, namely, that Balzac had no style, but you must not listen to what they say. First of all, you have to see the style. In some cases the style is in the centimeter, in others in the kilometer; when Michelangelo finished the frescoes in the Sistine Chapel, perhaps people also said that he had no style: they saw it from very close up (the scaffolding was still standing) and looked at a millimeter, which he had not painted. The dimensions of different things vary; written works can also be very different things.

82

One question is always or too often overlooked (and this leads many far astray):

. . . one must first know *where* the style is. The dome of St. Peter's Basilica has a style, just as a ring made by a jeweler can have a style; but no one demands that the stones be smooth.

It's the same with literature: just as you must consider it from various *distances*, you must read at different *speeds*. Has this been observed enough up to now? Each book should be assigned a number that indicates the speed at which the author would like to be read. (If 10 is the average speed, then works by Heraclitus, some late Goethe, Karl Kraus, and Hölderlin should be read at 1; Wallace's books should be given the number 1,000—and they would still not reveal any trace of style.) That Balzac can and *should* be read more quickly than other good writers (at the pace of 50 or 100—like Dostoevsky at the pace of 100 or 200), does not in any way mean that he has less style than another but only that he wrote on a different plane. His style may never be discernable to those who read exceptionally slowly: just as anyone a centimeter away from the ceiling of the Sistine Chapel will never discover Michelangelo's style.

[. . .]

84

The fact that someone can't write is no reason for him to imagine that he's a great critic. It would be as if someone unfit for mountain climbing who fell down the mountain were to present himself as a great aviator.

85

The only acceptable commentary on a work of art is parallel motions; an artistic production of as equal force as possible that attains the same level . . .

If only one could write a commentary on Hölderlin's: "Ripe is the fruit, dipped in fire, cooked / and tasted here on earth, and it is a law / that all things will enter, like snakes, prophetic / dreaming on the hills of heaven . . ."!

86

These important lines of Goethe's (as beautiful as they are important) are a contribution to the debate over whether a gulf separates humans from animals and are useful in the fight against theologians:[22]

You lead the ranks of living creatures
Before me and teach me to know my brothers
In quiet woods, in water and in air.

[. . .]

90

Karl Kraus.—"Among those born of women . . ." The others, the greater ones (but who, today is greater?) are not only born of woman

22. Cf. VII, 50, 92.

but of other, more ancient and more profound things: of the earth, of rivers, of the elemental; the act of their births was less clear and therefore their reach is greater.—Put more banally: Karl Kraus was not a less creative individual, but a more creative one; what lacked were connections.

91

John the Baptist is clearly characterized by the harrowing question: who was he? By contrast it is very clear who Jesus of Nazareth was, as it is with Bach, Hölderlin, and similar figures. Yet both Karl Kraus and D. H. Lawrence[23] are characterized by this same harrowing question of identity—albeit in very different areas.

92

Lawrence. His primary idea, if one can call it that, is false; but his secondary ideas and all that gleams through his primary idea are tremendous.

93

Hamsun

Without any doubt, his artistic reach is extensive enough to include his achievement of a style, a *voice* that is unmistakable. But why did he write so many books?

Balzac also wrote a great many books, even more than Hamsun. Yet whereas one feels the need to read all of Balzac's books, better readers don't feel this need with Hamsun's writing. This is because each of Balzac's books is a part of his oeuvre and one wants to read the body of his work to the end. But we got to the end of Hamsun's oeuvre long ago.

23. Cf. 15.

Geisler, the only person in *Growth of the Soil* of any interest, is treated ironically, set aside. And yet, Geisler is the only *real* person in this book: the rest are simply projections of *his* sensibility.

For critics it comes down to making distinctions. In his poetry, especially in his lyrical works, Hamsun certainly achieved some unrivaled things.

> Oh, there was something great about Isak; as it might be Israel, promised and ever deceived, but still believing.[24]

Why should he be competent in every area (as so often assumed)?—His knowledge is quite limited, without much breadth. His power is limited to a narrow field. (Geisler's speeches: just don't use them to formulate a philosophy! "The woods and mountains stand and watch . . .")

94

. . . Yet men don't want to be charmed, they want to be encouraged. Hamsun charms better than any other and then offers slight encouragement if any.

95

Hermann Hesse's work is for the most part conventional.

96

The greatest loss in German literature that one could imagine (aside from the absence of Hölderlin) would be if Goethe had died in middle age.

For which Goethe is the most relevant, the one with whom we

24. Knut Hamsun, *Growth of the Soil*, trans. Sverre Lyngstad (New York: Penguin Classics, 2007), p. 76. (Trans. note.)

have such a tremendous relationship? Perhaps the one who wrote *Werther*, or the one who had various relations with young women, who went skating, swam in the sea, traveled with Lavater and Stolberg, and accompanied Merck (fortunately!), etc.?

The *young* Goethe . . . is the old one.

97

Reading Goethe. Certain of Goethe's writings should not be read too often. From a distance we always think of the essential Goethe. But if one reads certain of his writings again (with less remove), one is inevitably surprised and disappointed to recognize the *face of chance.* The unspeakable clutter of time!

One has to recover from this shock, and recovery is possible with Goethe's *Faust*, especially Part II.

The writings of most other authors that have little meaning beyond the time they were written have not been preserved or are no longer accessible. Then again, Goethe wrote such an enormous amount. So much written in *ink!* Semi-scholarly, pedagogical; daily work that may have played an important, redemptive role for him but offers little reward for those of us who have looked it over and engaged with it deeply.

98

Goethe's "Prose Maxims" are unsurpassable. Such an unutterably *expansive* (far-reaching), *mild* light!

Space, acuity, and love are all present. — In other, similar works one is happy to discover acuity, or space. Only love is missing.

99

The books one should *always* have at hand are (five):

1. Spinoza's *Ethics*
2. Goethe's *Faust*
3. Goethe's *Maxims* and *West-Eastern Divan*
4. Montaigne's *Essays*
5. Lichtenberg (short texts)

100

Benvenuto Cellini's autobiography is extraordinarily dismal. A terrible feeling overcomes us at the sight of the constant hindrances he had to overcome in his work! This great suffering is the most essential motif running through the entire book. (And to think that it was Goethe, of all people, who brought this work to us—!)

101

The tale of the three tasks is a very good folk tale: note that it's not a morality tale in which the good are rewarded and the bad are punished as one might assume from a superficial reading. That the hero has put himself in the service of *the powers of nature* (or taken them into his service), not for the benefit of humankind, society, institutions or God—not for any benefit at all. (The birds. The elephants. The giants in the desert.) The tale is therefore completely true.[25]

102

The claim that Proust portrayed a specific society that existed in France before the First World War is either nonsense or a banality depending on one's meaning.

25. Cf. VII, 24, 25.

Some surface is necessary if one wishes to paint. For a fresco, one needs a wall. Had Michelangelo not been offered *that particular* wall (or ceiling), but another instead, could he not have painted his works just as well? For a Proust, the society is not the fresco, but the wall; a writer must speak of something; that something of which he speaks, however, is only the wall; *how* he speaks or what he expresses through his manner of speaking, that alone is the reality of art.

103

Heine. When I got hold of a copy of his prose (no need to waste words on his "poems"—confections for maids or other sentimental and conventional beings), I understood Karl Kraus's fury. Still, in this terrible prose there are here and there exceptions, even profound remarks, for example: "Only a great poet can recognize the poetry of his own age."

104

Thoughts on *Marxist* doctrine.

Seen from a certain elevation, what it lacks is the practical element. Yet another German system. I used to think that the practical element was its strength and that it was not a system at all (hence the "from a certain elevation"). Instead, the system magnificently presents a truth (which ensures its survival). What it lacks is the recognition of this sentence: "Man is a maniacal being."

—which is to say: lazy, prone to foreign illnesses, the symptoms of which we deem coincidental until we are ravaged by them. We consume poisons, or rather, the potency of poisons, their ability to replicate and spread (that an individual may happen on a belladonna plant and even consume it is assumed by this system as it is elsewhere. What this system does not recognize is that humans are fertile ground for the *joys* of empoisoning.)—It lacks recognition of man's sheer aptitude for self-poisoning.

105

Two Lenin quotes (*Internationale Literatur*, 1935, no.1):

. . . we must take all [. . .] science, technology, knowledge and art . . . But this science, technology and art are in the hands and heads of the experts.[26]

[Proletarian culture] is not clutched out of thin air; it is not an invention of those who call themselves experts in proletarian culture. That is all nonsense.[27]

106

In memory of Erich Mühsam (and many others whose names I don't know).

For most of its journey, this airplane flies at very high altitude, hidden behind clouds. Not a sound reaches your ears; your eyes can't catch a glimpse of it. And yet, with only the scarcest of data points, perhaps readings from a few instruments that determine one of its wings or fix a coordinate for a fraction of a second before it moves out of range: it's a machine with a motor steered by pilot. It lives, lives on, and continues its trajectory into the loneliest of realms . . .

[. . .]

108

"Unnecessary tragedies." As if they could be called tragedies! Awful incidents.

26. V. I. Lenin, *On Literature and Art.* (Moscow: Progress Publishers, 1970) p. 123, https://archive.org/stream/LeninOnLiteratureAndArt/Lenin%20on%20Literature%20and%20Art_djvu.txt. (Trans. note.)

27. Ibid. p. 141. (Trans. note).

109

"A few fortunate quotations." This kind of appreciation is precisely what reveals to me how far the author is from truly understanding the concept of quoting others.

110

"The unknown philosopher": but what philosopher is well-known—other than the authentic ones?

[. . .]

113

"Strictly speaking, one can say that the beautiful person is beautiful only for a moment." *Goethe*

114

From a retort:

"Whichever measure you use . . ." Take my measure only by the measure I use (used). No stricter measure!

115

Anyone who tries to write something new is no writer.

116

He wrote much faster than anyone else and had the latest information, yet was always dated. From this he concluded . . . that he must write even faster.

117

New proof that knowledge is not new but can only be recovered: one of Gide's fundamental ideas:

> And yet, is it not peculiar, he thought to himself, that it is precisely in trying to negate myself that I found the power I had so long desired?

Everyone knows this fundamental idea of Gide's. But this passage is from Balzac's story "The Seamy Side of History."

118

The Reader

Paul Valéry during a conference:

> . . . that is to say that they demand a kind of active collaboration of minds, a quite remarkable novelty and the essential trait of our Symbolism. It would, perhaps, be neither impossible nor wrong to deduce from the attitude of renunciation and negation I pointed out earlier the change I'm discussing, which consists, first, in taking as a partner of the writer, as reader, the individual chosen by the intellectual effort he is capable of; and then, as a second consequence we could, from this point on, offer to this hard-working and refined reader texts with no lack of difficulties or . . .
> (*Nouvelle Revue Française*, August 1936)

119

We must return one hundred times to Goethe's maxim:
"Not everyone who is given an incisive thought will become productive; he will most likely think of something entirely familiar."

120

The most beautiful passage written in our century:

> . . . As at the far-off time when her parents had chosen for her a bridegroom, she had the features delicately traced by purity and submission, the cheeks glowing with a chaste expectation, with a vision of happiness, with an innocent gaiety even, which the years had gradually destroyed. Life in withdrawing from her had taken with it the disillusionments of life. A smile seemed to be hovering on my grandmother's lips. On that funeral couch, death, like a sculptor of the Middle Ages, lays her down in the form of a young maiden.[28]

121

A *sequence.*—First you hear sounds of talking.—Then you see the crowd of thinkers.—Then, after two or three decades, little by little, you see the artistic power. (With Proust, for example, seen as the greatest writer of the century.)

But with some writers, it's the reverse: first you see an artistic power, possibly a great one; it fades, though the writer is still credited with intellectual importance; after more time has passed, you hear: it was just talk . . .

122

". . . persecution of genius fosters its influence." Tacitus[29]

123

Every true writer must think of this Bible verse: "Not everyone is seized by the word . . ."!

---

28. Proust, *The Guermantes Way*, trans. C. K. Scott Moncrieff (New Haven: Yale University Press, 2018), p. 379. (Trans. note.)

29. *Annals* IV, 35 trans. Alfred Church and William Brodribb (1876).

(On verifying the quote, I realized it's wrong. What it says in Matthew:19 is something significantly simpler: Non omnes capiunt verbum istud—not everyone accepts this word. I will leave the sentence as it was in my memory, subject to my unconscious collaboration.)

Should the writer destroy the word? This question cannot be left open for long or he's not a true writer but has already slipped from the sharp crest of his resolve down one side and taken the broad road that can be found *everywhere*, not the one narrow road of art.

Destroying the word so that the many can *apparently* make something of it cannot be his concern: but his concern is to bring something that will allow those who can reach it to climb even higher (have no fear, they will come, they will distinguish themselves from the many . . .)—and not just to climb higher where they are, but to develop their powers so they can climb higher in other realms as well.

Anyone aiming to satisfy the reader will never create art. Whom must art satisfy then? The entire world and even then its entire breadth can be caught only in the future.—Not everyone is seized by the word.

X

DREAM AND DREAMS

> A dream is a life which, combined with the rest of
> our existence, is what we call human life.
>
> *Georg Christoph Lichtenberg*

1

Dreams should also be *fulfilled*. Thus the *work* (every work!) is
also to a certain extent something social (that is, originating in relation to others, diminishing its own elevation.)

2

Half-asleep, I performed an experiment: could I learn to draw
from the images I saw in my dream? It worked. (According to my state
of half-sleep and still more according to my dream. This experiment
was (appeared to me to be) tremendously significant.

It was no easy task and I had never drawn it: a road winding
through uneven terrain so that the twists and turns overlapped. The
act of drawing it is nothing, my learning to draw by seeing it is nothing: but that I saw it so clearly in the dream that I, who didn't know
how to draw, could learn to draw from it as from nature, that is astonishing.

[. . .]

8

This recognition of the only possibility for "happiness" came to me in a dream or right after one: I was going up an enormously, giddily high ladder, very steep and difficult to climb. When I got to the top, I was meant to put a child on a sloping ledge. It was so terrifying, so difficult, almost too much. There was only the slightest chance that I would succeed—but I felt I would, that I had to. In any case, it signified all of life, the meaning of life: it was overwhelmingly clear that it had MEANING.

[. . .]

10

This struck me as astonishing: the spirit of my dreams always stays the same over the course of several days. Put differently: whatever remains constant in my dreams through all the changes over several days is what is most important.

[. . .]

15

First, a giant serpent of unparalleled size that I saw come through the ceiling in my room and disappear through the floor; more than ten meters long. Great danger in the house; no one else saw the serpent, only me. G. was working in the small room below mine; did the serpent have her in its sights? Great efforts to rescue her; but no one believed me.

Later, smaller snakes that attacked the cat.

Otherwise, there were marvelous but unbelievably small birds (the size of fleas) of various kinds, including brightly colored parakeet-like birds in a complicated cage and they were sure to thrive. Human stupidity had destroyed almost all of them because someone had poured buckets of water on the cage, thinking it empty; they'd paid no attention to my fearful cries of protest (I wasn't very close).

16

. . . a police officer was interrogating the suspects (men who performed small services for the police). One of them nervously asked if
he couldn't possibly pursue a career with the *regular* police force. The
officer answered, "Unfortunately not. Our regulations require proof
of *threefold spirit*. First, spirit in the usual academic sense (literature,
philosophy, etc.); second, spirit in everyday life, in politics, in worldly
affairs; third and most difficult, spirit in every particular situation,
even if you can't anticipate, not even by a minute."

[. . .]

18

A high-altitude ascent. A heavy snowfall had set in. I was meant
to be the guide. Tz. and a few others were already up in the hut. He
(like those with him) were better climbers than I'd expected; the fresh
snow made a particular passage difficult. — I myself see clearly in this
dream that mountain climbing (the technique of climbing) means
nothing other than intellectual thought. — "Yes," he says, nodding
wearily . . . He wasn't feeding them.

Up on the mountain (at an elevation about the same as the Jung-
fraujoch), Tz. was raising (in a large, fenced-in pasture) a rare breed of
large cat with beautiful, reddish-brown fur; there were a great many
and he was apparently raising them for their fur. — What did he feed
them with? "Yes . . . , well . . . ," he said and nodded wearily. He wasn't
feeding them. — How could he, since he barely had enough to feed
himself? (I felt a bit ashamed of my stupid question.) They were set
free now and again — the whole herd of them — in the adjacent, still
uncontrolled mountain forests. (Beech forests, bright, airy and filled
with light, boulders here and there; forests of luminous trunks — in
short, mountain forests as I remember from my childhood, from my
dreams.)

19

That the most beautiful things are just dreams is something I'm well aware of; but it's a matter of finding the ways that lead to these dreams . . .

[. . .]

24

"Incomparable dreams"—but dreams always seem incomparable.

I dreamed an entire book—with illustrations, too—that I'd written when I was younger (twenty at the most, more likely when I was eighteen) but had then forgotten, not considering it very good. I now retrieved the almost completely forgotten book and could read it like the work of another writer. The marvels it contained—mountains (the first of my childhood), the lively smoldering of love, and art—defied description!

25

While descending an endless staircase (I'd had to return for an object I'd forgotten), I suddenly recognized a statue, a kind of gargoyle, talking at me from the wall, as a human being.

[. . .]

29

Again and again, for weeks at a time, I mostly dream of myself writing.

This writing differs greatly: now wildly rushing and racing, always overtaken by writing that is yet more overwhelming, racing even faster, like waves of material crashing into each other over my head, so that I'm relieved to wake but I find myself in such an unpleasant mood that I have to refresh myself and wash. Now the writing is so dense, so powerful and victorious that when I awake (and even before then, presciently!), I'm certain I will *find* it written down on material paper, not just dream paper. First I have to convince myself—which always gives me a faint sense of vertigo, creates a sense of desolation and nausea—that there's nothing there, that the paper at my bedside is white and empty.

(Before there was landscape of mountains and valleys, with a cool, agreeable climate; now there's a fiery inner swarming—hence the feeling of nausea.)

Either writing rushed and drowned in the flood or victorious writing. Yet these are extreme cases and there are many levels in between. The laborious struggle to formulate a sentence, achieving one "I must keep" or "that will at least stand on the paper, stand there for all time though the rest may sink," which I then no longer understand even though I recall every word!, and still more intermediary and hybrid cases.

30

Someone should invent a device that can record what is written in dreams.

[. . .]

XI

ON DEATH

> Work is nothing other than translating what is
> mortal into what continues.

I, 51

1

The starting point:

The life of someone who has not settled his account with death
is not worth much.

How can someone who hasn't settled his account with death
live? How can you die properly if you haven't lived properly?

These verses contain death in its entirety:

> He who ever strives,
> Him we can redeem.

Is it surprising that most people, having lived so badly, die so
badly? (Lived badly: that is, always without true work.) Did a wise
man (who remained wise) ever die badly?

I have great regard for Ernst Robert Curtius's book on Balzac, except for one
passage on death, which he claims Balzac "did not understand." And what about *Le
Médecin de campagne?*

Can death be understood in any other way than through life (as happens in
Le Médecin de campagne)?—Just as life can only be understood through death.—
When someone is accused of not understanding death, the implication is that he
also does not understand life.

2

Time and again.—Yes, everything has already occurred (or: is always present somewhere). But I feel, with increasing urgency, the need to excavate from the rubble two or three *great* truths, the most basic things (for example, that the idea of death must be the beginning of all thought) and "impart" them to others.

This is art's purpose. Only through new *forms* can anything be "imparted": forms that correspond to each period's rhythm, language, terms, and references.

3

Surely only in thinking can we find an escape from the misery of this existence ("this"—as if there were any other!), and only in rigorous thinking at that.

—the supreme work: overcoming death by thinking many, almost all-encompassing things and effects . . . , achieving a complete harmony with things.

Mankind's earlier frenzied faith was a preliminary stage.

Earlier still there was an additional stage in making existence possible: should it be called blind existence? The animal phase; one renders death harmless by ignoring it.—From the subsequent stage of frenzied faith (with God, paradise, redemption) it was no longer possible to escape back to the earlier one. Similarly, now that the second stage has been undermined (through new knowledge), it's no longer possible to retreat to it either; one must struggle on to the next stage or the fear of death will remain.—No doubt some will continue to be born for whom the second stage is still possible, who are born blind. This is self-evident as the process of evolution does not advance along a single, unified front.

4

All thinkers throughout history have been preoccupied with overcoming death. There have always been some who, like Pascal, found escape into a kind of intoxication.

Intoxication is, after all, better than gouging out your eyes.

I see few new problems but I do see the old ones as terribly relevant—as new.

André Gide's great concern, the relationship of the individual to the social—certainly the central question of our century—what is it if not the question of the relationship of the subjective to the objective, the ancient question of overcoming death? A splendid answer has been given: by Spinoza.

5

Anxiety—A weighty word, suitable as the title of a great work.—He walks and walks—the key is to show how he ceaselessly walks—accompanied by anxiety, and yet he cannot escape this final fatality, which hovers before him. He walks *toward* it even as he wishes to elude it and is filled with anxiety.

6

There is only *one* evil: to not see the connection; for each individual is more than the effect of his actions.

If one does not see the connectedness and experiences anything that ostensibly has no effect as a lost cause—and such things are far more common than those with obvious effects—then death, especially the ever-present possibility of death, is a calamity so great it has no name.

7

The Highest

What is the greatest glory, the greatest happiness? When subjective thought changes to objective thought. That is exactly the moment in which one has conquered death; it is the same process; only in this way can death be conquered.

Most people think only subjectively: rather than dying, they are torn apart by torments. But there is also a number who always think objectively (admittedly not in every area of their existence, that is impossible and would be tantamount to dissolution, death; but in most areas; and these two groups have no connection); they are insignificant.

8

Variation:

The most glorious moment in our lives is when our thinking switches from the subjective to the objective.

(This moment must be repeated; there is no complete and definitive switch.—However there can be a kind of complete change. What is the life of a Spinoza if not such a change extended over its entire span?—And in the end, seeing more clearly and from a greater distance without being influenced by colors or conventional views: Balzac! Balzac's great *world vision*, rising above all pain from the deepest abysses.—And finally: all creation.)

9

He who can always draw a clear boundary between himself and others is no great mind.

[...]

13

He who has never been able to say, "Death, where is thy sting?" has no say.

Yet neither does a man who has never recognized that he will die one day.

[...]

17

If the first and greatest step toward true wisdom is being prepared for death at every moment, this does not mean one is summoning it as some of the so-called Romantics did, nor does it mean one is lauding or glorifying death but only: that one has settled one's accounts in all clarity.

At which moment is one most prepared? At the *height of life.* The more one's life declines, the more difficult it is to die. And the practical problem of death is that people have let their lives decline so much. — Compare Faust's death with Goethe's!

18

"*Should you prepare* for death?"

No! You must have accepted it and come to terms with it completely; — do not *study* death (there is nothing for us to study) but *begin* your thinking with it. You must take it as a foundation — like the fact that you exist. It is a complete and incontrovertible fact.

Whereas doctors and other specialists can study various aspects of death, only the simplest requirement is made of you: in all you do be conscious that death is a complete fact.

How your powers grow and find direction in this world! How the light of your vision will extend over the world!

Your actions have impact, you perceive colors, your life acquires *value.*

19

We can see only from constraint,
within a frame.
Our frame is death.

Katherine Mansfield was only able to perceive the full magnificence of the world through her illness.[1]

We are privileged and our privilege is that we do *not* see the whole. — Time and space exist so that we can see; without them we would see nothing.

[. . .]

24

(With regard to the WORLD, we must undergo same the experience as that of — unrequited — love in which: one must *let go* . . . then everything regains its grandeur. That said:)

We are always up to the level of previous situations and not, unfortunately, to the present one.

[. . .]

29

The only blissful feeling one can have on death's arrival is weariness.

The only legitimate feeling of a *positive* kind (of pleasure!) that one can have in the face of death: the light sense of exhaustion at the end of a work day.

The question, furthermore, the great question is being able to welcome death, to welcome, to bear it at all. There is an additional element: the *good* that can be connected with its arrival (so that it's not just not indifferent, but even good). *If* there is some good present, then the feeling is only one of weariness, just like the feeling right before falling asleep at the end of a stressful day. Is this adoration? Nothing can be further from it!

1. "There is no true intensity independent of the idea of death." Maurice Barrès.

30

He who is no longer productive dies quickly, or perhaps, strictly speaking, immediately.

31

But that is eternal life:
By their fruits ye shall know them.

32

"Life is only to be found in the will to transformation. — Life wants change yet maintains what is most important. Death wants stasis and achieves decay."[2]

If it die . . . ; that's how it is. Voltaire scoffed at this. Like so many things, he did not understand.

And yet, Voltaire . . . I hold him in great esteem . . . he surpasses other superficial writers. (Right now, it's not clear to me exactly how — perhaps simply because he was only superficial in some places.)

It's the *naïve* in Voltaire that pleases me. He has a naïve quality but also something far superior to his obvious naïveté.

33

Once again in other words:
Things must be measured *by their good qualities*, not by the negative.
(In writing as in life.)
"By the negative" means: "Here and there I did no evil. — I didn't get involved. — It could be worse." *This kind* of calculation is death.

2. *Nuancen und Details* II, 51.

34

Weariness is the beginning of the end.
[. . .]

36

Animals and Death

Animals, at least in general, have not yet discerned death; they have not formed an idea of it. Of this there is no doubt. A concept of death would express itself in fear every time it was evoked, that is, at the sight of a dead animal (that an animal is dead is something they readily perceive). But cats I've had the opportunity to observe reacted with indifference. — Just as those animals (i.e. simians) that carry off the cadavers do not display any other state. They may carry off the cadavers for another reason, in fact they *must* if not out of fear. (Perhaps they're disturbed in some way by the lifeless body or they mechanically provide the cadaver assistance just as they would have the living).

It's clear that only a wise man, a man who can comprehend death, can be stoic and that an animal would first need to reach the stage of recognition, which is that of fear. (Perhaps there are animals I haven't been able to observe that have already reached that stage.)

37

Why is it that children, when faced with death, war, imprisonment, or torture, do not (in general) react? Do they not see? Can they not imagine it (did I not see my grandfather laid out, dead?) They're familiar with suffering of all kinds in smaller measure. The explanation is simple: *they do not believe it.*

38

The Colors of Death

Funeral processions are black as coal and one suddenly realizes: the color is ridiculous in this situation. It's the only word that suits, fully and completely. This realization felt like redemption.

A color's status changes through the ages. And today black belongs only at carnival. (After several decades there, maybe it will regain its gravity.)

Which color should be assigned to death? Red, a raw shade of red, that would be something: a merciless encroachment on life.

Or an autumn pallor would be a good choice—a light pallor like the color of some horses or tent canvases—along with red; that would give a certain idea of death's reality, of its intrusive horror.—Or something similar:

In short, a carnival color! Colors become refreshed when they spend time at the carnival, they regain their innocence, are washed clean: they recover their strength and expressive power. And they undergo the reverse if, for a time, they have clad priests and such.

39

"No one can defeat me," one might say, adding: "One can only inflict hurt on me." What does that mean?

Any positive force is invincible.

What does "positive force" mean? Aren't all forces positive?

All forces are positive, but if you consist of many forces that all belong elsewhere and to which you do not belong, then these forces, positive in themselves, will not render you positive. You won't be able to depend on them in adversity for they're not yours; they will suffer, but you, who have become detached from them, are left with nothing and will die.

Thus "positive force" is the force that belongs to you; not things (forces) you perform as if a role but those that are you. For one can very well perform such roles and they are a force. Many exist without existing, twenty years, more, an entire lifetime. *But they can be killed.*

40

If you cannot see, if it's dark, if all is latent, if nothing appears in the world (hibernation, death), the decisive moment has not yet come. If you know: *something is happening*—it doesn't matter where or how or if anyone witnessed it; it could take place in darkest night!— that is everything.

[. . .]

43

Fear and Courage

Fear comes most often from ignorance but true courage is *the secure knowledge that you will not die* (knowledge that may well contain the recognition that if you do fail in the undertaking *after all*, it's of no consequence and no hindrance to a good life).

44

Death is actually not at all difficult to comprehend or, rather, there's little about it to comprehend. Everyone understands when it's explained: we must accept it without racking our brains; no one has ever faced any conditions other than these; *through* these very conditions we have access to the greatest glory; our lives consist of building within these limits, of doing our best work in order to transcend the personal and connect to the everlasting. In other words, we must enter into things and, in the rare moments we do, because our subjective thinking becomes objective, we experience the highest light that is accessible to us—: and the entire question is resolved into a clarity that puts us on equal footing with Montaigne's reflection that it is as foolish to lament the fact that we won't be alive a hundred years from now as it is to lament the fact that we weren't alive a hundred years ago. All who rise or are raised to the height of their powers understand this. Then they depart—and this knowledge disappears again.

This is a general example to show how knowledge cannot be preserved.

Our circumstances change and comprehension vanishes. Death is cunning and is ready to grab us by the sleeve . . .

What help is there?—First, by taking note that our new circumstances are weaker circumstances; then by being extremely productive there, in our new place, and by understanding that particular place, not fleeing it—! When we understand, we will once again understand death, we'll have access to it again. And so one can say:

Only life in all its strength can stand up to death.

XII

IMAGE

(Spirit–World–Reconciliation–The Real)

As long as we trust the image, we live.
Konrad Bänninger

It has been found again! What? Eternity.
Rimbaud

1

The Glittering Glass Stone

I was once obsessed with an image that was lucid and powerful, as compelling as a vivid dream, nearly a vision, and it brought me great pleasure:

A piece of glass or crystal, well carved, gleaming preposterously. Dusk is falling heavily over the world and it lies on the ground awash in a brown night—the sole light and life. Everything grows darker and darker, there are only a few slanting rays emerging from under the bottom layer of the clouds. The upper layers are like endlessly soft black-green cloaks spread over each other, darkening the world more and more. (These aren't the colors of Rembrandt, but of Titian and perhaps of El Greco.) And below, on the brown earth, the stone still lies, glittering boundlessly with even greater life.

2

There was no longer a single IMAGE to be found in his ashen interior.

That was his terrible fate.

3

They talk of "monotony." However, it's not monotony, it's emptiness.

. . . it's not monotony, that is, the repetition of the same reality, being fed the same food, but emptiness, in other words, the lack of reality, the lack of nourishment.

4

The apparent contradiction in philosophy:

A time came when they could no longer understand philosophy (perhaps the precise period can be found in Burckhardt's writings): they no longer saw what systems had in common, only their contradictions: they no longer understood philosophy itself (but didn't realize).

They were like children who say they no longer believe the possibility of one kind of music because what was begun in one form is not continued by another kind of music in the same form. There was Bach and . . . then comes Beethoven . . . "You see, in music nothing is certain."

—except for music, I reply.

5

We are, in part, acquainted with the monstrous. And when we comply with the laws of this life ("this": contemptuously not piously), then we do so only to became more familiar with the monstrous.

6

What greatness can there be in the man who is always at odds with fate?

Yes, *fighting against* it is something else entirely. But only one who is above it from the start.

7

To see that nothing changes and, without trembling, to work tirelessly for change in the face of the immutable, the arduous, the enormous,

to set out in the earliest morning hours for the summit—because of its splendor—which you won't even reach that evening because it changes before your eyes,

to read the end of Malraux's *Man's Fate* and be able to begin *there*,

this is what I wish for the young.

8

Age.—"I found being 27 terribly difficult."—That man there, at 50, found 40 to be a nice number just as you do 20. Do you see the secret? Where is youth? Was it at 40? Was it at 27? What we experience—we experience only as an *embodiment.* Our answer to the question of age depends on our perspective. Someone who is always looking back at his own youth is always old. Someone who always looks forward to his coming old age as bringing some greater fulfillment remains young at the age of 20 or 40 or 80.

[. . .]

10

Almost everything has a deeper meaning: God—the crusades of the Middle Ages—(by all appearances undertakings founded on the most egregious ideas of those dark times).

To write poetry means to restore that deeper meaning.

Almost everything has——: I do not say "everything: a stone on your path, every meal, each scrap of this burning paper"; we would die of exhaustion if we knew.

We select a few things from history to revive.

11

The gilding of distance.[1]—I was walking along streets, driven by various needs, without any means of support or social interaction; great obstacles impeded my production yesterday as they do today;—as counterpoint I think of our idealized image of the Ancients (always fully productive, surrounded, encouraged by others!) and suddenly remember that, as with prophetic visions, every time we imagine a face, picture an *image* of something, things contract in such a way that the unessential (whatever interrupts, is empty, or negates) falls away, leaving only what is particular. And this enabled me to recognize that my own course was the same as theirs.

12

Immutable in the mutable, like the moon in the terrestrial, the splendor of concrete objects passes into our interiors . . .

13

I, too, believe the world is for the most part good (positive).—So said a man after a long course—and it's not necessary to say "of

1. Cf. II, 281.

sorrow" because life is essentially sorrowful. — But happiness is not where one usually expects it: *to see how,* in all circumstances, *the spirit separates itself from all things,* that is happiness.

14

An inferior character and a superior spirit. (His character is inferior, but his spirit is great.)

15

Yes, only those who want change deserve my love.

Seen from the highest possible point, the world certainly may be wonderful — but it remains true that those who do not wish to improve this world do not deserve it.

16

KNOWLEDGE saves us; all else is confusion that is never correct.

"Knowledge": thought; all undertakings engendered by thought, paired with thought or become thought.

(This last three-part formulation is an obscure struggle; rather it's a difficult struggle for something still very obscure that will probably remain obscure.)

Action paired with thought, engendered by thought, one with thought in contrast to swampy activity done in animal blindness. (We can say we act with "animal blindness" when we act as animals — although animals are hardly blind.)

17

Are action and knowledge one? Or merely different physical states? — In any case, in wise men knowledge turns into action somewhat like water turns into ice (unnoticeably and without any intervention; it remains nothing but H$_2$O.

Vision and action become one at the highest level.

Action sharpens vision and vision sharpens action. And ever higher levels of knowledge manifest themselves in these two things: just as the more a conflagration manifests itself, the more it can consume. Its capacity does not simply increase proportionally: the *heat* rises as well and things that were previously inflammable begin to burn — the fire becomes infinite.

— The first action may even be (relatively) blind. Then the internal light increases; the spark of light contained in the first action (which was relatively blind) intensifies into light, which is vision; this vision increases action . . .

Perhaps Faust, or rather Goethe, didn't simply break off the well-known monologue on attempting translation, but ended intentionally with "In the beginning was the Act"?

18

It requires exceptional moral strength to put oneself in the position of another who is suffering the same kind of adversity but to a lesser degree (although for *him* it may be as severe) as oneself. It's much easier to understand another's *different* kind of adversity (assuming one is at all able to think of others): if our house burns down, can we understand the suffering of those whose homes have been swept away in a flood — or are even just damp? Someone who has no money can understand the pain of someone suffering from neuralgia: but it will be almost impossible for him to understand the distress of another with a monthly income of 100 guldens, even if this distress almost does the latter in. Someone suffering from an intense toothache doesn't want to hear someone else complain of a mild stomach upset — the former doesn't care that the chronic condition has brought the latter to despair. He refuses to understand and would even strike the digestive patient dead! But he would feel for someone suffering psychologically.

19

He understood the conditions, but no longer understood the results.

You can find certain people repulsive even though you understand where they've come from and the effect of circumstances.

Above all, it's not a question of *injustice* with regard to my rights but instead a different spirit

Theirs is a *different* spirit;[2] they are not wrong.

20

Memory. Memory is our highest capacity. There is no pure memory; but the pseudo-memory we call memory, that is, our capacity to strengthen those weakening areas of ourselves, those border areas of our being, is the most important capacity we have. When we develop it, it allows us to expand our being over a broad range. If we had no memory (impossible for the living), we would inhabit the briefest of moments, the mathematical moment. That is all we would know and experience. (In which case all thought, any relationship to others, and so on, would be completely impossible.)

21

Those who carry "a world" within (creative people) are not of a higher *rank* or on a higher level than others but are higher *quantities*.

[. . .]

2. On condition, of course, that they have a spirit.

23

Again and again what I once heard (years ago) about the moon comes to mind; I've wanted to write it down many times and now I finally must write; and if in the meantime it should no longer be true, it's still truer than true:

We know the landscapes of the moon better than certain areas of our own planet.

[. . .]

25

The extent of what we do *not* see is stunning.

I glimpsed a collection of bottles—they were just as they always are; smoke wafted through them, more precisely, between the bottles' necks. I watched the thin trails of smoke intently for they struck me as extraordinary, rich, marvelous. And suddenly (always "suddenly," this can't be a coincidence) I realized that most others couldn't see the smoke—I myself had not seen it earlier or, if it had been pointed out to me, I would merely have said, "yes, smoke" without really seeing it. I understood that a single point can become decisive . . . ; become the pivot point of consciousness . . . Surely there are always countless things we see without seeing.

26

He said:—I am the true guide, the spiritual guide, namely the guide through the intermediate realms.

27

The few advantages the Greek gods (who were almost human) had over us: magical powers and immortality.

But on closer examination: we have the former as well. The difficulty the gods had in working magic was disguised by their immortality. Their immortality, however, was conferred on them as an afterthought and for effect: to illustrate their magical powers and bring them vividly to the fore. How strenuous the struggle to master these powers actually is! For example, the many who have perished in the attempt to master flight in the thousands of years since Daedalus and the many who have been undone by the indolence inherent in mankind are less appealing than the myths.

28

World history is a precursor to the history of ideas.[3]

29

For great minds travel suddenly becomes unnecessary. (Kant, Proust, Socrates.) (And perhaps for the second greatest, distant travels are necessary.) For all that, woe to those who try to prevent travel when it is necessary!

30

. . . but intellectual capacity is this: to be able to take the side of what is distant.

[. . .]

35

It is absolutely clear to me that there is no God.
But there is the world, and that is wondrous enough.

3. Cf. 52.

36

X. is someone who believes in progress, a progress that will never be; and it's good so; the danger is that he might suffer a breakdown should he suddenly *see*, should he come to the view with which Malraux's great book[4] ends. Those of us who are immune know more:

we know we must transcend knowledge and turn to something other than knowledge (— as we had in youth): what is highest is not in thought, or more exactly, is *not in thought alone*. That's why Goethe said, "The best is not made clear by words."

"The best," dear X., "is not made clear by words." And here is a parody of the next sentence by Goethe, which goes right to the core of the most important connections: knowing that a pessimist (a *true* pessimist and they are rare) is a bad person is the highest knowledge.

37

The correction of a correction (of "the happy and golden childhood"):

Children are, in fact, happier — but only if "happiness" is properly understood when we speak of a *more elevated* happiness — because children have more imagination and are more productive than adults. (For: "We lack colorful images in our innermost souls: that is our affliction.")

38

Homer, too, in his most essential, did not want to amuse or entertain — we surely misconstrue his works because we lack historical understanding. Rather, he was compelled to express a spiritual reality. This certainly led to a heightening of colorfulness, of *apparent* playfulness: the flower blooms and has a perfume, too, and develops

4. *Man's Fate.*

an ever more intense perfume and color, symmetry, and artistic elements. Is it there for amusement? Is it a game?

It's all *one* vitality. There's no luxury, no pointless spinning of yarns. What justifiably seems so to us is soon stripped bare by History.

It's all spiritual vision, all an attempt to express an idea, to present an image of an entire world that is dawning: Rodin's "Balzac," like Balzac's own works and those of Heraclitus; in these we see it more clearly. It's absolutely the same in Shakespeare's works and in Homer's: Balzac serves as bridge[5] so we can understand that it *could not be* otherwise.

There is, no doubt, also a half-art that survives briefly on the crumbs of others.

It's only *that* true art that creates language; weak, commercial art (commercial in every sense) lives on for a time, in attenuated and counterfeit forms.

The carousel set up in the market square lives only from the sparks of life given by others, which it carries obliviously. Those others, the rare, true spiritual laborers: whether Epictetus, Praxiteles or Flaubert; Moses or Montaigne or—Pasteur. There is but a single spiritual profession: the serious one.

39

I never understand how people can distinguish art from philosophy so confidently.

These concepts are obviously useful for completely external distinctions (accordingly, Spinoza's *Ethics* can be designated as philosophy, Goethe's *Faust* or

---

5. "Life's dramas are not in the circumstances, but in feelings. They play out in our hearts or, if you prefer, in that immense sphere we should call the Spiritual World." Balzac, "Honorine"; "To be sure, the idea will always be more powerful than the fact." Balzac, "Massimilla Doni."

Balzac's *Human Comedy* as art): but how far do these external divisions get us? How insignificant and petty they are compared to these works' *internal* similarities!

Those who see an essential difference between great thinkers and great writers are neither thinkers nor writers.

40

All of art has never been anything but letters.

Letters for which only the sender is known, not the addressee.— The more wonderful one imagines the latter, the greater the love, the better the letters are.

"Dear reader! You must become the greatest of men: you aren't yet, but you must become so. In other words: I am working hard to write as well as possible."

41

But when I was ill, my literature did not recede into the distance like a dream; that is the touchstone.

42

How can anyone conceive of anything close to Spinoza's "adequate idea" as long as the opinion that philosophy is for philosophers has currency?

Theology is for theologians—what else would be left them? And philosophy is for human beings.

43

Great thinkers can be divided into two groups: those who provoke us to an (occasional) smile even in our admiration of their enormous accomplishments; and those in consideration of whom such smiles are impossible—just as we don't smile at the sight of nature or the saintly—: Spinoza.

44

Many, perhaps most men consider bodily pain to be a foreign body, an absolute; they do not know that it exists only in relation to a self, that one can regulate it, have a say in it.

[. . .]

48

Idiots claim: There is no truth! Because they are too lazy to fight for it.

The secret is: there definitely is one truth (one single and eternal truth—only most of the time, the *paths* that lead to it are taken to be the truth), but it must be fought for anew every day. It cannot be preserved and sold in jars at the pharmacy.

49

Legitimate possession and illegitimate possession.

Strictly speaking, there's no such thing as legitimate possession; it's simply greater creative powers. (There is, to be utterly precise, only illegitimate possession.)

There is no greater human possession than—more exactly, there is absolutely no other kind of human possession than—the ability to *take part* in the greatest possible array of things. (There can be no talk of possession. The sensual—sexual—is an example of this.)

Copulation: "Possession." Do you *have* it? What is it you have? Desire carries you from one "possession" to the next, but you never retain.

50

Humans can only steer life one way or another, not engender it.

Dedicated to the fools who believe that children are bound to their parents because their parents "gave them life," as if life can be given. Life exists already, it continues through us all. What you are capable of is a matter of consciousness, of will, of metamorphosis. One is bound to children only when one is devoted to them, to helping them, etc.

51

Blood ties: an absurd idea. It's not blood that creates bonds, but the mind. Similar experiences can create similar minds.

52

Once more: world history is but a precursor to cultural history and cultural history is a precursor to the history of ideas—that is, to the biography of the—unique—man.

This man has the characteristic of being immortal, like the Greek gods; it would be better to say that the Greek gods are immortal as he is, and in this regard are created in his image (whereas they share all other characteristics with random individual men).[6]

53

One thing must never be forgotten: that the same thing has different colors and different characteristics in different quantities. (Water ten centimeters deep is white, two meters of the same water is green or black. The fool stands on the shore and thinks the black liquid is ink; "because," he says, "water is white.") "The Ugly Duck-

6. Cf. 27.

ling" is a magnificent illustration of the confusion that arises when this is forgotten.[7]

54

If one would (could) explain *everything*, the result would be the same as nothing (all in its entirety = nothing).

Which leads me to Joseph Roth's excellent story "The Triumph of Beauty." Anger, at least some element of anger (anger is always a limitation) wrote this story: but the story is still good. There are sufficient circumstances and enough layers to the subject for the story not to seem stupid or too constructed. One could no doubt portray all the factors that determine the poor woman's condition as well as those that could improve her lot; and one could portray what determines those determining factors (there is, to be sure, not time enough for that, but this does not prevent us from imagining the process) and so on; everything that has ever existed in the world would eventually be drawn in. (There would no longer be any anger then and certainly no limitations.) Such a work would be meaningless; all works written in this fashion would resemble each other: form can only emerge through *limits* (that is, form which we can apprehend).

55

Many people are wary of psychology. They believe that revealing the sources of creativity would inhibit it or diminish the worth of what has been created.

Say an athletic record has been broken. "Yes, but it was *fear* that made him jump." Perhaps; that could well be. But I say, "Now, measure the jump."

Was it wrath that made Achilles the strongest of men? Nevertheless, he was the strongest.

What difference does it make if Goethe's "The Sorcerer's Ap-

7. Cf. 21.

prentice" inevitably leads to thoughts of certain base corporeal functions? If the poem is good, does that make it any less so?

Is a flower any less beautiful for being a sexual organ? How can it *become* any less beautiful for that, as it always was one (something no one can deny)?

56

The more advances in knowledge are made, the more clearly one can distinguish superior minds from weaker ones through one particular detail: weak minds will be more inclined to believe they will soon be done (that is: they will know everything). Strong minds will see the infinity of the world ever more clearly.

If two people are locked in a windowless room and always have been and never receive any news from the outside world: one stupid and one clever, they may have the same conception of the world's expanse; but when they are let out for the first time, their visions will differ radically: the idiot will think he'll soon reach the end, the other's conception of the vastness of the universe will expand.—And then, from the mountaintops, even more!

57

These two sentences express what is most important about *the imagination:*

1. Imagination is the ability to picture distant situations (situations different than our own) correctly—rather than inexactly as many claim (anyone is capable of that).

2. Imagination is not, as many claim, a luxury but one of the most important instruments in human "salvation," in life.

Edmond Jaloux's recognition (the emphasis is mine):
"To speak of man's solitude is a commonplace. Hebbel wrote in his journal: 'Living means being profoundly solitary.' It must be admitted that this solitude is an illusion like so many others because we would only be solitary if we were truly differ-

ent from everyone else. Reading proves that nothing is less true. We owe this illusion to our egoism, *our intellectual laziness, our stupidity* or our ill-will toward others . . ."[8]

58

It is a mercy, a wonder that in the end art expresses what each of us had in our natures, what was our particular capacity. This is not "natural," but amazing: for our efforts are almost always trained on something above or below, outside or within what is *ours* (one need only think of Hebbel or of what Schiller thought he was or wanted to achieve!). Our works are always much *deeper* than we suspect; — yet deeper in a different way than in the usual sense.

59

The finest thing about words is what they (usually) don't represent.

60

A splintering —
The birth of a mind.
[. . .]

62

". . . and the earth spun in the opposite direction":
Not at all! — This offers us a view of the gap between what God *would be* and what the world *is*.[9]

The most remarkable thing about this God business is that those who seriously affirm His existence and those who seriously deny it, understand each other very well.

8. *Nouvelles Littéraires*, 5/25/1935.
9. Cf. 35.

63

The most intelligent thing I ever heard of a God is: he walks among us in human form.

64

He went to such lengths that he could also distinguish the efforts Goethe made.

— only then, in my view, can one understand Goethe.

65

Mercy? This alone is a true image of mercy: children. That is, the fact that there *will always be* children, unspoiled beings. — In them, the higher possibilities of mankind are always offered us anew.[10]

66

The world is still young. As long as children remain children, the world will remain young. Woe is the time when children become as adults! (— as today's adults, arid beings, no longer able to change, in whom spirit dies.)

For the spirit, the world is always young. Spirit entails always being able to think of the morning — perpetual morning. At midday, the spirit thinks of the next morning. In the evening the spirit does not say, "good night," but thinks of the morning. In the morning, it thinks of the next morning. (Is that being harried? — because the same thing is precisely repeated, when one is always turned to what is coming,

10. Compare Konrad Bänninger's extraordinarily beautiful text "Geist des Werdens" (Spirit of Becoming) in the volume of the same name, which I only came across several years after writing this note.

one's line remains constant, one is filled with constancy, a constancy of the highest order, that is, the line of the spirit.)

67

Those who work in the realm of the intellect and the spirit always work on credit.

68

"My friends are far away."
Yes, they are very far, indeed.

69

The world is essentially a perpetual new beginning: this is an important truth that must never be forgotten.

Children, always being born into this world, endowed with enormous possibility, are an image and a part of this.

In the courtyard today I heard a dreadful folk song. The hideous screeching was enough to drive you insane. Who was the culprit? A child around five years old and the very same who, about two years ago or maybe less, had so beautifully sung in the early morning hours (on the other side of my wall, still in bed, when he had just woken) very simple melodies (of only three notes or so), in a fine, beatific voice, an *angelic* voice. (But now, adults have worked their influence on him, implanting their screeching and ghastly melodies in him.) And so you see, we all have the sublime. What is most essential? To preserve it as we grow for times when we are able to have an impact; to be reborn again as children when we are older.

70

The Prettiest Legs

They were the prettiest legs I'd ever seen, with the most attractive color and tone; when I got closer, I saw that this was because of the stockings. This incident provides the occasion for a marvelous examination and leads to a tremendous point of view. I should not have had to get *closer*. (Another time I notice the shapeliest legs and when I get closer, I see that they're not legs at all. Another time I see the loveliest young woman and when I awake, realize it was a dream.) For idiots, that is the end of the examination: "*That* was an illusion and *reality* . . ." Reality! Goethe found: "Our life is in light's colorful reflection." — For me there is no question in how to decide the question. I saw the most beautiful color, the prettiest legs, the loveliest woman. There's *none more beautiful*. Therefore, what I saw could not have been an illusion.

— Beware of false practical applications! If someone must travel, it's a mortal sin to hinder the journey under the pretext of so-called very highest knowledge! It is not to be used *that way*. The case of someone who no longer *needs* to travel is completely different. But to hinder someone who still *must* travel is a sin.

A story that can be told in few words about the most perfect erotic relationship belongs in this context. As a very beautiful woman walked past two friends, a woman who had a very regal gait (a regality not of power but enchantment; her posture was very straight but extremely supple, without any stiffness; her movements were very precise but she nonetheless seemed to float), one friend said to the other, "With this woman — but take care that she doesn't see us — I've had the most perfect relationship. It's the only relationship in which I've experienced only joy, not a single sorrow, in which I've received much and lost nothing." — "But now," the other said, "you've ended it—because you don't want her to see us." The first one smiled. (He looked dreamily into the past and reviewed all the days he had stood along her usual path in order to delight in, to feel elevated by her regal gait, now here, now there on her daily routes, which he knew. From this relationship, he'd obtained only what was indestructible. He'd taken only its essence.—He knew that all else with her would have been meager.)

He smiled: "I haven't, but she doesn't know me."

One must be warned about the terrible misuses such truths are put to. Cursed be those who would encourage or impose such a relationship on the young! The young must begin with material possession. In the beginning was the act. The afore-mentioned is the highest level and one cannot begin with the highest level. If one insists on it, the only result will torment and nullity; nothing but a *reduction* of one's being.

When you sit on the summit and see others writhing at the bottom of a dark, gloomy valley, you do not say to them: "Climbing is not the highest good.—Climbing is laborious. The steps are only there to be left behind. Abandon the climb. The high-est good is the radiance up top."

71

Travel is necessary even if only to convince oneself that else-where is also *not much.*

[. . .]

73

There is no greater miracle than a judiciously chosen word.

74

A *miracle.*—". . . is a sham." All art is a sham *if you don't have the strength* to cross the narrowest of footbridges . . .

For those who don't have the strength, it's a sham. (Without ex-ceptional strength you won't make it across the footbridge.)

75

How many times have I already observed this:
In order to find something, you must already have found it.
(But this should not be misunderstood.)

76

. . . everything through observation.
. . . he who is thinking an object, hardly need look at it again —
just one decisive look.

77

Travel. — Why should (must) one spend time in foreign lands?
What one sees there is not fundamentally different from what one
can learn about them; in fact, most people seldom or never see features as significant as those conveyed in good reportage,[11] other
books or even the oral reports of important individuals. (To see "nature itself" — what nonsense!) It is not, as many think, to have a *different* experience than one would at home instructing oneself through
available means but only because the *number* of significant features
one can apprehend is much greater.

78

Distant travels, aside from a few special fields of spiritual pursuit,
are not necessary for one's spiritual edification but are a question of
temperament, of disposition (and perhaps for that very reason connected to spiritual development).

Spinoza, a most expansive spirit, did not travel. The greatest spirit of antiquity,
if I am not mistaken, never left Ephesus.

11. At the moment, I know of only one good reporter: André Gide. I consider
his two books on Africa to be among his greatest works. Cf. II, 241, 242.

326   *Ludwig Hohl*

79

"He lives in a dream." Creative people must indeed remain in a dream. It comes down to the strength with which they can defend their dream.

Tomorrow's act and impact must always be today's dream.

In a newspaper this quote by Lenin: ". . . a bad Communist[12] who is unable to dream."

80

There is dissonance between these two laws:

1. that one may not *wait*, in other words that every activity must be complete; it must not be a preparation, but instead must fulfill the moment, must repose in itself. And
2. that every good action originating in a great idea at first sows confusion, causes damage, erodes conditions, and suspends the present—and the greater the idea, the more marked are these initial negative effects.

This dissonance gives rise to the necessity of imagination.

[. . .]

82

All great human capacities are easily misused; that does not prove that they weren't great capacities.

When the imagination works in a way that is meant to *replace* action—that paralyzes a possible action—it is misused.

In certain cases "action" can be set against imagination; in order for the imagination to be justified it must either lead to this action or be more than this action

12. Are they still able to dream today?

(more *action!*). This is the case in all true art. (Karl Kraus said: "The artist flees from life and emerges from this flight a victor.") The former is the case whenever great acts will come (Lenin). That which neither leads to action nor transcends it is bungling, the work of the fearful and the lazy.

83

Eternal task: to capture *it* (IT) in words that are always new. For words lose their substance, one after the other. (We *hear* the words of Spinoza but who *understands* them? How many understand the connection, the tremendousness, inherent in those commonly used words?)

84

Have men ever been so bereft of spirit as they are this year, so agitated (like birds before a storm), so devoid of knowledge of what is left and what right, so turned away from the real? While the common man claims that philosophers are lost in realms of effusion, in the unreal, and that the real is to be found in existence in the general world, the opposite is the case: they alone, those thinkers, especially the Greeks (to a lesser degree the Germans), but also Spinoza, Montaigne, and Goethe, have known reality, have *lived fully* (whereas the common man lives only in small spheres), and have lived *with* things. They have known what is simply called living (they have seen, known, willed), in contrast to others who have been whirled down the streets like dust before a storm (from "birth" to "death").

85

Will things change for the better? (—the course of the world again?)

But a true celebration is only possible in your understanding.

[. . .]

88

When I think back to my earliest consciousness—I was perhaps two years old at the time—that is, back to the earliest sense of consciousness I can remember, I find that consciousness was in no way different from my present consciousness. It was a consciousness of many fewer things but of the same kind.

89

Pascal—what limitation combined with such spiritual energy! A cripple—often atop the highest peaks but incapable of wanting life. Lichtenberg was also a cripple—my marvelous Lichtenberg! Gazing out beyond himself—the world goes on—he saw himself (not a captive of his own fear, which is the opposite of seeing oneself). And all the other *affirming spirits*, from Heraclitus to Goethe, whether as great as Spinoza and Montaigne or as simple as the childlike Voltaire! (I am speaking of him as spirit, not of his person.)

Every great spirit works like a torch, a flood light (in the night, for the general world is night); some are flood lights that illuminate the underworld; and they serve mankind, too. (Just as a lantern is hung at night where there is a pothole or a pile of debris on a road;—illuminating grim mountain crevasses, barren and impassible. There stands Pascal, he never left.) . . . but Voltaire is one of those who has won my love. Those who want change are the ones who love life.

90

Friend of God, enemy of the world!

91

"More light"—*or patience.*—They say that man has never had light in his room, only a tiny petrol lamp—how can you see anything, what can you do in those conditions?

But I say that with his small lamp (in gloomy Holland), this man ground lenses for binoculars and microscopes.

[. . .]

93

Katherine Mansfield always called out "I want to be *real*" — she who was more real than almost anyone else.

94

One cannot eliminate sorrow (not on the whole), but one must not suffer from sorrow.

[. . .]

96

Nothing you do should be preparation.

97

"I have a feeling often and often that it's dangerous to wait for things—"[13]

Yet imagination helps us with everything——helps us in the end even to imagine what we *have* (for that is the most difficult to imagine).

98

The spirit at its most elevated can no longer distinguish between mine and yours.

Precisely this inability to distinguish between mine and yours is spiritual elevation—the pious make an effort to not distinguish be-

13. Katherine Mansfield.

tween the two, but at that spiritual elevation, one no longer can distinguish between the two at all.

One identifies the course of one's own life with that of the world, the course of the world with that of one's own life.

There are only *degrees of separation*; so here, too, are only quantitative differences.

99

New art needs the old, my child, but that's not all:
Old images cannot survive if they are not refreshed by new ones.

100

He knew so many languages, he even knew the language of animals. He was familiar with each one. — But not philologically.

His ability to connect, imagination . . .

101

He observed a tempest in a water glass and discovered more than just the characteristics of a storm.

The true commitment to research is not bound to a subject: it always has one. Conversely, you can offer the lazy the seven seas . . .

102

We often hear of those who isolate themselves in sorrow; but to isolate yourself in joy, is that not something?

(The ability to isolate oneself — in today's world — joyless as it is — to preserve joy for an entire night —)

An accumulator — and do you believe that a man who can scatter sorrow to the four winds in his time is utterly magnificent and only magnificent?

103

Truths, like visions, cannot be stored up. What are utterances? Not much more than visions.

[. . .]

106

There is one area in existence, where one must be "faster than life."[14]

In connection with Geisler's words at the end of *Growth of the Soil:* ". . . they won't keep pace with life, but want to go faster"—words which I am intentionally misreading slightly or, more precisely, of which I am emphasizing only one aspect, at the expense of others in a way justified by the context.

—the area in existence where one must leap from one mathematical operation to another of a higher degree. Katherine Mansfield sensed this. She discussed the reasons for this and ways of achieving it in a letter dated 11 October 1922, a letter which is one of the most beautiful and most important ever written on account of the following passage.

A new way of being is not an easy thing to *live*. Thinking about it, preparing to meet the difficulties and so on, is one thing, meeting those difficulties another. I have to die to so much; I have to make such *big* changes. I feel the only thing to do is to get the dying over—to court it, almost. (Fearfully hard, that.) And then all hands to the business of being born again. What do I mean exactly? Let me give you an instance.

And here are the most significant lines:

. . . Looking back, my boat is almost swamped sometimes by the seas of sentiment. "Ah, what I have missed! How sweet it was, how dear, how warm, how simple,

14. Cf. II, 312 and 109.

how precious!" And I think of the garden at the Isola Bella and the furry bees and the house-wall so warm. But then I remember what we really felt there—the blanks, the silences, the anguish of continual misunderstanding. Were we positive, eager, real, alive? No, we were not. We were a nothingness shot with gleams of what might be. But no more. Well, I have to face everything as far as I can and see where I stand— what *remains*.

—"Leap from one mathematical operation to another of a higher degree": what I mean exactly is that salvation comes through knowledge. (Salvation through faith etc., is outdated.)

107

Lichtenberg was right: the concept of difficulty truly is foreign *to things*.

"The man of spirit must not even think of the word 'difficulty' as existing. Away with it!"—a man of spirit is among *things*.

108

He wants to make his lot in life easier and lets a burden drop, then everything becomes increasingly difficult.

He does not want to make his lot easier and takes on the burden that falls to him, takes on more and more, then everything becomes easier and easier.

109

Thinking of what the power—the decisive power—of *speech* is: the power to touch on realities, to stir up realities that are within the listener, that exist for him. How is this possible? Through the imagination.

I will say it again and again: the imagination does not create. The imagination heats up what is already there. *There is no creation.*

110

But: If you cannot work magic——then you are nothing; there is no hope.

111

He who cannot work magic is lost.

Variation: He who cannot work magic now is lost.
(The opposite of waiting for a miracle: therefore, he who does that is lost.)

112

Joy is less a natural phenomenon than a human creation: the greatest and most difficult.

113

Magic

(A keen and economically oriented thinker was speaking of "illusions.")

Of course, I can only dissuade others from illusions in general, from common illusions although they're related to what I see as closest to reality or even the only reality, the positive dream, but the dream is, in fact, something completely different: magic.

Do not wait for a miracle: He who waits for a miracle is lost. He who cannot work magic is lost.

"Is there such a thing as joy?" someone asks.[15] I can only point out that the question is wrong, meaningless. Joy, in adults (of sound mind) is not a natural phenomenon (like rain, for example, or your

15. Jean Giono.

hair color), or rather much less of a natural phenomenon than a human creation: the greatest and most difficult.

> You cannot go in search of joy. The mistake most people make is always going off in search of it.
> That is, you can go in search of it, but you won't find it. To find it, you must produce it.

114

I would like to hear what it is all great writers and all great thinkers agree on. For that must be the real.

Try to say it and you, too, will be one of them—you must merely succeed in *trying*. For if anyone ever succeeds in expressing it clearly, in producing the real in its *entirety* (instead of just touching on it), then we no longer need the others.

[. . .]

118

A creation of the spirit has reached its pinnacle when it begins to provide sustenance for itself (without becoming anemic!).

119

Journeys and landscapes.—Spinoza and Montaigne compared with high mountain ranges and southern seas.—The difference is only this: *we no longer have to go* into the high mountains or to the southern seas for when they're truly meaningful, it's because we have created them: we cannot create anything greater (than mountains or the sea). Yet through Spinoza's and Montaigne's works, we are raised from the depths on prodigious arms.

> Valéry recognizes this: "What we learn by reading the truly great writers are liberties."—And somewhere I read something very good by Brecht on nature: that one must be careful or one will get a fever from it . . . that it's unproductive.

120

Lack of knowledge is the abyss of all evils.

Of all kinds of evil: *no* evil can be more terrible than one: not recognizing evil. —
Where there is knowledge of them, evils are still evils — but they are not truly abysmal.

[. . .]

122

Hölderlin. He was walking in a forest. Dusk gradually overtook
the forest. It wasn't a terrible fate. Soon you'll hear them croaking
about misfortune. Nevertheless, the darkening of the forest was still
better than their wakefulness.

123

Landscapes. — I'm beginning to wonder if the mountains truly
are beneficial for the mind. They are stimulating — but the intensity is
suffocating. . . *The best climate does not incite but neutralizes.* Emptiness, but without opposition, an emptiness that spares the mind's
purity, prevents it from stiffness or over-exertion. The idea must do
it all, must retain its integrity — so that when nature is removed, it
doesn't become vulnerable, but real.

If the landscape (its quality and positive aspects) were so beneficial to the mind, it would be astonishing that so many of the greatest
thinkers have resided in awful landscapes. Is there a more desolate
landscape than Holland's? Spinoza always lived there. The landscape
around Paris is not much better and more great intelligences have resided there than in any other city.

Where are positive landscapes? The Mediterranean coast, the
alps. — The alps have not conveyed importance on anyone yet; but
Nietzsche did go insane a few years earlier than necessary because
of them.

Mountains: grimaces directed at the sky!

Our mind's creations are just such faces staring at the sky, teeth glittering. A bland, peaceful landscape does not intensify their staring, their delicate, fragile aspects, or their poison. But it does drive them to strengthen their solidity (with which they can then threaten the heavens more powerfully).

I believe the influence of spectacular nature on the mind's work is this: mistakes creep in and we excuse them.

One should be able to monitor the effects of high mountain ranges like desired doses of alcoholic liquors (abstaining when one wishes).

—But in the morning, when Nietzsche wakes in Sils-Maria, the dreadful, glittering mountains are there again——nothing cools the feverish, grimacing images of his dream . . .

But if someone wakes in the desert, his mind's gaping, towering creations, the figments of his dreams will disperse if he wishes or he will have to forge them into more solid shapes.

—and only ever new internal necessities will provide the impetus to strengthen them sufficiently to *withstand*. (Whatever has withstood the desert will withstand time.) Isn't Spinoza's work constructed this way?

[. . .]

128

Every great mind is a synthesis but does not know it. It emphasizes the analytical.

It leads us *across* and is therefore necessarily a synthesis, like a bridge. But the bridge does not know it. It says, "There!" and leads us across.

[. . .]

130

One who is truly far from others can no longer even say "you are far from me."

131

Miracles occur only when one has complete faith—or no faith at all. (Because both the one state and the other are so rare, miracles are rare.)

132

God

God is, above all, a product of human *inactivity*.

In passivity, will, action, and decision are separated into a bold idea somewhere in the cosmos, so that *one* thing acts, leads, decides: a gleaming, audacious image created and preserved by longing.

"God leads" comes from the fact that human beings do not lead when they could; people come up with and repeat this little sentence to preserve their dignity.

Everything they spend their lives denying condenses into the heavy idea of "God." And the bludgeon rains down upon them.

133

Others cannot teach you what *really* is.

134

And then, once again in the middle of the night, I understood Pascal as well as anyone can understand him. (It was not, of course,

with respect to the essential point I addressed in other passages.[16])
One can simply replace God with something else.

Besides, all great thinkers have suffered the same despair (to the
same or to a lesser degree, surely most to a lesser degree)—in the face
of *death*, the impermanence of all things, the military, the hopeless
stupidity of mankind (the ineffectual, the swamp).

They have faced it with ardor, too, and dedicated themselves
with the predominant force they all share to the redemptive *reality*
(which was mostly, if not always, marvelously solitary)—consider
Proust or D. H. Lawrence to see the endless realm of possibilities.
And the truly great politicians were . . . no different.

Whether God or idea, there is (psychologically) not much difference. It must simply be something that *defies our knowledge*.

135

To possess eternity, *in reality*, is to understand the old books;
achieving glory, creating "works" of one kind or another (which reach
or do not reach some form or other) depends on circumstances.

136

The man of spirit cannot offend any living creature.

For men of spirit are filled to the brim with life; and life respects
life.

This is a much more comprehensive concordance than, say, the
utilitarian concordance between humans and cows. It extends to
sleeping cats, to mice and beetles; if the man of spirit kills lice and
mosquitoes, he does it not as an insult, but with regret, as when he
kills animals to eat them, mows fields, chops down trees.

But he who can truly despise and offend animals, however

16. Cf. 89 and VII, 86.

small—beetles, snails, mice—is devoid of spirit. (It makes no difference if he does *not actually* harm the animals; he could do it)

> If I make an exception for dogs, it's not, strictly speaking, because of their animality but because their *human traits:* servility, sycophancy, duplicitousness, complete unproductivity.—All dogs are Catholic.
>
> Or Protestant. But not a single dog is Christian, or heathen, or human, or has spirit.

137

Many an idea is stale and barren in your eyes, but for me is still fruitful, still rooted in the earth and multiplying.

The past, for you, is worn out and done, but for me, is still open and full of unimagined potential.

138

If out of all of them, only Spinoza and Goethe were left: we would already (or still) have the essential.

Spinoza: the decisive audacity of the spirit.

Goethe: the prospect of infinite human possibilities, specifically the sensuous, incarnate prospect (expression, proof), so to speak, for an abstract version of this prospect is implied in Spinoza.

139

What attracts us to the old forms seems to shine with all the lights of poetry (Fascism's ardent devotion to the fatherland, which cannot be opposed with "advancement" or "fairness": new forms lack sensory aspects because the concepts are new and their poetry has not yet been created). What will lead to new forms does not yet have such lights and will be replaced by something completely different: distress.

And yet distress is not enough to create something truly great and wide-ranging; it requires that essentially creative power: imagination. — Perhaps it would be better to put it thus: *imagination is the manifestation of creative distress.*

"Creative distress": is there any other kind? Certainly, all distress can bring change; but what we call creative distress is able to transform not only the very moment, but also effect change beyond the moment (and not just causally!). It generates new *forms* that encompass a great many moments.

[. . .]

143

From a distance, a bumpy surface appears as smooth as polished metal.

"In the old days . . ." "The old days" was an ideal state of affairs. (Whatever the comparison.) — But only because you're not looking closely enough. In truth, there was a constant up and down, perpetual narrow escapes from calamity.

And today we can do the same.

144

The moment I took one of my biggest steps from solitude to non-solitude:

—when, at the age of thirty, in the room I will always remember, I first held a copy of Goethe's *Maxims and Reflections*; after the long obscurity, the extended period unremitting work in darkness, without any support, without any source of illumination; without any sign of approval from the outside *intellectual* world:

—such was the moment and it cannot be otherwise:

a crack forms in a rock ceiling, light trickles down, and all one has done is revealed as genuine.

145

In *this* period of his life he has enough of *something*—an erotic relationship, perhaps, or money—but he has lost what he'd previously had—an inner connection, for example, recognition, or health, or stability; *that* area of his life is now empty and filled with longing:

". . . so then he doesn't have this but he has that, it all balances out." *This is not true.*—Something new has been added. (A complement to the two; the image of the two missing halves as of the two present ones, a result of displacement; the recognition that each of the halves could be missing or could be present.)

. . . the real can be glimpsed through the constant change of the earthly.

[. . .]

148

The greatest, the solitary ones, are those who trust in the world —as in a brother.

149

Eternity looks in through the window, enormous, a face.

Just as a face suddenly appears at the window of the woodcutter's hut in the forest——the face of a wanderer; he had already been there for a long time while the woodcutter silently went about his business—at the hearth—, and he will remain for a long time.

[. . .]

151

"Impure, impure!" cried the angels of the middle order.
But a note resounded from the highest heaven:
"Pure."

152

All that you are, you will be one day.

153

At a decisive time, I was obsessed for days with this process:

You look with great concentration at the outline of rather distant hill or at the ripples in a line above the forest and you know: something is going to occur there, a *face* is being drawn. You just can't see it yet. Sometimes you think you've glimpsed it, and it's gone again; you don't see it yet, but you're working at it. We peer intently, trying to recognize it as soon as it appears. We not only focus our efforts there, but elsewhere as well: far below in one corner of the view, but also above in the clouds, here and there; but we only look with extreme concentration at the spot where it must soon appear, the spot where we are about to recognize the face (countenance). Whenever we think it has almost taken shape, it remains formless, we had merely forced our eyes into perceiving an illusion and the effort continues. Life is long and it now begins to seem long to us . . .

— But on one plane that extends from the earth to the zenith — as white as a canvas — only a small part of which, not even a hundredth of its surface, is covered by the ripples and spirals we are constantly focused on: on this tremendous plane rising from here over the forest and the top of the hill up to the clouds and all the way into the center of the heavens — on this plane, the face suddenly *appears*. All the lines, all the individual focal points of our work have joined together; what we were looking at is a small section of its expanse; it extends over and above and all around us; forest and hill and all things serve and served it, entered into it; and its formidable contours rise to the zenith.

For us humans, the connections and the dynamic are clearer, much clearer than the dimensions; — we have often observed already how the prophets' predictions proved true — only the dates were wrong.

TRANSLATOR'S ACKNOWLEDGMENTS

I would like to extend my deepest thanks to the John Simon Guggenheim Foundation and the Fondation Jan Michalski for a residency in Montricher that allowed me repeated forays into the Ludwig Hohl archives held by the Swiss National Library in Bern. Magnus Wieland of the Schweizer Nationalbibliothek, Hugo Sarbach, and Rainer Michael Mason provided invaluable guidance, advice, and encouragement in my quest to bring *The Notes* into English.

INDEX OF NAMES

The Roman numeral indicates the section, the Arabic digit the number of the note. The following abbreviations have been used: A = Appendix (to Section VII); E = Epigraph; P = Author's Preface; I = Introduction. Mythical and literary figures are not named.

346 *Index of Names*

Giono, Jean, XII, 113.
Goethe, Johann Wolfgang von, *P*, *I*, I,
    17, 19, 43; II, 30, 35, 36, 40, 42, 70,
    71, 102, 103, 133, 188, 206, 208, 235,
    264, 273, 280, 304, 305; III, E; 14,
    27; IV, E; 3, 10, 21; V, *E*; 1, 30, 32,
    38, 40; VI, 5, 30, 31, 48; VII, 50, 78,
    91, 139, 154; VIII, 1, 23, 33, 79, 81;
    IX, 1, 42, 45, 55, 67, 69, 75, 82, 86,
    96, 97, 98, 99, 100, 113, 119; XI, 1,
    17; XII, 17, 36, 39, 55, 64, 70, 84,
    89, 104, 138, 144.
Van Gogh, I, 14; II, 228; V, 13; VII, 135.
Gotthelf, VIII, 81.
El Greco, XII, 1.
Green, Julien, VI, 5.
Gryphius, Andreas, VI, 20; IX, 26.

Hamann, Johann Georg, II, 273.
Hamsun, Knut, I, 43; II, 72, 103, 264,
    312; IX, 9, 17, 93, 94; XII, 106.
Hebbel, Christian Friedrich, II, 153,
    161, 272; V, 13; VI, 5, 6; VII, 8, 97;
    XII, 57, 58.
Hebel, Johann Peter, VIII, 81.
Heine, IX, 103.
Heraclitus, I, *E*, 42; II, 2, 170, 235, 273;
    IV, 4; VI, 20; VIII, 1; IX, 25, 55, 82;
    XII, 38, 78, 89.
Hesse, Hermann, II, 130; IX, 63, 95.
Hölderlin, Friedrich, *P*, I, 37; II, 22, 89,
    154, 273; III, 14; IV, 21; V, 30, 38;
    VI, 20, 27; VII, 139; IX, 55, 75, 82,
    85, 91, 96; XII, 122.
Homer, IV, 10; XII, 38.
Hugo, Victor, V, 32.

Jaloux, Edmond, XII, 57.
Jean Paul, IX, 20.

Jesus of Nazareth, IX, 91.
John the Baptist, IX, 15, 91.

Kafka, Franz, V, E; VI, 30.
Kant, Immanuel, I, 17; II, 89; XII, 29.
Keller, Gottfried, IX, 10.
Kierkegaard, Søren, II, 76.
Kleist, Heinrich von, II, 30, 36.
Klopstock, Friedrich Gottlob, V, 13;
    IX, 26.
Koelsch, Adolf, VI, 20.
Kraus, Karl, *P*, II, 56; V, 32; VI, *E*, 2, 5,
    17, 19; VIII, 1; IX, 51, 73, 82, 90, 91,
    103; XII, 82.

La Rochefoucauld, François de, IX,
    69.
Lavater, Johann Kaspar, IX, 96.
Lawrence, D. H., II, 23, 103, 171; IV, 2;
    IX, 15, 16, 17, 91, 92; XII, 134.
Lenin, Vladimir, I, 17; II, 27, 81, 200,
    206; VII, 38; IX, 105; XII, 79, 82.
Leonardo da Vinci, II, 103.
Lichtenberg, Georg Christoph, *P*, *I*, II,
    198, 206, 235, 273; IV, 1, 18; V, 13,
    25; VI, 17, 30, 31, 48; VII, *E*, 94, 97,
    125; VIII, 1, 117; IX, *E*, 20, 55, 69,
    71, 75, 99; X, M; XII, 89, 107.
Lorenzo the Magnificent, II, 276.
Lot, Fernand, I, 3.
Luther, Martin, I, 20; II, 132, 264.

Mallarmé, Stéphane, VI, 4.
Malraux, André, II, 157; IX, 5; XII,
    7, 36.
Mann, Heinrich, II, 257.
Mann, Thomas, *P*, I, 17; II, *E*, 103, 200;
    V, 32; VI, 5, 20; VII, 121; IX, 22.
Mansfield, Katherine, I, 1; V, 30, 31,

GENERAL INDEX

Abyss: in each false step II, 8.

Accesses: new VII, 129.

Accomplishment: radiance of I, 25; gratitude for II, 149; impediment of II, 183; and idleness II, 206; and self-discipline II, 294; and utmost effort II, 196; and sorrow II, 254; external conditions II, 272; and its explanation XII, 55.

Action: and knowledge I, 47, 48, 49; II, 264; XII, 16, 17; the great act I, 18, 19, 20, 24; the small act I, 18, 19, 20; good deed II, 12, 97; and imagination XII, 82; and inactivity II, 286; positive I, 32; and goodwill.

Activity, the active: truly active I, 31; false II, 52; one feeds another II, 118; doing one to do the other II, 143; authentic II, 267; must be legitimate VII, 22; hindering legitimate activity? VII, 23; suspends the present XII, 80; writing and talking III, 3; inactive man I, 34.

Admiration: and love II, 124.

Adults: and children XII, 66, 69.

Adventure: unproductive II, 133.

Advice: three levels in offering II, 10.

Affirmation: the great yes and the small no XII, 61; II, 234.

Age: simplicity of II, 2; and wisdom II, 103; determining age XII, 8.

Aging: growing older not wiser II, 103; becoming brittle II, 303.

Airplane: flight of IX, 106.

Alcohol: and prayer VII, 51; distilling a finer spirit from VII, 127.

Animal: humans and VII, 91, 92; IX, 86; blind as XII, 16; respect of XII, 136; naming VII, 97; and death XI, 3, 36; estimation VII, 91; species: dogs IV, 9; VIII, 112, 130; XII, 136.

Armor: in distress II, 260.

Art: offers affirmation II, 32, 119; spiritual task II, 32; as ambler's walk II, 106; criterion for real art II, 171; essence of IX, 72; location of V, 3; dimension of V, 25; and interior and exterior V, 6; means bringing the few great truths to others XI, 2; what art is V, 5, 6, 35; more action XII, 82; learning in II, 172; V, 28; two fundamental elements of V, 30; and subject V, 14; and material V, 15; VI, 6, 7, 8, 21; VII, 123; and composition VI, 6, 15; VII, 76; and form II, 81; and art of storytelling VI, 16; as substitute for activity; as one's own expression V, 38; as letters VII, 131; XII, 40; and seriousness V, 40; taking stock in II, 127; where artfulness ends VII, 78; either plagiarism or non-plagiarism

Art: (continued)
VI, 30; starting point for any training IV, 3; criticism of IX, 85; and
life V, 1, 4, 5; and personal worth
IX, 44; and nature V, 2; and the
business of art XII, 38; and social
environment VI, 1, 3; and the
masses VI, 1, 2, 3; and miracles XII,
73, 74; and philosophy VII, 118;
XII, 39.

Artist: merely a greater quantity II, 119;
as typical case V, 1; great V, 23; true
V, 28; pretentious V, 32; relationship to environment II, 153; dependence of II, 273; finding the right
shade of color II, 222; and politicians II, 253; facing subject matter,
content, and form IV, 3.

Artwork: acceptable commentary, IX,
85.

Atheist: Spinoza as IX, 21, 31; no easy
thing IX, 31.

Autobiographical: genesis of the
Notes P; relation to journals VII,
A I; theme of the day VII, 139; not
speaking in the morning VII, 140;
rising early VII, 141; physical exercise VII, 141; turning away from
the difficult VII, 142; of working
methods VII, 144; everything is
work VII, 150; relation to correspondence VII, 151; reaction of
readers VII, 152; writing under pressure VII, 153; I can only develop
my methods in resistance VII, 155;
daily chronicle VII, 163; chisel-
ing sentences VII, 162; incapable
of waiting VII, 164; speaking with
Katherine Mansfield VII, 166; de-

veloping my own thinking VII, 166;
needing friends in this world VII,
167; that I will have readers VII,
168; typing up the notes VII, 169;
material conditions VII, 172; power
of meditation VII, 174; my work
will never reach completion VII,
175; bearing perfect witness VII,
176; no aphorisms *P*, VIII, 7 footnote; tremendous change in my
way of thinking VIII, 23; do I write
things filled with rage? VIII, 112;
relation to literature IX, I; Montaigne, Lichtenberg, Spinoza IX,
21, 21; those to whom I am most
grateful IX, 55; individual dreams
X, 15, 18; earliest consciousness XII,
88; step out of solitude XII, 144.

Automatic: movement I, 17.

the *Bad:* deciding what is II, 85; out-
numbering II, 97; and laziness II,
186.

Beauty: of diamonds VII, 81; of glass
marbles VII, 82

Beginning: not difficult II, 219; somewhere II, 108.

Being: all that you are, you will be XII,
152.

Belief: others and own strength II, 44;
and strength II, 63, and knowledge
II, 263, and knowing II, 292; frenzied and death XI, 3.

the *Best:* and words XI, 34.

Birth: not bringing anything with you
I, 45.

Blindness: of the seer II, 310; VII,
83; enhances vision VII, 119; 120;
capable of II, 314.

has disappeared II, 244; product
of environment and personality II,
42; appallingly stupid? II, 128; and
nature II, 140; and animal VII, 50,
91, 92; IX, 86; and change II, 193;
of the future II, 193; human dignity
and dignity of books IV, 7.
Humility: "whosoever exalteth himself . . ." VII, 94.

I: seeing oneself II, 269; speaking of
oneself II, 270.
Idea: great idea and small ideas I, 18,
19, 20, 24; great idea and good
thought II, 73; night-idea and
morning idea VII, 154.
Identity: and quantity XII, 27, 53.
Idiot: and delusions of grandeur II,
202.
Idleness: as prerequisite to accomplishment II, 206.
Ignorance: and judgment II, 252.
Illegality: of the great II, 81.
Illness: acquiring I, 17; inactive man I,
34; and health II, 4; and struggle
II, 48; causes II, 120; and healing
is everything II, 229; as touchstone
XII, 41.
Image, images: colorful I,1; XII, 37;
constant flow toward us of I, 43;
and expanse VII, 3; as an absolute
II, 87; of God II, 238; none in one's
interior terrible fate XII, 2.
Imagination: as mastery over the far-
away VII, 70; XII, 57; action XII,
82; most important about XII, 57;
necessity of XII, 80; helps with
everything XII, 97; ability to connect XII, 100; does not create XII,

109; manifestation of creative
distress.
Immutable: and changing I, 46; II, 2;
XII, 12.
Indigence: temporary and lasting II,
259; put oneself in another's XII,
18.
Individual: relation to the social XI, 4.
Individual images: glittering glass stone
XII, 1; a face being drawn XII, 153.
Initial stage: spirit II, 208; and end
stage II, 318.
Insight: and insights VII, 10, 11.
Inspiration: and composition VII, 76.
Instruction: and preparation II, 210;
and language II, 211.
Intolerance: of the newly arrived VII, 6.
Intoxication: escape into a kind of
XI, 4.
Intuition: relation to the past II, 40.
Inventing stories: and art II, 32.
Isolation: bitterest II, 293; ability to
isolate oneself XII, 102 (—> alone,
solitude).

Journalist: writer and science IX, 44.
Joy: and sorrow II, 57; and progress XII,
104; most difficult human creation
XII, 112, 113.
Judging: others II, 191; oneself II, 192.

Kasernenstraße: as allegory VII, 17.
King: royal element VII, 121.
Knowledge: and work I, 15; as true work
I, 29; turns into action I, 47; right
act I, 48; descending from above
II, 109; creates strangeness II, 139;
and resisting II, 142; paths of II,
151; of everything XII, 54; mistakes

Knowledge: (continued)
about I, 44; as the highest I, 48, 49; and good will II, 83; as antidote to power II, 181; and one's conditions II, 259; and belief II, 263; and action II, 264; XII, 16, 17; not transmissible VII, 165; cannot be preserved XI, 44; lack of is the abyss of all evil XII, 120; types of II, 200; partial II, 237; scope of II, 264; having much II, 287; and belief II, 292; degrees of intensity of III, 5; is not what is highest XII, 36.

Landscape: positive XII, 123.
Laziness: today I, 3; in you II, 54; of human beings II, 128; same as stupidity II, 188, II, 302; and evil II, 186; and talent II, 264.
Learning: and simplicity II, 209, 210; and what has been learned II, 264; in art V, 28.
Legacy: and posterity II, 203.
Letters: and daily life VII, 35, calamity of writing VII, 151; as writing VII, 131; XII, 40.
Life: brevity of I, 1; and death XI, 1, 17, 18, 44; quantity of I, 3; one's own I, 1, 8; monstrousness of XII, 5; eternal XI, 31; changing I, 20; and change II, 135; XI, 32; not preparation II, 138; essentially sorrowful XII, 13; a pursuit II, 48; as enhancement of life II, 58; we are but participants XII, 9; we can only steer, not engender XII, 50; only life delights life; beauty and atrophy I, 43; counting bad and happy moments II, 13; not that hard I, 20; II, 128; question of

the meaning of II, 22, 23; respect for XII, 136; and productivity II, 60; and life sciences IV, 14; and geometric methods II, 179: and art V, 1, 4, 5; as art product II, 119; not without political principle II, 88.
Light: of night II, 14; and action II, 53; absolute II, 156.
Limits: give rise to form XII, 54.
Lineage: in art V, 31.
Literary: heart-warming IX, 75.
Literary criticism: IX, 10.
Location: those who have no II, 133; effect of particular VII, 20, 31.
Logos: mystery of II, 105.
Look: one is enough VII, 68.
Losing position: I, 35.
Lot in life: to ease XII, 108.
Love: for mankind I, 19; higher beings VII, 69; and the meaning of life II, 22, 23; divine love II, 114; unrequited XI, 24; more than admiration II, 124; as excuse VII, 1; "most prostituted word" II, 171.

Madness: kinds of II, 291; and spirit VII, 135, 136.
Magic: when you can't work magic XII, 110, 111, 113.
Masses: and art VI, 1, 2, 3.
Mathematics: pure mathematics cannot bloom II, 27.
Meaning: and outer life VII, 117; question of the meaning of life II, 22; of senses I, 50; and words V, 11; almost everything has a deeper XII, 10.
Meaninglessness: as danger II, 203.
Measurability: and life II, 306.
Measure: and measureless principle II,

123; of things II, 250; measure with my measure IX, 114.

Meditation: power of VII, 174.

Memory: wonder of II, 40; highest capacity XII, 20.

Mercy: image of mercy XII, 6.

Merit: or fidelity II, 133.

Message: disguised IV, 13 (—> com- munication).

Messiah: explanation of II, 46.

Metal: your sentences should be like VI, 47, 48.

Method: of work I, 10; methods of the practical II, 300.

Miracle: origin of II, 232; and food II, 272; parallels to art XII, 73, 74; do not wait for XII, 111, 113; only occur when XII, 131.

Mirror: everywhere II, 110.

Misdeeds: acceptance of II, 216.

Mistakes: of great men IX, 43.

Modesty: of the literati VII, 85.

Monstrous: in "this" life XII, 5.

Moods: foul II, 315; "just a mood" VII, 126.

Moon: traveling to II, 104.

Moon forest and hedgehog forest: VII, 20, 24, 31, 76, 134; IX, 91, 52; XI, 35.

Morality: and ethical basis II, 187; and changing the world II, 283.

Mountain climbing as image of small acts I, 25, 26; as image of self-encounter I, 27; as image of the path II, 11; as image of writing II, 90; VII, 130; where mountains no longer have anything to teach II, 172; as image of decision II, 298; as image of path to the highest VII, 128; as image of thought X, 18.

Mountains: grimaces directed at the sky XII, 123.

Movement: central point II, 70; ade- quate and inadequate II, 172; and rest II, 184, 185; VII, 20.

Mr. Jones: a definition I,14; and work I, 14; Mrs. Jones and work I, 17; and solid ground I, 13, 14; three-stage I, 22; and development II, 294.

Music: possibility of XII, 4; pharma- cists and VIII, 55.

Mystery: neither loving nor denying II, 289.

What cannot be *Named:* in poetry IV, 2.

Narrative: art of VI, 16.

Nationality: and nationalism IX, 30.

Nature: and man II, 140; and waste II, 225, 281; and art V, 2; and motion VII, 20; influence on the mind XII, 123.

Natures: and the work XII, 58.

Necessity: place of II, 139; and freedom II, 206.

Negative: measuring by the negative is death XI, 33.

New/novelty: old and new art and images XII, 99; new writing IX, 115, 116, 117; of intellectual discovery IX, 1.

Night: removing light from II, 14; over the ocean II, 15; seeing farther at II, 39; of night fosters ideas VII, 154.

Nourishment: as the absolute II, 248.

Novel: captures readers VI, 10; help for learning foreign language VI, 11; because one must still write VI, 12; what is desirable for the novel today VI, 30.

no II, 197, 218; XII, 80; and defini-
tiveness II, 221; danger of III, 1;
XII, 96; for preparation VII, 13; for
death XI, 18.

Present: and past II, 40; being at level
of XI, 24.

Preserving: one's knowledge II, 70.

Production: we grow only through VII,
20; without production one soon
dies XI, 30.

Productivity: one lives through II, 269;
enjoying pleasures is also VII, 21;
pinnacle of spiritual XII, 118; and
life II, 60; and production II, 144;
IX, 29.

Prognoses: as test of one's vision II,
28, 29.

Progress: value as such II, 57; and pes-
simism XII, 36; and joy XII, 104.

Proof: as context II, 179; bringing into
relation VII, 116.

Prose: and poetry VI, 3; and material
VI, 4; methodical VI, 46, 47.

Prosperous: duty to be II, 25, 118, 144.

Proverbs: use of II, 68; VI, 34.

Psychology/psychologists: false and
non-psychologists II, 74; diminishment of accomplishment? XII, 55;
two groups of II, 74.

Punctuation: meaning of III, 7.

Purity: and impurity XII, 151.

Quantity: artist as greater II, 119; and
identity XII, 27, 53.

Question: changing II, 18; badly formulated II, 290.

Quoting: and writing VI, 31; how it
should be understood VII, 139;
IX, 109.

Rapture: living in constant II, 118.

Reader: the true IV, 1, 2, 5, 6, 18; loving
the reader while writing IV, 15; and
artist VI, 2; bad VI, 9; VIII, 132;
future readers of *Nuances and Details* VIII, 110.

Reading: and writing IV, 1, 4, 18; XII,
105; good IV, 18; at different speeds
IX, 82; much and little IV, 11; fruits
of IX, 52; what have you read? IV,
10; experience of reading IV, 17;
personal experience of IV, 15; how
the inferior man reads IV, 9.

Real: as the inexpressible IV, 2; where
is the? VII, 170; on which all great
writers and thinkers agree XII, 114;
glimpsed through the constant
change of the earthly XII, 145.

Reason: and the world II, 130.

Recognition: not achievable II, 256,
and fame II, 256, 273; sequence of
IX, 121.

Reconciliation: premature reconciliation of the Swiss IX, 10, 11.

Religion: its genesis II, 125; and spiritual dignity II, 163; and truth II,
205.

Reproaches: offensive II, 255.

Research: true commitment to XII,
101.

Resistance: each step is an overcoming
of I, 25; and power II, 60, 131, 132;
as measure of spirit II, 189; against
time IV, 21; methods of VII, 155;
locus of II, 249.

Rest: and movement II, 184; VII, 20;
kills VII, 20; humans will never be
able to VII, 23.

Revelation: and psychology II, 239.

Revolution: a period of constant II, 208.

Revolutionaries: made of heavy material II, 132.

Reward: must be found within II, 24; not for I, 33; II, 57, 220.

Rightness: right or wrong VIII, 133.

Road: (path) recognizing I, 36.

Rock: most divine VI, 48.

Run-up: (cf. preparation) avoid, II, 217.

Saint: sanctioned one II, 164; and life II, 165.

Salvation: through knowledge XII, 106.

Saved: beware II, 116; IX, 1.

Say: and repeat II, 216.

School: and mind II, 82; effect of II, 210; and voluntariness II, 206.

Sciences: consecrated II, 81; taking stock in II, 127; and knowledge II, 288; writer, journalist, and scientist IX, 44.

Sculpture: material is all VI, 28.

Seeing: stars by night and by day VII, 4; and having time II, 299; VII, 85, 89; and action XII, 17; and not seeing XII, 25; law's life XII, 46.

Self-criticism: of the writer II, 67.

Self-discipline: and achievement II, 194.

Senses: knowledge and action I, 50.

Shame: as protection VII, 140.

Short stories: city of night watchmen VII, 2; the frozen man VII, 11; no more train VII, 12; story of a king VII, 13; on giving VII, 15; education VII, 15; tavern on Kasernenstraße VII, 17; the man who was carried great distances in a dream VII, 138; patrols in the desert IX, 24;

the art critic IX, 42; perfect erotic relationship XIII, 70; three men arguing VII, 10; of the churl VII, 29.

Significant: risk inherent in II, 41.

Silence: and talking III, 7, 10, 11, 13, 15; and chatter III, 19, 21; is golden III, 8; none is significant III, 10; enjoyment of III, 11; who is permitted to remain silent? III, 14; eternal III, 12.

Simple: and the complicated II, 282; VII, 49.

Sin: and awareness II, 183.

Single: step is arduous I, 25; and the whole I, 26; II, 175, 176; and change I, 23.

Sleep: turn toward powerful production VII, 20; not an end in itself VII, 21.

Small: things teach greater ones II, 150.

Social: work as social X, 1; relation of individual to XI, 4.

Socialism: and genius I. 29; II, 227; and spirit II, 145; types of VII, 26; and communication IX, 16.

Solitude: of night II, 15; forms of II, 59.

Sophism: and technology II, 129.

Sorrow: and struggle II, 48; overcoming II, 94, 111, 167; cannot be shared II, 157; greatest II, 167; arrival of II, 168; what we make of II, 169; accomplishment II, 254; last and greatest II, 293; tragic II, 294; life is essentially XII, 13; not suffer from XII, 94.

Speaker: kinds of III, 22, 24, 27; and public appearances III, 23; distance from politician III, 24.

Specialists: and universality II, 253.

Speed: of reading at different IX, 82.

LUDWIG HOHL was born in Netstal, Switzerland, in 1904. He lived in Paris, Vienna, and The Hague in his twenties. He returned to Biel in 1937, then settled in Geneva where he lived in a basement apartment and worked as a writer, initially publishing his works only in newspapers. Although Hohl was revered by writers such as Friedrich Dürrenmatt, Max Frisch, Elias Canetti, and Peter Handke, he lived most of his life in relative obscurity, finding recognition only late in his final years when he won a number of awards, including the Prize of the Schweizer Schillerstiftung in 1970 and 1976, the Robert Walser Centenary Prize in 1978, and the Petrarca-Prize in 1980. He is best known for his 831-page magnum opus *Die Notizen* (*The Notes*). Hohl died in Geneva in 1980.

TESS LEWIS is a writer and translator from French and German. Her translations include works by Peter Handke, Walter Benjamin, Anselm Kiefer, Christine Angot, and Philippe Jaccottet. Her essays on European literature have appeared in *The American Scholar, Partisan Review*, the *Wall Street Journal*, the *Hudson Review, Bookforum*, and others. Tess Lewis has won multiple awards, including the 2017 PEN Translation Award, the Austrian Cultural Forum NY Translation Prize, a Max Geilinger Award, and most recently a Guggenheim Fellowship to translate Ludwig Hohl's *Notes*. She has served as co-chair of the PEN America Translation Committee and is an advisory editor for the *Hudson Review*.

JOSHUA COHEN is the author of six novels, along with collections of short fiction and nonfiction. Called "a major American writer" by the *New York Times* and "an extraordinary prose stylist, surely one of the most prodigious at work in American fiction today" by the *New Yorker*, he was awarded the 2013 Matanel Prize for Jewish Writers, and in 2017 was named one of *Granta*'s Best Young American Novelists. His most recent novel is *The Netanyahus*.